AF305055

Where
Tourists Seldom
Tread

Also by Chris Moss

LANCASHIRE: EXPLORING THE HISTORIC COUNTY
THAT MADE THE MODERN WORLD

SMOOTHLY FROM HARROW: A COMPENDIUM FOR
THE LONDON COMMUTER

WALES COAST PATH: TENBY TO SWANSEA

PATAGONIA: A CULTURAL HISTORY

TIME OUT FLIGHT-FREE EUROPE (EDITOR)

Where Tourists Seldom Tread

Postcards from Bypassed Britain

Chris Moss

First published by Guardian Faber in 2026
Guardian Faber is an imprint of Faber & Faber Ltd
The Bindery, 51 Hatton Garden
London EC1N 8HN

Guardian is a registered trademark of
Guardian News & Media Ltd
Kings Place, 90 York Way, London N1 9GU

Typeset by Faber & Faber Limited
Printed in the UK by CPI Group (UK) Ltd, Croydon, CR0 4YY

Map illustration © Joe McLaren, 2026
Photographs © Chris Moss, 2026

Quotation from *The World Turned Upside Down* by Christopher Hill
published by Penguin. Copyright © Christopher Hill, 1972, 1975.
Reprinted by permission of Penguin Books Limited.

Quotation from *Londonstani* reprinted by permission
of HarperCollins Publishers Ltd © 2007 Gautam Malkani

A CIP record for this book
is available from the British Library

ISBN 978–1–783–35317–0

Printed and bound in the UK on FSC® certified paper in line with our continuing
commitment to ethical business practices, sustainability and the environment.
For further information see faber.co.uk/environmental-policy

Our authorised representative in the EU for product safety is
Easy Access System Europe, Mustamäe tee 50, 10621 Tallinn, Estonia
gpsr.requests@easproject.com

2 4 6 8 10 9 7 5 3 1

Contents

Map   vii

Introduction   1

1 Logistical Daydream: Warrington   11

2 Under the Arches: Stockport   25

3 Shafts of Shadow: Birkenhead and New Brighton   35

4 Changing Tracks: Crewe   51

5 Border Capital: Wrexham   63

6 Black Country Rocks: Wolverhampton, Walsall and Dudley   77

7 Vagabonds and Chartists: Newport   93

8 Tin Cry: Redruth and Camborne   107

9 Cider with Barbellion: Barnstaple   121

10 Short Flights from London: Hounslow, Croydon, Gillingham, Wokingham, Surbiton, Slough   131

11 Ghost Story: Jaywick   151

12 Memory Haven: Harwich   159

13 Back to the River: Ipswich   171

14 To the Sky, to Infinity: Boston   185

15 Northbound: Doncaster   195

16 Estates of Mind: Gateshead   207

17 Silver and Gold: Wick and Thurso   219

18 New Wave, Auld Punk: East Kilbride and Paisley   229

19 End of the Road: Barrow-in-Furness   241

20 Alternative Ulsters: Armagh and Enniskillen   251

21 Castaways: Douglas and Ramsey   267

22 Radical Angles: Nelson and Colne   281

23 First Canal, First Railway, First Home,
        Last Walk: St Helens   297

Epilogue: Martians and Postcards   313

Acknowledgements   319

Further Reading   321

Index   325

Thurso
Wick
Paisley
East Kilbride
Gateshead
Armagh
Enniskillen
Ramsey
Barrow-in-Furness
Douglas
Colne
Nelson
St. Helens
New Brighton
Stockport
Doncaster
Warrington
Birkenhead
Crewe
Wrexham
Boston
Wolverhampton
Walsall
Dudley
Ipswich
Harwich
Jaywick
Newport
Hounslow
Slough
Croydon
Wokingham
Gillingham
Surbiton
Barnstaple
Redruth
Camborne

Introduction

Most of those [cities] which were once great are small today:
and those which in my own lifetime have grown to greatness,
were small enough in the old days.

Herodotus (*c*.484–*c*.425 BC)

Know most of the rooms of thy native country before
thou goest over the threshold thereof.

Thomas Fuller (1608–1661)

Since the world is on a delusional course, we must adopt
a delusional standpoint towards the world.

Jean Baudrillard (1929–2007)

Take your pick. Dubrovnik or Doncaster? Corfu or Crewe? A safari in Kenya or an abandoned zoo on the Isle of Man?

Some places are fixed in the imagination as holiday destinations. A relative minority, they are regarded as rich in heritage or history, gastronomy or scenic beauty. Or, at least, abundant in crowds and queues. They're where lots of people go.

Other places are deemed too plain, rundown, functional or funless to be worthy of anyone's leisure time. At least by the mass of people, and the market. If you've picked up this book and are contemplating using it to plan a day out or a longer break, you're in a minority. But our little group of offbeat excursionists is growing, and I believe we're on the right side of history – which increasingly demands we use free time creatively and with an accent on curiosity, and try to make our travels greener, cleaner and more local.

After the pandemic lockdowns, I realised I wanted to explore the UK, partly to cut down my flying and reduce my carbon footprint; also, I wanted to come home, in an expansive sense. The idea of reconnecting with your own country sounds simple enough, yet how many people really make an effort to do it? I had lived overseas from 1991 to 2001 and, working as a journalist who specialised in foreign travel, spent much of the following two decades visiting faraway destinations. I knew Patagonia better than I did south London, Devon, Carmarthenshire – all places where I lived during that period.

When it came to reacquainting myself with Britain, I wanted to write about less obvious places. This was a reflex more than a mission. During all those years of foreign travel, I'd often sought out the marginal or at least less reported edges of towns and cities. I caught local buses and alighted at random stops, drawn by obscure, hard-to-read sites rather than places where I could spend money or tick a box. I walked long distances through residential areas, industrial estates and inter-urban districts, dawdling and drifting rather than set on reaching any destination. I enjoyed reading books about supposedly humdrum towns and once anchoring, now abandoned factories, and watching old BBC films featuring architecture and planning critic Ian Nairn enthusing about industrial cities and 'football towns'.

My first column for the *Guardian* on improbable, bypassed, unloved (any adjective I choose will offend someone) British holiday destinations was published in January 2022. The editor Andy Pietrasik capped it with the headline 'Where Tourists Seldom Tread', a nod to E. M. Forster's 1905 novel *Where Angels Fear to Tread*. Forster wrote about travel in several works of fiction and non-fiction, believing its pursuit involved risks worth taking. He set stories in India, Italy and South Africa, jolting the complacent British reader out of their comfort zone.

He never wrote about St Helens or Wolverhampton, though. And all the books by, for and about flâneurs emanated from Paris, or else London, Berlin and New York.

When I published the first postcards from non-obvious towns, some *Guardian* readers wondered if I was being provocative or sardonic. But my intentions were, while hopefully not overly earnest, quite sincere. I actually do believe that domestic travel and visiting places on our doorsteps have a lot to give – in terms of enlightenment, history, culture and entertainment.

My approach in this book isn't uncritical, but it's broadly hopeful. Our towns attract plenty of negative press for their declining high streets, underfunded public services, social inequalities, homeless populations and potholed roads. This is as it should be; the news media's main job is to speak truth to power and show politicians where they are failing. Simplistic formulations, however, like 'Broken Britain' and 'left-behind' towns, serve to generate shame without leading to solutions. The internet fizzes with negativity. Local newspapers, much reduced these days, highlight crime, decrepitude and nostalgia-laced reminiscences to generate clicks on their websites. Most Facebook community groups bristle with anger, intolerance and petty moans. The satire of 'Crap Towns' – that very nineties, London-centric josh that everywhere else was awful – has spawned copycat online forums that denigrate the places where most of the pessimistic posters were raised or, in fact, still live. Type the name of a town into Google followed by 'is', and the search engine often autocompletes with 'a dump'. The internet's default slant is pejorative.

Gloomy headlines are not the full story and, anyway, a visitor's needs are not the same as a resident's. When I visit a town, any town, I am looking for a mood or feeling. I want to know its stories, which means more than current affairs and recent history, though they of course matter. I want to know when it was built and why. Britain is full of ancient places – Ipswich is twice as old as Machu Picchu – and ordinary-looking high streets boast houses, pubs and shops from Shakespeare's time or older. Many of us take such antiquity for granted, unlike foreign tourists who swoon over our stone bridges, medieval alleyways and head-banging oak-beamed inns.

Many British towns date their main period of growth from around 1800, when industrial development turned villages and scattered parishes into major centres, necessitating sizeable workplaces, civic buildings, amenities and lots of housing. This process was socially convulsive. Then, gradually from around 1920 and more precipitously after the Second World War, the industrial revolution came to an end – and a comparably dramatic period of change ensued.

In those cases where a town lacks, say, architectural charm, protected heritage sites and independent retail, that is a fundamental part of its story. Learning to look at what is missing is vital.

This book is principally concerned with towns and small cities in the UK. The largest metropolises are always in the news. Rural idylls are fashionable with the metropolitan set and wealthy retirees. But most people live and work in towns. Only a handful ordinarily qualify as tourist destinations, but towns are everywhere. It was only when

I began to make a list of the names of towns I might cover in the *Guardian* column that I realised there were hundreds I didn't know at all, except as universities I didn't go to (Keele, Lampeter) or military barracks (Catterick, Aldershot) or racecourses (Doncaster, Uttoxeter, Newton Abbot) or places I had passed through, time and again, without stopping (Crewe, Stockport, Port Talbot).

To date, I have written about eighty such places for the *Guardian*. For this book I have selected roughly half of that number – some grouped in regions – and expanded the texts in an attempt to slow down and dig a little deeper. Of course, they remain only extended postcards; superficiality is inevitable when you are a day tripper or weekend visitor, passing through. Any depth or insight gleaned is down to reading others' texts, helpful locals and luck. I chose some places I already knew well, to keep my travel budget under control and to compare my responses in familiar towns to what I saw and felt in those that were new to me.

This book is part field guide, part travelogue. A lot of travel writing, especially about less celebrated places, is written from the perspective of 'I went so you don't have to'. My hope is that readers will want to visit the places I have included once they have read my accounts. Pevsner and all the wonderful old-school gazetteers gave previous generations of domestic travellers stately mansions, ivy-walled churches and manicured gardens and parks to look out for on their road and bus trips to Wells, Canterbury and Edinburgh. If this book gets people looking for the same, as well as the overlooked sites, in Camborne, Gateshead, Paisley and Croydon, I will consider it to be a success.

Tourism is in crisis. It's an ouroboros of consumption and self-destruction. We fly far too much around our climate-crisis-threatened planet. We drive unthinkingly; motorways and road maps encourage blinkered travel, satnavs a kind of spatial blindness. Buses and railways service cities, just about, but fail to link up communities. Overtourism is destroying everything once considered beautiful; it punishes the

   where tourists seldom tread

traveller as much as it does the UNESCO-garlanded wonder or 'Instagrammable' beach. Second homes and holiday lets are a blight the world over. There are many Britons who have been to Dubai or Cancun several times, but don't, when it comes to worthwhile domestic destinations, know their Preston from their Pontefract, or the second-nearest town to them, or the fact that they actually dwell in a place brimming with secret histories and unsung cultural value. Meanwhile, travel media – newspapers, glossy magazines, guidebooks, blogs – go to great lengths to unearth remarkable, 'unspoiled' places, never acknowledging the absurdity of their position. In any case, most so-called discoveries are repackagings, or bare-faced lies.

Unknown destinations are all around us. Philip Larkin was thinking about Hull when he wrote 'Where only salesmen and relations come'. I was always envious of travelling salesmen (do they still exist?), MPs, footballers, music bands, rep actors and Avon ladies. They get to tour districts, regions, towns, sometimes travel the length and breadth of the country, including its least touristy places – at least for a day or two, to ply their trade. Travel seems to me to be a human need – some residual urge from our common nomadic past, perhaps. What could be better than an occupation that requires you to be mobile, while also allowing you to explore your own land and people? We can't all be travelling salespeople, but we can play at being one for our holidays.

None of the towns in this book has an overtourism problem. But they are all worthy of visitors; they are all intriguing, complex, multifaceted. Some I found hard to decipher, to navigate, to like. Others seemed to me like forgotten marvels. I would depart, wondering to myself: how has the tourism industry, so predatory and greedy, missed this amazing place?

In a way they're all beautiful. Dylan Thomas called Swansea 'an ugly, lovely town'. Both adjectives can be simultaneously true. When we describe a place as beautiful, or ugly, we are making lots of value judgements. We are comparing it with others. We are falling victim to

Stratford-upon-Avon syndrome, a bias towards the famous, the tweely picturesque, the old, the safe.

Ugliness has as many forms as beauty, and it too is in the eye of the beholder. The ugliest place in England for me is Belgravia, London, that haut-bourgeois ghetto of privilege and entitlement, where monotonous facades and security cameras sneer down at empty pavements. For me, in a way, Belgravia is 'a dump'. But I'd still go there to see it, understand it, know it.

In fact, I'd go anywhere – and always find some loveliness, some beauty, even in the ruins.

A manifesto for getting the most out of Britain's tourist-free towns

1 Heritage is everything a society inherits. It includes the recent, the useless, the vacant. Everything is potentially interesting and instructive. What Pevsner, the National Trust and Historic England proffer are merely the prettiest bits.

2 Be curious. Matthew Arnold wrote that curiosity was a 'liberal and intelligent eagerness about things' and a laudable desire to 'see things as they are'. He thought it an attitude the English misunderstood and often lacked, unlike the French. *Allons flâner!*

3 Edgelands, wastelands and ruderal-spattered ruins aren't the preserve of self-styled psychogeographers or YouTubing urban explorers. Overlooked and undersold places deserve to be mainstream destinations.

4 There are more than 1,300 towns in the UK; more than 38 million people live in them. The average Britain lives in a town or a suburb. You probably live in one, used to live in one, and work and/or shop in one. Respect towns. Own them.

5 When a person is tired of London, or Manchester, for that matter, they become more alive, more aware, more thoughtful. Every shortcoming you observe outside the metropolis is partly the responsibility of the metropolis. Every quiet town is sending its workers and shoppers, and its money, to a city.

6 Make notes, take photographs, meet people; treating a town like a project, working towards a personal impression, takes practice but repays the effort.

7 The high street is dead, they say. The British high street, as we know it, is about two hundred years old. Going to town *to shop* became an activity for the masses around a century ago. A town is more than its retail strips and boxes, however full or vacant.

8 Support local museums, galleries, parks and heritage spaces, but never end your experience there. The official, curated versions of a town are never the whole story.

9 Nothing is boring. Cobblestones aren't boring. Seventies blocks of flats aren't boring. Empty brownfields aren't boring. Boredom isn't boring.

10 Tell your friends to swap Tenerife and Timbuktu for Barrow, or Wrexham, or Walsall, or Colne . . . Britain is their oyster. Flight-free. Local. Walkable. Wondrous.

where tourists seldom tread

1
Logistical Daydream
Warrington

I t's not so much a mist as a whitish murk, a weakness of light due to the late season and lowering sky. Mirroring the grasping raised hands of wintry trees are bare branches plunged into still water, in turn reflected there. I think of flooded forests on the upper Amazon. But I'm in Warrington.

It's December 2021. I've come to visit a familiar town and take a circular walk along the banks of the River Mersey and the Manchester Ship Canal, great watercourses widely ignored – certainly by travel writers and tourist boards – and, from the evidence of the deserted footpaths, by Warringtonians. It's a Saturday afternoon. Across from the riverside path are semis in mud-brown brick, a shade familiar from childhood, of strangers' houses. I peer intermittently into front windows but they are dark and secretive. I imagine residents seated beside hearths, reading supplements, more probably surfing the net, wondering about a holiday away from the pandemic and the pall of winter.

The river is on the romantic southside. I arrived from the opposite direction, via Newton-le-Willows and Winwick and acres of housing estates. Warrington was designated a New Town in 1968. It didn't lead to noteworthy architecture or eye-catching and innovative planning, but it did produce lots of housing to the north and west of the town. It's now Cheshire's largest conurbation, twice as populous as Chester. Warrington's inner edges are cookie-cutter Anglo-American: roads, roundabouts, strip malls, fast-food outlets, big boxes, big car parks filled with big cars. There's a new bus station that's so underwhelming it's almost invisible. I glance up a side street and see a solid polychrome brick building, formerly a Cheshire Lines railway warehouse. It's an apartment block, the frontage handsome and solid.

The centre is vaguely as I recall it. I came to Warrington's shops with my dad occasionally during my teens, and recognise the general contours. It's somewhat dishevelled, with a few hints of Victoriana and, aside from the town hall's golden gates – forged at Coalbrookdale Ironworks in Ironbridge no less – has no truck with looks. Though on Bridge Street there's a swirly pavement like the ones along Copacabana beach, part of a 'River of Life' memorial to the two boys killed by the IRA bomb in 1993; that, and Eddy Shah, were the only times Warrington was much in the news. A rubbish piece of street art looks like green skittles, alluding to nothing. There's a sign for a 'cultural quarter'. Every town centre must have its quarters, usually five or more of them.

The Barley Mow pub, built in 1561, is a rare Tudor trinket in a town that's tended to translate 'development' into 'demolition'. Outside the old inn they have erected an al-fresco food truck with picnic benches. Everyone's in puffer jackets and bob-hats, eating burgers or pizza and drinking fizzy drinks or beer, shivering, vaping, smartphoning. There's a steady traffic of shoppers and strollers – the standard twenty-first-century Saturday mêlée of single parents with kids in tow, couples, elderly women, plastic-bag carriers, middle-aged people on mobility scooters, sweary teens.

I hesitate to say much about the shops. We have lots of towns still to visit. How many shuttered or charity or chain stores can we walk past without getting despondent? And the river beckons. Mid-sized town shopping centres are, the standard narrative runs, all the same, all full of empty units. But Tolstoy's claim about unhappy families works for retail spaces too; sadness and emptiness vary from town to town. Warrington's shopping heart is desultory, uninspiring, but it hasn't given up. After passing the Golden Square arcade I find myself on a modish piazza, Time Square, dominated by a faux market hall that's actually a food court. Est. 1255, opened July 2020.

Down by the riverside is a statue of Oliver Cromwell clutching a sword and a Bible, by the London sculptor John Bell, also made at Iron-bridge and originally displayed at the 1862 International Exhibition in London. It was presented to the town in 1899 by local councillor Frederick Monks to mark the 300th anniversary of the Lord Protector's birth. There was, unsurprisingly, opposition from the local Irish community, but it's a fitting location in some respects. Warrington Bridge, across the road, saw action during the English Civil Wars. In 1643 the 7th Earl of Derby used the town as a base for Royalist operations; when a retreat was necessary, he ordered Warrington to be set on fire to stall the Parliamentarians. The Royalists surrendered here in 1648 following the Battle of Winwick. Three years later, Charles II's Scots forces repelled the Parliamentary militia led by Thomas Harrison and John Lambert, forcing them to retreat south. The 7th Earl crossed the bridge again in the same year, on his way to Bolton, where he would be beheaded at the Man and Scythe Inn, owned at the time by his family, for his part in a massacre.

Behind Cromwell is an almost elegant, vaguely Georgian building claiming to be Warrington Academy, opened in 1757. At that time, only Anglicans were allowed to study at Oxford and Cambridge. Warrington was elected to be the site for a new academy thanks to the drive of local dissenting minister John Seddon, and because of its useful connections to the region's two cities. Paid for by subscriptions from local and colonial merchants – and attended by the scions of plantations where slavery was practised – it would train ministers for the Nonconformist chapels and meeting houses that had recently sprung up across England. The enlightened curriculum included foreign languages, English literature, history, natural history, chemistry and physics, as well as classics and divinity. Several of its tutors were men of some standing, most notably Joseph Priestley, a polymath credited with discovering 'dephlogisticated air' – oxygen – in 1774 and inventing fizzy water.

The academy lasted only until 1783, but it had significant impact on intellectual life in the North-West. It was refounded, and relocated, in 1786 as the Manchester Academy, its staff subsequently travelling to York, back to Manchester and down to London, before the institution finally became Manchester College, Oxford. Former students founded the Manchester Literary and Philosophical Society and the Liverpool Academy of Arts. Its tutors presided over the Warrington

Circulating Library, created in 1760. Leading schools, including Macclesfield Grammar and Manchester Grammar, were inspired by Warrington Academy to add modern subjects, such as languages, mathematics and bookkeeping, to their curricula. Thomas Robert Malthus, who had studied at the Warrington Academy in its last year, would go on to write foundational works of political economy and population. There is some evidence the Jacobin martyr Jean-Paul Marat spent time at the academy, possibly teaching French or working as an assistant to Priestley.

In the second half of the eighteenth century Warrington was nicknamed the 'Athens of the North'. When Jeremy Bentham recalled visiting in the summer of 1764 with his father, he described the town as 'classical ground'. Warrington might have become a northern Oxford, an Edinburgh on the Mersey.

In *The World Turned Upside Down*, his magisterial account of religious movements at the time of the Civil Wars, Christopher Hill writes, 'There was . . . another revolution which never happened, though from time to time it threatened. This might have established communal property, a far wider democracy in political and legal institutions, might have disestablished the state church and rejected the Protestant ethic.' What might England have become if the republic had prospered and lost its puritanical venom? Warrington Academy might have played a part in the revolution.

In 1981, the listed academy building on Bridge Street was lifted from its foundations and moved nineteen metres north on rollers in order to widen the road. Its structure fatally damaged, it was destroyed and completely rebuilt. The delisted building we see now is a block of 'supported living apartments' called the Academy.

———

For the traveller heading north in the industrial era, Lancashire's smoking, dinning, teeming sprawl began at Warrington. Coalfields and the textile belt lay just beyond the town, but here there were mills and tanning factories, copperworks and ironworks, sugar refiners, boat-builders and breweries (Greenall Whitley and Walkers).

Close to Bank Quay station is the Unilever factory, which closed in 2020. The aroma of wort and mashed grains used to compete with the vapours produced by Crosfields soap factory. A brand called Perfection Soap had turned Crosfields into one of the pre-eminent soap producers in the country by the 1860s. In 1884, William Lever brazenly built a plant right next door, to begin production of his Sunlight soap. 'Soap wars' ensued. Lever Brothers, miles ahead in marketing and packaging, was the victor. The factory, scheduled for demolition, is a green and grey hulk of a building somewhat enlivened by Pompidou-esque tubes. But people here feel a deep saudade for the chemical-industrial past. For decades Warrington smelled of soap powder; if it stung the nostrils and made the eyes smart, everyone agreed it smelt of 'washing day'. Clean air is healthy but here it signifies mothballing. The Friends of Warrington Transporter Bridge keep up a lively campaign to preserve a 1916 steel rail bridge built for Crosfields at Bank Quay, though it now moves nothing from nowhere to nowhere.

The southside of town has qualities to counter post-industrial ruination and vacancy. The Mersey is narrow and shallow at Warrington, which explains why the Romans built an encampment at Wilderspool, and, perhaps, why Lancastrians and Cestrians ignore it. In Liverpool, the Mersey is a harbinger of the sea and history. Inland, it's an afterthought. Despite this, I slow down and breathe more freely when I arrive on the riverside.

The Woolston New Cut, now an ecology trail, was built to shave off one of the river's great meanders. The vegetation is stinging nettles, docks, brambles, reeds – *Flora lancastriana* that can handle the short, chilly days and that probably flourished even when the waterway was cluttered with chemical works, a tannery and an abattoir. There are railings, puddles and cinder tracks. I catch glimpses of light industrial units on the near bank. When I climb briefly to higher ground, there's a view down to a weir and suddenly the river is bigger and wilder. A huge raft of tufted ducks drift and dabble in the currents below. I pass two stoners sitting on a lump of hardstanding. One leans back into the prickly tangle behind him.

As I arrive at the north bank of the Manchester Ship Canal, I catch the dark rumble of the M6. Warrington sits at the heart of a motorway network as dense as that of Los Angeles. This is partly because James Drake, the man who invented British motorways, was Lancashire's county surveyor and bridgemaster, but it's also a recent iteration of an age-old avidness for logistics. Roman roads criss-crossed here. Some of the world's oldest railways meet near Warrington. The Manchester Ship Canal was the finale to a century and half of building navigable waterways. As I walk, I pass under and over several bridges. I slip by Latchford Locks – one for ocean-going vessels, a smaller lock for barges, coasters and tugs. Across the canal, people's gardens reach the water's edge. It must be magnificent when a large ship passes, a rare occurrence now. A sign says Powder Mill Road, after a gunpowder mill built in 1755 by Liverpool merchant John Stanton, primarily for the slave trade. The sulphur came from Genoa in galleys which were fitted with oar ports to row up the Mersey.

Warrington Town's ground is beside the canal. Like the more successful rugby league team, the football club is known as the Wire or Wires. Wire-making was Warrington's industrial USP. At the end of the seventeenth century, Thomas Patten, whose family had built considerable wealth trading tobacco, sugar and tea, invested in making the lower Mersey navigable to facilitate the import of copper ore from Ireland, Cornwall and Anglesey and the export of brass wire. Demand came from several markets: jute sailcloth, manufactured in Liverpool and Dundee, was strengthened by incorporating wire into the warp; paper could be dewatered using wire mesh; later on, the Davy lamp needed flame-arresting gauze to help prevent firedamp explosions underground. In 1811, Warrington-born James Locker was the first person to use the steam-powered loom to weave wire mesh. During the course of the nineteenth century, four big wire-making firms – Greenings, Rylands, Monks of Whitecross and Locker – became the town's biggest employers.

Wire was used to make pins. It was fiddly work, drawing out the brass wire, straightening it on pegs, cutting it into fixed lengths, pointing them and riveting on the pinheads, made from small spirals of wire. Children of both sexes were employed in pin factories, some starting as young as age five. They worked long hours with few breaks, and suffered from eye trouble and earache, probably caused by the head-shaking equipment; they were beaten if they didn't work and beaten while on the job.

The rugby team was renamed Warrington Wolves in 1997, and you hear Wolves as often as Wires. The old Wire pub was renamed the Wolves. A popular nightspot was Club Wired (a cannabis farm was seized there in 2015). The local FM radio station was called Wire. Now it's Greatest Hits Radio Liverpool & the North West. Locker still makes wire.

Industry is often imagined as glorious, Brunelian, large-scale. Wire is everywhere and unnoticed, essential and critical. Communications cables, power and light, and traps for rats.

I think Warrington is seen as boring by most people, at best. The west Lancashire plain is flat and here it has been mostly paved over. There is neither grinding poverty nor auspicious wealth. Manchester and Liverpool are almost exactly twenty miles to the east and west, respectively. They drain the town's workforce, ingest its disposable income, ignore it equally. But Warrington is a portal between the Cheshire fields and one of the most built-up areas in Europe, and between the South and the North; the fast train to London doesn't stop after Bank Quay. Warrington has always been halfway to elsewhere, a logistics hub long before everywhere else became logistics hubs. Bypasses abound. I've sometimes wondered if it was a sense of constant traffic, in all directions but inward, that turned me into an inveterate traveller.

When I leave the canal at Stockton Heath I'm tired and a little lonely. The murk has condensed into mizzle. The December daylight, never generous, has dwindled. I want to walk quickly through town this time without looking around or thinking too much. Baudrillard writes, 'One of the pleasures of travel is to dive into places where others are compelled to live and come out unscathed, full of the malicious pleasure of abandoning them to their fate.'

This is only part of the truth. I was born five miles north of Warrington. It was the town to which my village, Burtonwood, became attached from 1974, when local government borders changed and it slipped from Lancashire into Cheshire. WA was my postcode. My secondary school was even closer to Warrington than our bungalow. Teachers told us to add 'Near Warrington' to our addresses.

Home is a slippery word. It's a house, a place, a region, a country, a continent. The house in Burtonwood was sold in 1984, but an older brother and his wife still live in the village, as does a life-long friend. It has almost been drawn into Warrington's orbit. The ageing New Town became an octopus, stretching out tentacles of closes and crescents and greying the green belt.

Can you travel so close to home? Isn't travel escape from home? Unlike Baudrillard, wherever I have gone, near or far, I've always expended some time and emotions considering what it would be like to live – and work – and have a cat, and maybe a wife and children – in that new place. Homesickness becomes home-yearning. Briefly, while in Warrington, I imagine the me that never left, living in one of the dark-brick semi-detached houses just over from the Mersey Way footpath, by the hearth, not going for a walk on this cold Saturday. And I think of all the shoppers and idlers as my people. I could have been a stoner on the canal. I remember a song by Firehose I used to listen to with my oldest childhood friend, the one who lives in Burtonwood, and the lyric 'Make your bed a big briar, thorns of chemical wire'.

There's a good reason I'm starting the book in this town. All my journeys began close by, whether holidays, long walks with friends, outings on my Suzuki moped. All my earliest life-changing journeys were initiated at Warrington Bank Quay station, in the shadow of the soap factory. Many adventures ended there.

Warrington isn't just any town. It's all the towns and cities I've been to. The Manchester Ship is the Panama and Suez; the Mersey is the Plata, Mekong, Congo. By the weir I watched a cormorant skimming and a stork rising like an old C-54 Skymaster from Burtonwood air base. The thrum of the motorway. A distant train off to London. The gloom-hued canal, the rushing dirt-coloured river, and the great iron girders and steel spans. History flows through everything.

2
Under the Arches
Stockport

I t's a slow, oft-stopping, twice-changing train ride from Clitheroe, where I live, to Stockport. Forty-one miles. Two hours. A journey across Lancashire's eastern flank, only half the county's length. Northern Rail is fully capable of making it longer. Non-city-dwelling provincials using public transport have had to embrace C. S. Lewis's hopeful suggestion: 'The great thing, if one can, is to stop regarding all the unpleasant things as interruptions of one's "own", or "real" life. The truth is of course that what one calls the interruptions are precisely one's real life – the life God is sending one day by day.'

Possessing no books on Stockport, I thought about taking one about Manchester with me to pass the time. But on flicking through my most recent acquisition, I saw the names Erasmus, Factory and Wilson, and decided: I know that story. Doesn't everyone? Instead I read *Stat*, a little DIY magazine produced by Pete Mercer, which had chosen Stockport as the theme for its tenth issue. Inside was a profile of Maruja, a 'jazz punk, art rock, post-hardcore' trio from the town. It featured a pixellated image of the Stockport Pyramid by Cillian Mcilvenna, whose praxis was to portray buildings as an antidote to 'growing up in the north on the internet'. It celebrated the Luddites and non-urban radicalism. The mag's motto, for this issue, was 'Abolish Manchester'.

The last leg of the journey took me away from Piccadilly on an empty London-bound Avanti. 'Welcome on board. Due to a technical issue I'm unable to do speciality coffees.' We passed the twin colossi of the then-stillborn Co-op Live and Man City's masted bowl, through scruffy greenish belt and into Stockport, or, rather, on to Stockport, as arrival is by means of its mighty viaduct – the great drawbridge between ancient Stokeport, or Stopford, or Stockford, and its brash neighbour.

Towns close to major cities can – especially to outsiders – seem invisible, lost, swamped. Almost 300,000 people call Stockport home, but its history has been overshadowed by Manchester's, its economy made subservient. The vast blob of Greater Manchester has absorbed five hundred square miles of human geography and history. For most drivers on the M60 ring road, Stockport is another turn-off to ignore. Only the viaduct, overhead, declares something significant thereabouts.

Built with eleven million bricks at the dawn of the railway age, it's long and sturdy rather than beautiful, but it adds a dash of drama across the gaping canyon of the Mersey. When you're on it, everything else looks shabby and unplanned, as if the town ran out of ideas after all the bricklaying. When you're off it, down below, it's the thing you most want to look at – but the viaduct flirts, teases and ultimately frustrates, as you never get to see all the span-arches, are unable to walk the length of it, and – worst of all – Stockport council has allowed a firm called Capital & Centric to 'develop' Weir Mill, which translates as: erect a fourteen-storey tower violating the view of the viaduct for everyone else.

L. S. Lowry drew and painted the structure several times. An un-dated, atypical oil, *The Viaduct*, places the bridge low down in the background, along with two rows of terraced cottages and, centrally and larger, a pub, towards which three men are resolutely walking. Sky and land are off-white, frigid-looking, as so often in Lowry's works. Three options face the three men: home, nothingness, alcohol.

Alert to the fact it's impossible to take it in at a sweep, Lowry used it as a backdrop in his 1955 bird's-eye composite *Industrial Landscape*. Even here it shrinks beneath much taller chimneys and a huge slag-heap. The viaduct, along with the elegiac sound of whistling trains, had a brief but pivotal cameo in Tony Richardson's 1961 film *A Taste of Honey*. Jo (Rita Tushingham) tells Geoff (Murray Melvin) she is pregnant. He tells her you can get rid of babies and gives lots of other unwanted advice about the right thing to do and how she'll be judged by others. She bridles, declaring, 'I am an extraordinary person.' Geoff is won round and they run through an arch, as he shouts, 'We're unique, unrivalled, we're bloody marvellous!' The scene is now available as a postcard.

I took a roundabout route to the town centre. Stockport's architecture is a muddle of grand red-brick and pale stone buildings and newer

 where tourists seldom tread

municipal bits and pieces. The Queen Anne-style further education college is big and bold. The porticoed War Memorial Art Gallery, in bloodless Portland stone, is definitely better fitted for mourning than mooching. Stopford House, built in 1975, is clad in deep-grey aggregate precast panels of varying coarseness. It's a slab of a building – cool brutalism for aficionados, I suppose, but standing there alone it looks like a misstep. (Its exterior was used for the police station in *Life on Mars*.) A guidepost on the A6 (which I later find out is listed) reminds me I'm 6½ miles from Manchester and 182½ miles from London. Buxton and Chester are also marked. Stockport tilts towards its Roman past and rural environs. New signage points one way towards the courts, council and police, and in the other to the town-centre shops. I got my first glimpse of the viaduct after fifteen minutes.

Look up at first and second floors in Stockport and you see signs of Victorian attention to detail. It was an important textile town, with specialist mills for hats and silk throwing, some of which survive. The contemporary conformation of shops and roads detracts from the topography, but the town evolved around a ford on the Mersey before it bifurcates into the Tame and Goyt rivers; the flowing waters washed the yarns and cloths and powered the early looms. The confluence is buried away below the M60, but sudden changes of street level and short, sharp brews are reminders of the riverine setting. The most arresting building in the centre is the Plaza, an art deco theatre designed by William Thornley in 1929 and built in 1932–3. The faience-tiled facade is high and flat, echoing the cliff face to which the structure is bolted; two fluted pilasters shoot towards the sky. When I go inside, they're playing jazz and old-time showtunes. The tea-shop-cum-restaurant on the first floor has period decor, gold and green. I am taken aback by the genteel atmosphere and the care taken in the interior's conservation. Originally built as a Super Cinema, the Plaza was a bingo hall for a spell, before closing completely in 1998. A charitable trust and army of volunteers raised £3 million to set in motion a recovery plan. Brenda, a waitress there, told me, 'If it wasn't for the volunteers, it wouldn't be like this. It would be a Wetherspoons probably. I've been here twenty-odd years since it reopened and I started out pulling six-inch nails out of the wall. We've torn up carpets. You name it, we've done it.'

It was 11.40 a.m., so I declined the champagne celebration tea and opted for an ordinary cuppa (with a strainer, milk, no lemon), and smoked salmon with scrambled eggs. The place was fully booked for lunch. Another friendly volunteer, Tommy, showed me the auditorium and the Mighty Compton Organ, with its glass panels depicting a stylised sunburst.

The real sun was out so I skirted the shopping centre. The small stores on the rows at its edges were short stories. Mint Nails, Vape Town, Earful, In & Out: Consuming Passions, Upward Frog. (Only In & Out was shuttered.) The Underbanks, the smart retail area during the nineteenth century, felt medieval. It had the shadows, textures and human scale lacking in twentieth- and twenty-first-century Stockport, and was a little ghetto of hip, cool and independent: a bakery, coffee, barbers' and a speakeasy owned by the Blossoms singer Tom Ogden and his wife Katie. Stairways connect it to the marketplace above. A castle once stood here, high on a promontory. A market has been held in the space formerly occupied by its bailey since the thirteenth century. The wrought-iron structure is a bare-boned beauty. When it boasted only a roof, it was nicknamed the 'glass umbrella'; Ephraim Marks – brother of one of the founders of Marks & Spencer – added walls to his shop to shield customers from draughts. The rest of the market was soon enclosed. Looming over all is Robinsons Brewery on Lower Hillgate, a handsome fortress of ale-making, decorated with a unicorn for the Unicorn Inn that William Robinson bought in 1838. The plant was being wound up. Cranes hovered. Expect a co-work space, apartments, offices or a mix of these. Nearby crept another stairway, Coopers Brow. I took it but was dumped back in the scruffy present so bolted back to the Underbanks.

　　　　　　　　　　　where tourists seldom tread

In Rare Mags I had an espresso and perused the periodicals. Print isn't dead – it's gone underground and upmarket. I bought a tiny booklet by Manchester chronicler Dave Haslam about Grace Jones's visit to Stockport to work with A Certain Ratio (I know, more Manc music myth-making . . .) and – having enjoyed *Stat* on the way in – asked Holly, the owner-manager, to choose me a random read for the train home. She had been installed there six years, so it looks like the business, admittedly quite niche, is working. She says she's fallen out of love with Manchester because 'it's a bit shit'. She means the vaulting skyline, the corporate takeover, the rents, the reality that Stockport is more likely to attract cultural entrepreneurs than Ancoats these days.

The stairways have made me think of two other paintings. Nearby I found Crowther Street, where the steps persuaded Lowry – whose natural tendency was receding flat planes and marionette people in profile – to depict a curving perspective. Even on these paintings, very few of the figures are looking at one another. I photographed the steps before ascending them – momentarily experiencing a sensation of walking into an artwork – to make my way slowly back to the station.

In 1983, Frankie Vaughan released a song titled 'Stockport' in response to a newspaper competition. It's a well-crafted if silly effort (all proceeds went to a charity), with a sub-Sinatra refrain: 'I'm going back to Stockport / There's nowhere that can beat it / That's right, I tell you, Stockport / You want me to repeat it / Well, it's S.T.O.C.K.P.O.R.T / Stockport, Stockport, it's the place for me.'

Was Stockport considered the surest antithesis of New York or Paris, or Phoenix or Jackson, a place name worthy only of derision? The song was recorded at the Plaza by a mobile unit from the local recording studio, Strawberry, owned by 10cc. The same engineers worked with Joy Division and Happy Mondays. A sense of place seeped into both bands' music. The former channelled the dark arches of the viaduct and Lowry's bleached wastelands. The latter's songs evoke the transit and clutter of the town under the hesitant, cloud-chased sun. But that was the seventies and eighties; another town.

Today, Antony Szmierek's 'The Great Pyramid of Stockport' tries to wring meaning from that specific building, and while it's not my kind of tune, it speaks to the randomness of what has happened to Stockport's built environment.

Some Stopfordians say their town is the UK's 'karaoke capital', hitched to a claim by sometime local shopkeeper Roy Brooke, that he had invented a 'Sing-a-long Machine' in 1973. Japan had already developed the concept twice by then, but Brooke's website (mrkaraoke.co.uk) says 'Japan became involved with the marketing of his concept in 1976 and at this time Roy Brooke then "*adopted*" [his italics] the name "Karaoke".' The word translates – appositely – as 'orchestra void'. Twelve pub teams meet every Monday to compete in the Stockport Fun Karaoke League. A well-attended venue is the Blossoms pub, after which the local indie band is named – known for their karaoke-style Smiths set at Glastonbury, fronted by Rick Astley.

Sometimes all modern music sounds like a pastiche of the past. Sometimes I wonder if Manchester isn't a singalong city, plundering musical heritage to cover up its architecture–culture–community voids. Sometimes I wear a hat and silk gloves, and then Stockport really is the place for me.

Abolish karaoke. Raise the drawbridge.

3
Shafts of Shadow
Birkenhead and New Brighton

The other side had always been a great mystery. On visits to Liverpool I could never resist standing at the Pier Head to wonder at Birkenhead. The dark monolith beside the water. The weather-filled sky. The brown, frothing river. Liverpool is not my city, but was always the one closest to home. A familiar place, albeit with frayed edges and strange secrets. Birkenhead was a complete unknown.

I used the tunnels to go west to Wales, and to come home to Lancashire, but never stopped. One evening I caught the ferry to Belfast. We pushed away and I could make out details even with the declining sun in my eyes. Birkenhead's skyline was all towers, domes and spires. Nothing imposing. No architectural statements, but, here and there, buildings with a hint of thoughtfulness, reaching skyward. The ship rounded the corner and there was a beach and a bluff, and soon the Irish Sea took over.

————

Port Sunlight is a shock after a morning on the malevolent motorways, the heaving A41 and a drive past Stanlow's oil refineries, chemical plants, fertiliser manufacturers and uranium-enrichment factory. Then a single left turn and all is calm, easy on the eye, hushed and expansive. The road traffic dwindles to almost nothing. Pedestrians walk small dogs, push large prams. Neat flower beds line grass verges. There's free parking in front of the Beaux-Arts art gallery. Everything feels quite natural – and wholly planned.

The model village, created by William Hesketh Lever in 1888 – when his Warrington site proved insufficient – is named after a brand of laundry soap produced at the neighbouring factory. Lever wanted to create a *rus in urbe* that would win over his workers – an airy, healthful place in which to live and labour, sunny even when the Irish Sea sky was stubbornly grey. As he explained in a 1915 lecture, 'Art and Beauty and the City': 'The picture of a cottage crowned with a thatched roof, and with clinging ivy and climbing roses and a small garden foreground suggesting old-fashioned perfume of flowers, and a home in which dwell content and happiness, appeals straight to the heart of each of us, and there are few that can resist its quiet, peaceful influence for good.' There was a ready supply of hands, river transport, the Manchester Ship Canal was under construction, and there were good roads and direct rail links to Chester and London.

I joined a walking tour that took us along broad, tree-lined avenues with ample pavements, through neat gardens and past bowling greens. Port Sunlight's houses come in numerous styles. Warrington architect William Owen designed the first twenty-eight houses, on Bolton Road and Greendale Road, with a Tudor flavour. He was also responsible for the village's first community building, Gladstone Hall (now a theatre), which opened in 1891. Such amenities were key to Lever's vision. There was a school, hospital, neo-Gothic church and a post office (now the Tudor Rose Tea Rooms, flanked by red K6 telephone boxes). A young Edwin Lutyens adorned four houses on Corniche Road with Venetian windows and hanging tiles. There are turreted Belgian-style houses on Windy Bank and Flemish gables on Park Road. The Arts and Crafts-influenced Bridge Cottage, where Lever and his wife lived for a spell, is a melange of leaded windows, pebbled walls and a grand entrance. Architecture students must be in their element, ticking off jettying, Doric columns, oriel windows, pantiled roofs, diapers, mullions and heraldic touches. Add a flurry of monuments, including a sphinx, sundials, a huge Grade I listed war memorial and the grand obelisk of the Leverhulme memorial, as well as more of the vintage telephone boxes, and sometimes it felt like a Portmeirion-meets-Seahaven fantasy. But ordinary people always lived – still live – in these houses.

Port Sunlight influenced Ebenezer Howard's Garden City movement. William Lever, born in Bolton, spent his later years in Hampstead. No doubt he enjoyed seeing Raymond Unwin's Garden Suburb down the road from his mansion, the Hill. The New Towns reworked some of the same principles. But Port Sunlight is anchored in the collective memory of pre-industrial villages. It's not about newness at all.

               where tourists seldom tread

I spent the night in the former Temperance Hotel, now the Bridge Inn. I had an early night; there's not a lot to do in Utopia come nightfall.

———

I wanted to walk into Birkenhead along the riverbank. Promising signs for a Wirral Circular Trail pointed the way. After Port Sunlight, the late-twentieth-century housing looked drab and the tree-less straight streets unkind, exposed. There had been heavy climate-change rain and the park areas in front of the terraces were sodden. Where the vegetation became unruly, I could hear the whirr of plant machinery beyond the hedges. The footpath eventually took me to the edge of the Mersey. The hardstanding was broken, the holes filled with puddles and mud.

Across the water: Liverpool. It looked, as always, stately and proud – designed to impress. UNESCO withdrew its World Heritage stamp, claiming newbuilds detract from the waterfront's profile. But the city doesn't care, with its monumental cathedrals, Three Graces, the Radio City tower, stadiums, ranks of red terraces. Birkenheaders have this view all the time, the view of the departing ship. But it's nothing less than wondrous to a visiting wool.

Overlooking the crumbling path – which maps say is Rock Ferry Promenade – are romantically dishevelled big houses. They remind me of Havana's mansions, in that they look damp, overgrown, under-funded and perhaps squatted by multiple occupiers. Decline is a kind of revolution, I suppose. Nathaniel Hawthorne lived on this row when he was American consul in Liverpool. His diary captures the area's exclusivity and opulence:

Rock Park, as the locality is called, is private property, and is now nearly covered with residences for professional people, merchants, and others of the upper middling class . . . It is the quietest place imaginable, there being a police station at the entrance, and the officer on duty allows no ragged or ill-looking person to pass. There being a toll, it precludes all

shafts of shadow

unnecessary passage of carriages; and never were there more noiseless streets than those that give access to these pretty residences. On either side there is thick shrubbery, with glimpses through it of the ornamented portals, or into the trim gardens with smooth-shaven lawns, of no large extent, but still affording reasonable breathing space. They are really an improvement on anything, save what the very rich can enjoy, in America.

The decay of these elegant residences is only the smallest change. South of Birkenhead, the Wirral has been filleted by the A41 and the M53. The traffic noise is insistent. The air is rich in particulate matter. At the end of the pocked promenade my way is barred by the Tranmere Oil Terminal. I double back and pass through a housing estate and then, after crossing the car park of a KFC and a couple of dangerous junctions (the Wirral Circular Trail is routinely intersected by major roads), I am in a densely occupied industrial zone: flooring and heating supplies, car-hire enterprises, an aggregate yard, a timber yard, cylinder-gas suppliers, sign makers, maritime services, modular manufacturers for the nuclear sector, Cammell Laird's huge shed, and a new half-a-million square-foot shed under construction which announces itself as the Arc Royal 'cross-docked logistics facility'. It's breezy, with the shore winds funnelled between the large boxy buildings. I'm the sole walker on this side of the chain-link fencing.

The roads pay tribute to ships and shipbuilding. Campbeltown Road. Alabama Way. Valiant Way. Unicorn Way is barred off so I am forced on to the A-road again. Over the bypass is the Rock Retail Park. Packed double-deckers pass, bound for the Cheshire Oaks shopping centre. A riotous roost of starlings tries to drown out the vans and cars in the sycamores outside Home Bargains. On another island is a monument to the Mersey tunnel: a golden drill on top of a charcoal-coloured column. Originally it was a lamp pillar, illuminating the way to the tunnel.

My next right takes me to the ruins of Birkenhead Priory. The monks operated the first ferry service; perhaps Gawain used it to cross from the 'wyldrenesse of wyrale' on his epic journey to the Green Chapel. The priory, with a chapter house dating from the mid-twelfth century, is the oldest building in Merseyside, but looks lost among garages and gyms. Rising up behind are two warships docked for repairs, their clean deathly grey stark behind the time-blackened sandstone.

Round the corner is a sign for the Grand Admiral Miguel Grau Walk, recently opened to mark Wirral's status as Borough of Culture for 2024. Grau is Peru's foremost naval hero, admired for his treatment of enemies as much as his leadership during the War of the Pacific against Chile. The honour is also due to the fact the flagship he commanded, the *Huáscar*, launched in 1865, was built by Cammell Laird.

The shipyard is not the force it was; more ships were built between 1910 and 1913 than have been built since 1975. It was quite an event in 2023 when it was announced the first new Mersey ferry in sixty years would be built at Cammell Laird. It will be the sixteenth Mersey ferry and the 1,395th ship built at the facility.

Along the now well-paved riverside path are extraordinarily bland, cheap-looking orange buildings, housing and offices in the same Lego style. There are signs for HM Land Registry and the Official Receiver. Nonetheless, a sign tells me I'm on a maritime heritage trail, and in the murky brown water, lapping against slimy seaweed-covered cyclopean stone walls, I can divine the reflections of chandlers and ropemakers, stevedores and sailors. There's a model of an ancient submarine, transit sheds behind a high palisade fence, an attraction called the U-Boat Story that's closed for repair. I catch sight of a Midland Railway office building (Birkenhead once had trains to the capital that didn't pass through Liverpool) and the tower of the former town hall with its copper dome on top, my first cupola of the day. There's stencil art above a hard-to-read metal sign laid into the floor about HMS *Birkenhead* and the Birkenhead drill: 'Women and children first!' Two frontages are painted with local celebrities: Glenda Jackson with her two Oscars; Paul O'Grady and his alter ego Lily Savage.

But nothing can compete with the Woodside ventilation tower – the 210-foot high, brown-brick windowless oblong that I have looked at, from afar, more often than any other landmark on the Mersey. Designed by Herbert Rowse and completed in 1934, it's a sublime expression of form meeting function. A system of fans and ducts forces fresh air underground into the two-mile-long Queensway Tunnel and evacuates toxic exhaust gases into the ether where they won't harm humans.

Guy Debord wrote, with wilful imprecision, of the 'beauty of situations'. These have nothing to do with the picturesque and are borne in the unconscious, in a playful encounter of watcher and site, perhaps from the juxtaposition of a ruin and a relic, an industrial site and a palace. The ventilator tower looks like a church – like the Anglican cathedral across the water – or a high temple of some obscure cult. On its front and rear are vertical art deco-style reliefs depicting the same form as the lamp pillar. In this age of repurposing, it looks as if it ought to be, like London's Tate Modern, converted into an art gallery, but it's filled with noisy machinery and filthy fumes. Rowse was influenced by the Expressionist take on pre-Columbian forms he had seen in Dénes György and Nikolaus Menyhért's pavilion for the 1929 Barcelona International Exposition. But he took radical symmetry to new heights. The Woodside shaft won him the 1937 RIBA bronze medal. Rowse built two further ventilation stations in Birkenhead: a twin-towered building on Sidney Street and one at Taylor Street to serve the former Dock Exit, which was closed in 1965. He was also responsible for the shaft-crowned George's Dock Building in Liverpool – also magnificent, but conservatively clad in Portland stone – as well as the Philharmonic Hall and India Buildings. Woodside is his masterpiece. The staid brown brickwork draws the light out of the sky. It is structural engineering as shadow-lith. I touch the building, not out of reverence but because something hitherto seen only at a wide river's distance has become tangible, at last.

       where tourists seldom tread

I walk around old Morpeth Dock, part of the Great Float – the tidal inlet that mirrors the long-since buried inlet in Liverpool. It's bordered with aromatic honeysuckle. I see the top of one of the eye-catching towers I'd spied from the ferry: the Central Hydraulic Tower by J. B. Hartley, son of the legendary dock-builder Jesse Hartley, providing the power to open lock gates and raise bridges on the wharves. It's based on the Palazzo Vecchio in the Piazza della Signoria in Florence. I cross a bascule bridge with a bell attached and make my way into town.

I've read that Hamilton Square is second only to Trafalgar Square for the number of Grade I listed buildings at a single site. In 1825 Scottish shipbuilder William Laird commissioned Scottish architect James Gillespie Graham to build a square of townhouses surrounded by further residential streets as impressive as those of Edinburgh New Town. Sited on high ground above the docks, it was to be visible from the river – and, with opera glasses, from the Liverpool waterfront. Only the square was completed, a slump in British trade leading to recession. Now Hamilton Square stands as a grandiose, unfinished idea that nobody knows how to use. Tenanting the cold, grubby Georgian houses are the inevitable solicitors, financial advisers and property and management companies, but a block away are offices for care charities – rape crisis, men's mental health – Thai massage, Thai cafés, Turkish barbers. One local writer who said he visited Hamilton Square in his youth likened the classical grandeur to a de Chirico painting. Passing bin trucks blow that particular image out of my head. I recall the dull gloom of empty public spaces during the darkest days of the pandemic.

A walk away is a shopping area with an eighties-era strip of outlets, a dead market hall and a bus station painted in Merseytravel regulation yellow. Nothing suggests I should loiter. I use my phone to locate the park. The route takes me down a long, straight jugular filled with more pounding traffic. The cross-streets are long rows of red-brick terraces. Beyond are distant bursts of foliage and a gentle rise in the land. The green, bucolic, wealthier Wirral of the west.

Birkenhead Park, opened in 1847, was the first park to be built with public money. It was laid out by Joseph Paxton, best known for his work on the gardens at Chatsworth House, and offers native and exotic trees, lodges, ponds, rock gardens, serpentine paths, bridges, 'probably' the oldest brick-built cricket pavilion in the world, and a boathouse. American landscape architect Frederick Law Olmsted, visiting in 1850, took ideas from Birkenhead when designing Central Park in New York.

I eat my picnic on a bench. A few Chinese tourists hover around the artificial lake, bustling with Canada geese.

Birkenhead Park and Birkenhead Docks opened on the same day, on Easter Monday 5 April 1847. A few days later the *Illustrated London News* summed up the event as follows:

Birkenhead may fairly be looked upon as of Liverpool lineage and alliance, and having been literally called into life by that leviathan of trade itself in its effort towards finding an ampler field for the accommodation and convenience of its overgrown trade. Birkenhead will now become a sort of chapel of ease for the redundant commerce of the mother port, and probably there is no port in the kingdom, not excepting Liverpool itself, that presents such grand natural facilities. A few years hence, and Birkenhead will become a second Liverpool, launched upon the Mersey; for time was when, at the beginning of the eighteenth century, Liverpool itself, now the entrepôt of all our trade with the Americas and Indies, was simply a fishing village.

In 2024, I can't escape the feeling that the shinier right bank of the Mersey is draining all energy and capital, even at the risk of spoiling itself with artless newbuild. The inner-city hinterlands above the ridge of hills fringing Liverpool are patchily regenerated and certainly not gentrified. Birkenhead is severed from the source in a different way. It's not post-industrial so much as post-civic, post-commercial, post-social. It has degenerated into a concrete desert of warehouses,

       where tourists seldom tread

engineering shops, car parks and roads and railways. Not so much a sister port as a barely seaworthy ship that's drifting away from the mother-city.

———

Seaside memories are passed down with cracked buckets and bendy spades. When I was very little, in the early seventies, we used to have days out in Southport and Blackpool – but my mum always talked about New Brighton. It signified her own childhood, before marriage, work, kids. But we never visited, as if she wanted to protect some memory.

I went for the first time in the summer of 2023. It was a glorious, hot, cloudless day. I was struck by the casual drama of the front: the epic promenade; the castle on the corner, a defence battery built in the 1820s; the sturdy white lighthouse; and the great sweep of the beach, with families and couples and dog walkers enjoying the abundance of space. Across the water, the cranes and docks of Liverpool. From 1900 to 1919, the resort had a tower that was the tallest building in Britain; the views of the Isle of Man and Ireland would have been stupendous. It was demolished but the ballroom at its base, despite fires, survived until 1969; the Beatles played there many times.

Decline came to New Brighton after the war, and ferries to Liverpool stopped in 1971. Martin Parr satirised the place and its working-class visitors in his 1986 show, *The Last Resort*. Buying a split and cod at Perch Fish Bar, I couldn't help recalling his caricatures, but back outside, the light was Mediterranean, and people were friendly, relaxed, happy.

Beside one of the concrete benches built into the sea wall was a blue plaque dedicated to Malcolm Lowry, who was born at 13 North Drive in New Brighton. Unveiled in 2019 on what would have been the writer's 110th birthday, it quotes from his best-known work, *Under the Volcano*: 'The smoke of freighters outward bound from Liverpool hung low on the horizon.' It's a simple line, evoking the pull of travel for someone who feels marooned on the Wirral Peninsula. The theme ripples through his debut novel, *Ultramarine*, along with memories of Birkenhead and Wallasey. Cammell Laird, the Great Float and the Mersey ferry are namechecked, as the young narrator, Dana Hilliot, tries to fit in on his first voyage as a mess-boy on the freighter *Oedipus Tyrannus*. Hilliot is a thinly disguised alter ego. In 1927, Lowry left school to sail as a coal trimmer aboard a freighter bound for the East. He spent the rest of his life travelling, drinking and writing. The narrator in *Ultramarine*, for all the trials and tribulations he suffers as the sensitive new boy flung into the midst of an aggressive environment, emerges from the experience convinced he made the right choice in going to sea; that the human spirit is enriched and made yet more tender, compassionate and good by exposing itself to the elements. However, in *Under the Volcano*, the protagonist, Geoffrey Firmin – an alcoholic British consul living in Mexico – asks, 'What's the use of escaping from ourselves?' Travel and drinking involve self-deception. The poem 'Trinity' reflects on the interconnectedness of place, memory and being:

Imprisoned in a Liverpool of self
I haunt the gutted arcades of the past.
Where it lies on some high forgotten shelf
I find what I was looking for at last.
But now the shelf has turned into a mast
And now the mast into an uptorn tree
Where one sways crucified twixt two of me.

New Brighton is nothing like old Brighton, or any other seaside resort I know. It has a fairground and a few arcades, but I wasn't aware of them. It isn't swamped with tourists and hasn't the estate agents' enticements to turn into a hell of second homes and holiday lets. There are no hordes, no hype. Just views, space to think and breathe. Mum's secret is intact. Perhaps it was a first love, or something inchoate, unconsummated. Or a particular memory of her own mother, who died

                               where tourists seldom tread

when she was young. Or a long walk along the prom was enough to set her dreaming about something other than school and the confines of home. For the Wirral's wide-open north shore is curiously liberating and sometimes the idea of escape is voyage enough.

4
Changing Tracks
Crewe

InterCity

Crewe is not a railway town. It is *the* railway town. Historian Asa Briggs names Crewe, along with Barrow-in-Furness and Middlesbrough, as one of the 'new English communities of the nineteenth century', 'as new as the cities of the British Empire'. Iron, coal, chemicals and cotton would give birth to many such towns. In Crewe's case, a new community would coalesce around transport, around the manufacture of trains and the movement of goods and people.

Most people who have been to Crewe station have never been to Crewe. When I first visited the town I'd been through it hundreds of times, seen it through smeared, smutty windows, in snow and sunshine, to the music of diesel and electric, Sprinter and high-speed train, watched it dwindle in appearance and importance – like someone getting older and losing a sense of purpose. When the trains from Warrington stopped stopping there, I felt almost guilty as we sped through.

In the eighteenth century, there was a village nearby, now called Crewe Green, which evolved out of the settlement of Creu, mentioned in the Domesday Book; the name derives from the Old Welsh word 'criu', meaning 'weir' or 'crossing'. It was part of an ancient parish, Barthomley, which survives in the name of an unofficial service area at junction 16 of the M6.

The Grand Junction Railway Company opened its Liverpool to Birmingham line in 1837 and moved the railway works from Edge Hill in Liverpool to Crewe. An early example of what would become the Crewe-type locomotive, *Columbine*, came out of the works in 1843; the beautiful, glossy black engine, topped by a brass steam dome, is on display at London's Science Museum. The new town grew around the station and engineering workshops. The railway bosses owned and controlled everything. They supplied gas and water, built workers' housing, opened public baths, a library and Mechanics Institute, and endowed and erected a church. The glorious Queen's Park, which opened to the public in 1888, was laid out by Francis Webb, who was both loco designer and builder, and served as mayor, becoming known as the 'King of Crewe'. His Jumbo-class locomotive *Charles Dickens* clocked up more than two million miles powering the 8.30 a.m. Manchester to London, and 4 p.m. return, nearly every day for 20 years.

A grand cheese hall opened – butter and bacon warehouses followed – as did several textiles factories, including Compton's, which made uniforms for railway workers, police and soldiers. It was while employed at the latter that Ada Nield Chew, socialist, author and suffragist, campaigned, by means of anonymous letters to the *Crewe Chronicle*, for fair pay and treatment for women, equal to their male colleagues, rather than a 'lingering, dying wage' and being charged for tea breaks. Her name is inscribed on the statue of Millicent Fawcett that was unveiled in Parliament Square in 2018, but local women want their own statue of Ada right here in Crewe.

Crewe was 'a veritable railway colony', as George Findlay, general manager of the London and North Western Railway, put it. By the 1870s, the town's population had swollen to 43,000; in April 1931, King George V and Queen Mary came to inspect the new Royal Train. From the start, Crewe operated a division of labour with as many as nineteen different trades including: smiths and their strikers; moulders and their assistant dressers and casters; pattern makers and coppersmiths; boilermaking trades of platers, riveters and 'holders-up'; turners; coachbuilders and engine fitters. More than 8,000 locomotives would come out of the works. They were robust and elegant, and named after classical heroes: *Atalanta, Erebus, Fortuna.* Liveries of blackberry black, maroon and 'plum and spilt milk' evoked artistry and affluence; twelve-wheeled dining cars aided passenger comfort and eased digestion.

The tracks were as busy as the workshops. Until 1923, the LNWR was the largest railway in Britain. It had been formed in 1846 by the merger of the Grand Junction, London and Birmingham, and Manchester and Birmingham railways. The main line ran from London

    where tourists seldom tread

Euston to Carlisle, where traffic was passed on to its Scottish partner. Other major lines ran to Holyhead, continuing by mail steamer to Kingstown (Dun Laoghaire) or by company steamer to Dublin or Greenore; to Liverpool; through Manchester to Leeds; to Peterborough; and to Merthyr Tydfil and Swansea in South Wales. At its peak, the company ran a route mileage of more than 1,500 miles. By 1913, just before the First World War, it employed 111,000 people. Serving the backbone of the nation, the LNWR was known as the 'Premier Line'. It could claim the Liverpool and Manchester – where the modern age of intercity transport began – as its origin story. It was the largest joint stock company in the United Kingdom (and for decades the world), collecting a greater revenue than any other company.

The station was the first to have its own adjacent railway hotel, the Crewe Arms. Thanks to a privileged location, close to the Midlands and ideally positioned to distribute trains to the populous North-West, it was as busy as a grand city terminus. In the 1890s, a thousand trains passed through Crewe every 24 hours. Sleeper, freight and Royal Mail trains ran through the night. Many Creweans worked on the railways, in the signal boxes, marshalling yards and sidings, or as drivers and guards. They supported Crewe Alexandra, 'The Railwaymen'. Two of the men assaulted by the Great Train Robbers, Jack Mills and David Whitby, were from Crewe. In Ronald Harwood's celebrated play *The Dresser*, the character known only as Her Ladyship declares: 'I'm sick of cold railway trains, cold waiting rooms, cold Sundays in Crewe and cold food late at night. I'm sick of packing and unpacking and darning tights.' Changing, waiting, shivering. Salesmen, entertainers, students, squaddies, sitting under yellow lights, standing at the lonely ends of platforms, faces sometimes sad, often bored, at times expectant.

Crewe is fixed in the national consciousness.

The wind-down of Crewe Works began in the seventies and eighties. Buildings were razed to create space for a supermarket and houses. The western wall, an immense red-brick curtain that had contained two miles of workshops, was torn down in 2020; it was a potent symbol, for generations of Crewe workers, of the freedom to travel for the masses, service, craftsmanship, history and local pride. A short film inspired by it won a History Channel prize. A large area – formerly the London, Midland and Scottish railway yard – was set aside for the Crewe Heritage Centre.

There, in the company of mainly men and boys, I drove a Class 43 HST, better known as the InterCity 125. I walked through the tartan-moquetted, once-tilting carriages of an Advanced Passenger Train to get to the buffet car, to admire the boxes of No 6 and Embassy Red. For dinner on Wednesday 12 December 1984, the set menu was: asparagus soup, choice of chilled orange, grapefruit or tomato juice, steak and parsley potatoes, coffee and mandarin cream gateau, cheese board and Maxpax coffee with mints. I climbed the stairs to visit two signal boxes – one manned by an ex-banker turned railfan, who invited me to pull a lever and switch the points – and rode on a miniature railway from Spider Bridge, the old footbridge between the works and station, to Forge End, on a track tucked between the West Coast Main Line and a Tesco supermarket.

Inside the heritage centre's large sheds are assorted bits of rolling stock, ticket machines, signage, components only aficionados properly comprehend (such as the Caprotti poppet valve), old bicycles, a bust of Webb, lots of information boards, steam-puffing paintings by Harry Watson, and train sets of assorted scale.

The trainspotter and the model train-constructor embody two distinct modes of fantasy. The former travels by stealing numbers from the sides of engines – be they vintage beauties or modern EMUs – and, in return, lobbing his soul onto the first carriage. The latter, not content with this world, builds a microcosm rich in tiny details, loosely representative of reality but with transport as its core raison d'être. A whole room is taken up by a large train set sited in an idealised North American factory-scape, with snow-covered fir trees, vintage cars and a busy main street; Crewe is represented by a building bearing the

 where tourists seldom tread

name of Mornflake, the long-established local oat-milling firm. All the people are frozen; the only thing that moves, when a button is pressed, is the little train. Verisimilitude is not what we're after here. A Virgin Train will pause for a Mallard or a Rocket, or a grinning Thomas, to pass – not once but a thousand times. The endless circle of loco life. But working engine drivers and guards are often fans, too. Railways excite people in so many different ways. I talked shop with the men switching the miniature points, checking wiring and managing sound effects. They were kindly, gentle people. I experienced a joyous flicker of a memory from childhood when toy-worlds – Hot Wheels, Airfix Motor Racing, Subbuteo, model-making – filled the horizon and entire novels of stories and subplots took place without anything much happening.

All the time, at Crewe, you can hear big, powerful, quotidian trains passing through just a hundred yards away.

The railway company's monopoly was broken in 1938 when the Crewe Corporation Act was passed. In the same year the potato fields of Merrill's farm were chosen for the construction of a shadow factory – removed from the Luftwaffe-luring ports and cities – to manufacture Rolls-Royce Merlin aero-engines. After the war, car production began, turning out dream machines like Bentley Mark VIs and Rolls-Royce Silver Dawns. For some reason, in Crewe, motors of the latter marque were always Royces, never geezer-ish Rollers. Today, the Bentayga and Continental GT are designed, assembled and painted at Crewe. Crewe also happens to be the UK and perhaps global centre of ice-cream van production. New e-vans sell for £142,245. John Cooper Clarke tells a joke about a man who wants a Silver Cloud and ends up with a hula-hoop. I like to imagine a spivvy Cestrian or one of Alderley Edge's millionaire footballers messing up his online order form and ending up driving not a royal blue Bentley but a pink and white Mondial Lusso van, kitted out with Rapida X soft ice cream machine, back to his gated pile, 'Row, Row, Row Your Boat' echoing round the leafy private roads.

I hate cars, most of the time. I love trains – the idea of them, increasingly, and the reality, sadly, decreasingly. In December 2021, the vestigial Crewe Works – part of Alstom – signed a deal to co-produce 54 trains for HS2. In October 2023 Rishi Sunak scrapped the line from Birmingham to Crewe and Manchester; the money was to be used to fill potholes. Labour has not publicly confirmed any plans to build the section to Crewe. In truth, lines north of Crewe, and east and west, are more urgently needed. HS2 was always going to be a siphon into London.

After visiting the underwhelming front of the station, I walked to Crewe. A fair hike: fifteen minutes or so. Crewe was a junction more than it was ever a station for Creweans. There was little need to detrain people close to town. Indeed, given the need for a dozen or so platforms and scores of sidings, and all the expanding works, it made sense to grow the town centre elsewhere.

Crewe has little in the way of listed buildings. The railways bankrolled those that are eye-catching: St Barnabas's, designed by the Lancaster firm of Paley and Austin and paid for by the LNWR; the Gothic Revival tower of Christ Church, built for the Grand Junction Railway in 1877; the last few railway workers' cottages on Betley, Dorfold, Tollitt and Victoria streets – the symmetries are exquisite and clever landscaping has made the streets car-free; the sole surviving manager's house at 47 Delamere Street. A lot of the town centre was at the post-demolition phase of redevelopment. A bus station, a library and the Queensway shopping centre had been flattened and whatever was coming next hadn't made it off the drawing board. Other buildings were boarded up, waiting for the wrecking crews. Large car parks built for newish shopping and fast food units resembled the gaps left by demolition; I don't think I have ever seen an emptier-looking town.

The market hall once warehoused two thousand tonnes of Cheshire cheese. Popular all over the country and especially with the Royal Navy in the pre-railway era, it was manufactured hard enough to be transported by cart and boat. With the coming of the iron horse, it could be consumed fresher and crumblier. There's a small cheese shop in the hall but most people are seated at benches, enjoying ramen, coffee, pizza, kebabs; others are browsing vinyl records or having their beards shaved. The space feels underused, as if the town's general air of vacancy has drifted inside.

Victoria Wood's 1996 episode of the BBC's *Great Railway Journeys* was titled, lyrically, 'Crewe to Crewe'. When I was a regular user of the West Coast Main Line, my trains to London Euston always stopped at Crewe. I thought of it as the end of the North. The announcement as the train shuddered to a stop was an inventory of British towns, unlived lives I might have led: Derby, Nottingham, Stoke, Chester and North Wales, Cardiff, Wolverhampton, Shrewsbury, Wrexham, Edinburgh, boat trains, seaside trains, football specials. And Warrington, Wigan North Western, Preston – services back to where I'd started, place names that sounded stranger with each passing mile. I studied the faces of those alighting to board shorter, folksier trains. People changing at Crewe were hippyish, hirsute, kind, wholesome. The corruptible continued, with me, to the capital.

5

Border Capital
Wrexham

Pistyll Rhaeadr and Wrexham steeple,
Snowdon's mountain without its people,
Overton yew trees, St Winefride's well,
Llangollen bridge and Gresford bells.

Anon, probably a tourist, late eighteenth century

PARTH
Cyfyngedig
Restricted
ZONE
Unrhyw bryd
At any time
EAGLES MEADOW
DÔL ERYROD
Your Space

Regent House of Flowers
Charisma

Wreckers have had a ball in Wrexham. The Victorian St Mark's church, which had a 200-foot spire, was destroyed in 1959. The 1909 Hippodrome theatre/cinema, gutted by a fire in 2008, has gone. A brutalist police station was pulled down in 2020. A mock-Tudor vegetable market was demolished to make way for a BHS, now also extinct. Manchester, Birmingham and Yorkshire Squares, where trading in textiles, hardware and leather from those regions took place, have disappeared; nineteenth-century sources also cite Sheffield and Bradford Squares. In 2022, the old Rhosddu vicarage was removed, despite local protests. An eighteenth-century Moreton pub was cleared to make way for housing, again in the face of local opposition. The 150-stall open-air market (formerly a beast market) was closed to make way for a Tesco. Fewer than half the stalls moved to a new space, which was in turn usurped by an Asda and subsequently Eagles Meadow, a Spanish Steps-themed shopping centre. The mall ousting the mart was merely the latest re-purposing. Old Ordnance Survey (OS) maps show a horse repository at the site. A US army division parked its cars there. All towns have ghost buildings. Augmented reality might one day make past layers simultaneously viewable.

Yet, walk around central Wrexham, as I did in July 2024, and the energy is palpable. I constantly step over and around building sites. Regeneration is rife; city status – granted in 2022 at the fourth time of asking – appears to have attracted investment. The old commercial core – High Street, Town Hill and Abbot Street – is a clamorous, obstacle-strewn mess of machines and men at work. You can't see shut-tered shops for the dust.

Given the above absences, I'm on the lookout for old things, elusive, and allusive, survivors. Bank Street, an alleyway, feels like a secret. Marubbi's Temperance Bar, opened originally at a nearby location in 1896 and at this site since 1936 (warm Vimto is its speciality), stands across a tiny square from a jeweller's that opened in 1932. This will be my breakfast stop tomorrow. The General Market (formerly the Butter Market, for dairy produce), built in 1879 in the area's famous Ruabon brick, faces the rear entrance of a Butcher's Market; the latter's facade is a neo-Jacobean jewel. Workmen are hammering and hewing inside both sites. A row of seventeenth-century timber-framed shops on Chester Street – originally cottages – look semi-rural and refined.

I sometimes wonder if Wales hasn't been too heedful of Gerald's famous prescription – issued principally to himself – that it's necessary to 'give celebrity to a cottage' in order not to disappoint those looking for palaces and temples. St Giles' church dazzles anyone who makes it to Wrexham. Tall, voluminous, richly decorated, built in Cefn sandstone – moodily soot-darkened (perhaps the sandblasters can be kept at bay) – it stands mighty and magnificent on the top of Town Hill. St Giles' would impress in a carefully conserved Italian city. In Wrexham it is immense, and a powerful reminder that the town was Wales's largest in the seventeenth and eighteenth centuries. The ornate wrought-iron gates to the churchyard lie at the end of a side street off the main shopping drag. One minute: New Look, Nationwide, Chequer's Cocktail Bar and Figo's Pizza Palace. The next: glory and death, art and eternal life. I rest on a bench. British towns are short on both tranquillity and fee-free places to sit; St Giles' churchyard is soothing and solitary-friendly.

Entombed nearby are the remains of Elihu Yale – misspelled Eliugh – of university fame. American-born, he could trace his ancestry to Plas Grono, a country house near Wrexham. His name is celebrated in the local Wetherspoons. The ersatz pub chain follows the same formula wherever it lands: buy a building that would impress Pevsner; rename it after a local legend; serve cheap ale at all hours and offer catering along pub-grub lines. No music. No familiar bar staff. No meetings with strangers. Yale was governor-president of the British East India Company in Madras (present-day Chennai), where he amassed a vast private fortune through dubiously acquired diamonds, while trading in slaves. Celebrate that, Wetherspoons!

There are further examples of ecclesiastical prominence. The two Gothic standouts are the Roman Catholic cathedral by Edward Welby Pugin (his only building in Wales) and the Ruabon red-brick Presbyterian church by William Beddoe Rees, with its distinctive belltower. A glassy Methodist church on Regent Street might seem at first glance lost – it's sited above a row of shops – but strikes me as thoroughly modern. Shall I buy a pasty or take steps to enter paradise?

A grand High Victorian Gothic archway on Hope Street leads nowhere. Commissioned by Scottish-born engineer William Low, it was the turnstiled entrance to the Art Treasures & Industrial Exhibition of North Wales, held in 1876. Similar art shows were mounted in Dublin and Manchester to advertise local wealth and cultural sophistication. One highlight was made locally: the Wrexham Tailor's Quilt by military master tailor James Williams (*c*.1818–95) of 8 College Street. The pieced composition depicts biblical scenes – Adam naming the animals, Jonah and the whale, Noah's ark with a dove bearing an olive branch – as well as Thomas Telford's Menai Suspension Bridge, a Chinese pagoda and the Cefn Viaduct, complete with a passing steam train. Where the glass-and-iron exhibition hall once stood is now parking bays and the backsides of shops. A relief and plaque inside the arch remind us Low, who had a wealth of experience in mining, drew the first plans for a tunnel to France; it didn't get beyond geophysical studies, but Low's twin-bore concept was adopted in the eventual Channel Tunnel.

The Soames Brewery Chimney, erected in 1894, stands stranded at the foot of Yorke Street. Industrial towns were once forests of chimneys. The few remaining are, if not beautiful, bracing and suggestive; they soar away from the flat boxes and twisted road networks of now. The Nag's Head, nearby, started brewing here in the 1830s and was later used as a boardroom when Soames was merged into the Border Breweries.

Drink has long been important in Wrexham. 'Lager Town' was its nickname for years, adopted as the handle for CB radio users. At one time there were nineteen breweries. In his richly detailed memoir-cum-cultural history *Real Wrexham*, Grahame Davies refers to the Owain Cyfeiliog literary society which used to meet at the Belmont Hotel, a local pub. The only work to survive by Owain Cyfeiliog aka Owain ap Gruffud ap Maredudd (*c*.1130–97) is 'Owain's Drinking-horn'. Regarded as a classic, it toasts bravery, camaraderie and the dead:

Fill the horn with foaming liquor,
Fill it up my boy, be quicker;
Hence away, despair and sorrow!
Time enough to sigh to-morrow.
Let the brimming goblet smile,
And Ednyfed's cares beguile.

According to George Borrow, who travelled through Wales in 1854, the only Welsh Wrexham inhabitants had was 'cwrw da' – good beer.

I visited a dozen pubs and there were another dozen I might have tried. Town pubs each have their own atmosphere, hanging like a second sign over the doorway: the Heavy Drinkers; the Would-Be Bohemians; the Conspirers; the Lost and Lonely. I'm not a lager drinker but I made an exception. In 1882, two German-born entrepreneurs based in Manchester, Ivan Levinstein and Otto Isler, decide to try to recreate the lager taste they were missing in their adopted homeland of tepid bitter and flat mild. They chose Wrexham to make use of the River Gwenfro's fresh water and exploit its hillsides to ease construction of underground cellars where fermenting ale could be insulated from external heat. Pilsener-style lager likes a cold environment. The temperature proved harder to control than they expected and the beer was tainted. The initial business failed but another German immigrant, Robert Graesser – who had established a chemical works at nearby Acrefair – came up with a solution using mechanical refrigeration. As locals were used to warmer, darker ale, the Wrexham Lager Brewing Company concentrated on London and the export market. Wrexham

               where tourists seldom tread

Lager was sent to Australia, Bermuda, Brazil, Ceylon and China and quaffed on ocean liners operated by the White Star Line – including *Titanic*. When Lord Kitchener entered the city of Khartoum in Sudan in 1898 a stock of Wrexham Lager was found in the deceased General Gordon's palace.

The only architectural vestige of the enterprise is a somewhat Tyrolean building on Central Road, now home to a financial-advice firm. The Wrexham Lager brand was reborn in 2011. I had a bottle at the Ty Pawb market with a beef and ale pie, and a pint of draft with a chicken bhuna at Indian restaurant IJazz. I can vouch for its authentic lagerness: refreshing, acidic, forgettable. It always was. That's why the local Temperance Society approved: 'The Wrexham Lager Brewery has been successful in producing a light, pilsner lager, which not only refreshes, but acts as a tonic in cases of weak digestion and is almost non-intoxicating.'

My sense of the frontier between my Lancashire/Cheshire homeland and North Wales was largely defined when I was very small and taken on holiday to Rhyl, Colwyn Bay, Prestatyn and Llandudno. Runcorn Bridge was 'the border', as far as I was concerned. Wales was less exotic than exciting, connected principally with the sea, beaches, chocolate milk and chalets. I was not yet ten, but my narrow view of Cymru was similar to that of the adults ferrying me: a land of leisure, consumption, rest and general unseriousness. Centuries of disrespect, verging on disdain, have led to a chasmal lack of imagination in the English attitude to its ancient, quasi-foreign neighbour – not so different in essence to the ignorance and arrogance shown by 'Americans' for América [*sic*].

Wrexham is unpackaged Wales. It is an archetypal border town, lying east of parts of England and Offa's Dyke. The city is seen, from both sides of the frontier, as the poor piggy in the middle of Shrewsbury and Chester. It stands apart, with fields on all sides and hills and mountains to cross to reach other Welsh conurbations. From Cardiff it takes longer by train than London. I drove the A483 Swansea to Manchester road many times when living in south-west Wales a decade ago. I never considered pausing at Wrexham. It was the kind of place you bypassed.

Yet the border town of Wrexham was also once a centre, a nexus, an industrial crucible. There were coal and iron ore in Ponciau, Rhos and Llwyn Einion, limestone quarries at Minera, charcoal from the woods around Coedpoeth and waterpower from the Clywedog. By the late eighteenth century, the Bersham ironworks – recently taken over by Cumbrian John 'Iron-Mad' Wilkinson – ran night and day, turning out state-of-the-art cannon parts and steam-engine cylinders. Wilkinson sank his own coal mines and expanded operations to Brymbo Steelworks. Myths whirled around him: he discovered coal tar and coal gas; he founded Wilkinson's Sword; he built the Iron Bridge in Shropshire. None were true but he was a legend to the locals who worked for him and the many thousands who clocked on in later generations.

Industry and armaments often overlap. Pillboxes and remnants of random defensive structures festooned with vegetation litter the area chosen for Wrexham's Royal Ordnance Factory. Rail networks and a ready supply of labour made it a natural choice for a factory producing cordite for shells. Part of the area was used subsequently to build the UK's second-largest industrial estate and largest prison, HMP Berwyn.

The Racecourse Ground looms above Wrexham General station. Manager Phil Parkinson's face is daubed on a fence outside the Turf pub. Street art idolising striker Paul Mullin covers the gable wall of the Fat Boar. Shop windows showcase themed T-shirts. A painting of Rob McElhenney in the style of Kate Winslet's nude drawing in the 1997 movie *Titanic* hangs at the Tŷ Pawb gallery. It was given to him on his forty-seventh birthday by Wrexham AFC co-owner Ryan Reynolds. Amid the road tearing-up and building work, hoardings on Henblas Street declare that the Ryan Rodney Reynolds Memorial Park is under construction – apparently a gift from McElhenney to Reynolds for *his* forty-seventh birthday. This is where the Hippodrome cinema used to stand.

Football would seem to have given Wrexham a new sense of identity, of importance, of mattering to the wider world. The Disney+ series *Welcome to Wrexham* is unwatchable, at least for a neutral. It is not about the game. It isn't about Wrexham. It's about two celebrities having bro-fun through the commodification of football and its supporters. Vast amounts of lip service have been paid to the show, including by erudite locals, out of gratitude for 'putting Wrexham on the map' as well as reviving the ambitions of the long-struggling club. But I can't shake off the feeling that the relationship, for all its putative positives, is ironic and whimsical. There's plenty of circumstantial evidence. *Deadpool* is a parody of a Marvel superhero; the TV-subservient, money-obsessed English football league is a parody of sport; the American celebrities are parodies of genuine football fans. If you want to think about how Americans see Wales, then think about how you see America. They hold the telescope the other way round; Wrexham is a quaint and quirky dot on a twee green landscape far, far away.

As Terry Eagleton wrote in the *Guardian* in 2010, 'Modern societies deny men and women the experience of solidarity, which football provides to the point of collective delirium.' Like carnival, church, Roman circus and gladiatorial arena, football strokes tender scars in the human soul. It triggers so much that has been lost, shrivelled, debauched, ridiculed. Eagleton's chief argument is that all this wizardry is at the service of capitalism and populism. 'Football these days is the opium of the people, not to speak of their crack cocaine . . . Nobody serious about political change can shirk the fact that the game has to be abolished.'

Or reformed. Or amateurised. Or something. The prominence of football across the UK is a devastating sign of a pan-national lack of hope, a fixation with a mono-sport, to go with the mono-agriculture, mono-high streets, mono-politics. Headlines like 'Club Necaxa's backers purchased 5% of Wrexham AFC in April 2024 and both owners, in turn, purchased a minority stake in Club Necaxa' should freak fans out for their deadpan surreality.

But the town's footballing past is woven into so much else. For most of its history, Wrexham was one of only four Welsh clubs in the English league. It kicked above its weight in cup encounters, beating First Division titans Newcastle in 1978 and Arsenal in 1992. Thanks to successes in the Welsh Cup, it routinely qualified for the European Cup Winners' Cup. The club, formed in 1872, is one of the oldest in Wales. The Racecourse was a major venue for soccer internationals until Cardiff's Millennium Stadium supplanted it.

Mitchell and Kenyon, the Blackburn moving-picture pioneers, shot one of the oldest international football encounters when they filmed Wales vs Ireland in 1906 at the Racecourse. Four of the eight goals scored (in a 4–4 draw) were recorded for posterity. Claims this is the oldest extant soccer film in the world are wide of the mark, but they may have captured the first football injury on film, when an Irish striker collapses after apparently pulling a hamstring in his right leg.

Wrexham Museum is being refurbished to house a national football museum and a new space for its local history collections. The working name for the project is 'Museum of Two Halves'. Let's hope the non-footballing "half" doesn't get hoofed to the margins. Perhaps the curators can reclaim the beautiful quilt – currently at St Fagans, Cardiff – to remind visitors that history is multi-faceted, interwoven, full of patches and strands.

Waiting for the train home on the platform at General station, I noticed the word 'hiraeth' on a window, painted there by artist Sophia Leadill as part of an artist-in-residence project. Somewhere between hiraeth's grief and longing and the aggressive hype of the football-crazed present lies a more interesting, time-skewing story of a town morphing into a city, of ruins mingled with regeneration, of lager fantasies and vaulting church dreams, of dead miners and opera (and folk) singers.

In 1998, Wrexham offered itself as home for the new National Assembly for Wales. But Cardiff got the Senedd, along with everything else. Wrexham and its region were not chosen as sites for the founding

                    where tourists seldom tread

constituent colleges of the University of Wales. There is no National Museum outreach in the town. The BBC chose Bangor for its North Wales headquarters despite the far larger population in the north-east.

At the 2007 National Eisteddfod in Mold, Flintshire, the late historian John Davies observed,

There is a tendency – in the south in particular, but also perhaps in the north-west – to consider the north-east to be a rather detached part of Wales, or, indeed, to be more of an adjunct of Merseyside than an integral part of the Welsh nation . . . The region has not had its share of Welsh institutions, not because it is an unsuitable place in which to locate such institutions, but because we in the rest of Wales have connived in the region's marginalisation.

He pointed out that the first written evidence of any area of Wales is Tacitus's account of the Roman attack upon the Deceangli/Tegeingl, who lived between the Dee and the Clwyd. The large military camp discovered in 1975 at Rhyn Park, ten miles south of Wrexham, indicate the scale of the Roman preparations and the degree of resistance they were expecting.

Davies added: 'The Eliseg pillar in Llangollen; the constant toing and froing between the Kingdoms of Wales and England in this part of the world during the Middle Ages which helped define what we today know as modern Wales; the home of Owain Glyndŵr – this all before even thinking of the huge role the area and its people played over the last five hundred years.'

Borderlands are porous, tense, contested. Glyndŵr was most fully alive waging war on these fringes. Wrexham, where mountain meets plain, stone abuts brick, accents and languages merge and meet, is hard to define, to summarise, to pin down. Borderland vagueness is sometimes perceived as non-place. Wrexonians are not considered as Welsh as West Walians or North Walians, or even South Walians, as if distance from England or proximity to the sea or to the recently crowned capital city intensifies nationhood. But Wales was birthed at and from and through its border – in acts of resistance, bloody battles, hill forts and the earthwork of Offa's Dyke. Wrexham can't be disappeared by those who disdain its chronic in-betweenness any more than it can by those who swing the wrecking ball.

6
Black Country Rocks
Wolverhampton, Walsall and Dudley

It had appeared over night.
A black shadow on the scrub,
galloping above the gates
of the derelict factories

From 'Black Country' by Liz Berry

The Black Country is as vaguely comprehended by outsiders as it is passionately intuited by insiders. Motorways – most people's introduction to the region – are linear, raised or culverted, avoidance mechanisms, even as they knife through the heart of a place. The centre of Birmingham is hard to place at speed. Its satellites are confusing up close. Trains, entering from all angles, ascribe names to the blur at their stations: Snow Hill, Shirley, Four Oaks, Bilbrook. Bucolic towns, specious suburbs, neither, both?

Wolverhampton is my 'in'. Approaching from the north by rail, it's where the green turns grey, though not unrelentingly. A canal, sidings, riotous quantities of buddleia, garish splashes of graffiti. I see one of the region's signature equestrian sculptures, cantering across a platform. Liz Berry's giant black horse, rising from shallow coal outcrops and deep belonging, is its poetic analogue.

There's drama and romanticism when you're on the move, perhaps rooted in childhood. Nothing was more exciting to the young Wystan Hugh Auden than a train ride through the West Midlands' industrial landscape of smoking chimneys and huge warehouses: 'Clearer than Scafell Pike, my heart has stamped on / The view from Birmingham to Wolverhampton'. A seriously built-up area will produce different emotions in different people at different times. I live in a set-apart farmhouse; I've not been out for two weeks. I can feel my shins twitching.

Wolverhampton became a city in 2000. It looks like it's been one for much longer. It has imposing civic buildings, a substantial railway station, a capacious multiplatform bus station. It has an Afro market, a Punjabi sweets shop, Caribbean restaurants, a Polish deli, an Asian grocer's, a Ukrainian church. My first stop is the Spanish-sounding Posada, a proper city pub. I've been told the Black Country still drinks mild – the man behind the bar tells me he bought a keg for some discerning CAMRA chaps, but they had two halves and never came back, and he was left with a drink no one wanted. Perhaps I'm not in the real Black Country yet? T. E. Lawrence drank at the Posada while based in Wolverhampton, where he was overseeing the assembly of a new batch of RAF boat engines at Henry Meadows Ltd. He called the town 'squalid' and a 'cess-pit' – his lodgings were allegedly bug-infested – adding that it had 'the worst mannered local press of my experience!'

Across the road is the city's art gallery, which has the UK's largest Pop Art collection outside London. Curator David Rodgers began collecting in the late 1960s, when the style was new and controversial – and pieces affordable. Parts of the media thought he was squandering public money, running stories with headlines like 'Gallery Bid for Pants Picture' (Richard Hamilton's *Adonis in Y fronts*) and '£1,800 Up In Smoke' (Peter Blake's *Cigarette Pack*). Rodgers was called 'a rebel leader of the arts'. Clearly, he was a visionary. I spend an hour all by myself with several dozen lurid, vital works, including a 1964 Warhol oil, *Jacqueline*, and one of his Campbell's Soup screenprints, Roy Lichtenstein's *Purist Painting with Bottles* (1975) and Pauline Boty's tender portrait of Marilyn Monroe, *Colour Her Gone* (1962). Captions by local LGBTQ+ residents give the exhibition a queer slant.

The genius of Pop Art was to turn dross and ephemera – promotional posters, magazine covers, press photos, packaging – into something lasting and worthy of attention. It revealed context by removing it, made the dully familiar unignorable. It's user-friendly, unlike much conceptual and abstract art. Patrick Caulfield's 1971 painting *Tandoori Restaurant* – in shades of turmeric and saffron – truly belongs here in the West Midlands.

A temporary exhibition is devoted to design in football. Another crowd-pleaser. Molineux Stadium is five minutes' walk from the gallery and Wolves' team colours and Marvel-style wolf badge are all over the room. Displays mix vintage shirts and local memorabilia with ancient leather balls, managers' set-piece routines, goalkeeper gloves and old blueprints for new grandstands at Anfield and Arsenal.

Messi's shirt is framed behind glass, as are Lauren Hemp's boots. An unintentional second Pop Art space – and a lot busier.

Wolverhampton's motto is 'Out of darkness cometh light'. The Black Country was once 'the workshop of the world'. A platitude and a cliché hiding so much soot and noise, suffering and graft. Areas had specialisms, as did genders and age groups. There were women chain-makers in Cradley Heath, Sandwell. Children started making nails from the age of seven. Wolverhampton was known for its keys, horseshoes and locks (the Chubb Building is a prominent landmark), as well as grease, beer and kitchen furniture. Japanning (adding a decorative black lacquer finish) was a huge trade. A cabinet on the first floor of the gallery is filled with exquisite brooches, belt buckles, rosaries, buttons and pendants made in Bilston, once a powerhouse of decorative enamel production. It was also home to houseware brand Beldray. Out of darkness came beauty, and piles of ironing. In the same room is a small but arresting group of Black Country landscapes. Edwin Butler Bayliss's canvases are smoke, smudge and shadow; most figures have their backs to us; none have eyes or mouths. Robert Perry's *Synthetic Chemical Factory* (1989) keeps a safe distance from the flaring toxic emissions. A 1977 photograph by Nick Hedges shows a works football match, with tiny human figures playing under the looming Bilston steel plant.

Ed Isaacs, a retired Wolverhampton council-housing officer who has reinvented himself as an urban sketcher, meets me for a coffee in the gallery's smart café. He shows me drawings of Lidl stores, branches of Greggs, parked cars, landfill sites, street furniture, tubing and piping and the esoteric bits of infrastructure that jut out from weeds and behind railings across any town. In his faithful renderings of surfaces and straight lines are depths and fissures, human and geographical. He calls his late-life vocation 'obsessive markmaking'. There's an evolving tradition of West Midlands New Impressionism; the works of Isaacs, Tom Hicks, David Rayson and George Shaw make you want to walk to see the actual places, as Monet-worshippers go to Rouen or Van Gogh fans to Arles. Pop Art again – the familiar, seen afresh – splicing neatly with the boom in urban and suburban hiking. I share a brief saunter with Andy Howlett and Fiona Cullinan from Walkspace, a cooperative of artists and creatives that undertakes everything from gentle strolls to 'hardcore psychogeography' in a bid to transform the way West Midlanders look at their surroundings. We chat until we come to a monolith in West Park. It's a glacial erratic, which travelled here from North Wales on an ice sheet. The group's public walks map the points where these are found; anything to fracture the sprawl and make the ignored visible.

There are buses plying the six miles from Wolverhampton to Walsall but the train is more fun – it performs a great loop around the region, passing through stations in Smethwick, Tipton, Birmingham, Oldbury, Aston, more besides. I ride on it a few times and begin to feel quite at home – always a turning point in a stay in a new town.

———

I was never a smelly, grebo, greaser or headbanger, though I occasionally performed the thumbs-in-the-belt-loops, elbow-winging dance with other ten-year-olds at village-hall discos. In my teens, I preferred self-conscious indie music and the middle periods of Reed, Pop and Bowie. One of the latter's least-typical early-seventies songs is a filler on *The Man Who Sold the World* titled 'Black Country Rock'. It's a heavy, bluesy number, a nod to the honest, rocking, big-guitar sound of the West Midlands. The origins of Black Sabbath, Led Zeppelin, Band of Joy, Napalm Death, Godflesh, the drumming third of Emerson, Lake and Palmer, Roy Wood and the Move, Chicken Shack, ELO, Cloven Hoof, can be traced directly to the region. The rock heritage in turn can be sourced in the banging and clanging and general sonorousness of the small workshops that powered the industrial revolution in these parts – as contrasted with

   where tourists seldom tread

the mega-mills and mass-production-oriented mines of the north. Boulton & Watt steam engines, made at Smethwick, were not much used locally. This simple fact explains the famous sprawl. It also, arguably, makes West Midlanders more independently minded and self-sufficient than the factory-processed drones of Lancashire and the West and South Ridings of Yorkshire or the suited, soft-skinned ciphers of the capital.

The name of Walsall, like that of Walby, Walton and Wales, derives from the Anglo-Saxon word for 'stranger', or 'foreigner'. It was once the 'valley of the Welsh'. There is something of the outsider in all rockers. As fashions have changed and sped up, folk, reggae, Northern soul, ska and two-tone, New Romanticism, British Bhangra and techno have come and gone, sweeping up a generation, at most – but heavy rock and metal, and to a lesser extent prog, have endured. Legends from the sixties still decorate the back panels of de-sleeved denims on Black Country high streets.

Walsall's origins as a settlement lie in the Middle Ages, when loriners (saddlers' ironmongers) fashioned equestrian items such as stirrups, bits, buckles, spurs and harness mounts. They were the first to exploit local ores, including high-grade iron, coal, charcoal and limestone. Leather-cutters, especially bridle-makers, tapped the obvious synergies by setting up in the area. The trade grew steadily and boomed in the nineteenth century. With the arrival of the motor car, leatherworkers switched to travelling bags, hatboxes and wallets. Hobby horse-riding in recent years has rebooted the saddlery sector. According to *The Field*, Walsall 'has more saddlers and leather goods makers than any other place in northern Europe'. Walsall FC are known as 'The Saddlers' (and are currently managed by Mat Sadler). The art of manufactured leather wearables extended to humans. On the back of the loriners' long contribution to local commerce, there was also a thriving metalworks sector, producing nails, pots, pans and locks. Foundries opened to produce rivet iron, pig iron and steel plates and bars for heavy industry.

Over on the Beechdale Housing Estate, the dreams of young men like Rob Halford and Noddy Holder were filled with the harsh noises and hellish soot and a different kind of leather – studded, black, zip-filled, tasselled, shiny. Slade were softer and more commercial, turning out masterpieces like 'Pouk Hill' and the plangent seasonal classic 'Merry Xmas Everybody' (Hodder penned the lyrics in his childhood bedroom after a night out at a Wolverhampton pub). Judas Priest, Halford's band, were the ultimate Walsall leather-clad metalheads. As Halford sings on 'Deal With the Devil', his origin-story hymn, 'Forged in the Black Country / Under blood red skies / We all had our dream to realise'.

We tend to decode towns through maps, guidebooks, texts, photographs. Walsall can perhaps best be approached aurally.

Like Wolverhampton, Walsall is home to an impressive art collection. The New Art Gallery was nominated for a RIBA Stirling Prize in 2000; its workmanlike exterior belies the warm interiors (panels of Douglas fir, leather handrails on the stairs). I listen to my Black Country playlist while wandering through its rooms. The exhibitions (supported by workshops and residencies) are dashingly eclectic, riffing on the subjects that matter here: class, belonging, identity, queer and trans culture, disability, the South Asian diaspora, West African connections, eco-activism and local creativity. The gallery is the resting place of the Kathleen Garman collection, a mini-Tate of European masterpieces and sculptures by her husband, Jacob Epstein. So transfiguring is the space – briefly, sickeningly, threatened with closure in 2016 due to public funding cuts – that you wish it could spill its contents out into the wider world. I discovered Turner's watercolour *Clitheroe Castle*, a humble fortification close to my current home, and *Rain Over Dartmoor* by Yasmin David, Garman's niece. When I lived in Totnes, prior to Clitheroe, I often escaped to the western flanks of Dartmoor, to walk in the filthy weather she renders so well. Seeing your homes in art galleries allows you to check in on memories.

A window between two paintings shows me Walsall's new canal-side developments, framed like a work of contemporary hyperrealism. 'Ron Next Door' by Ron's Neighbours – an eighties band that draws together many of the region's musical strands and splices them with a spoken word field recording of a voice, Ron's, in the mellifluous local accent – fills my head and I am intoxicated, deeply content and everywhere at the same time.

————

Duncan Edwards's powerful tree trunk of a right leg swings back, ready to kick the ball into the rain, down the hill. Model player, paragon of Black Country respectability and imperturbability, a 'real-life Roy of the Rovers' (so said Terry Venables), and pre-telly, his myth is as surely set as his bronze quiff. He didn't grow old, turn sour, turn to drink. In Dudley a road and a leisure centre are named for him, and the church of St Francis's stained-glass windows depict him protected by a saint and a crusader. In *Best and Edwards*, his remarkable book about footballing fame and tragedy, Gordon Burn quotes Robert Musil: 'There is nothing as invisible as monuments'. Despite the Edwards statue's prominent location on the edge of Dudley's market square – it's the first thing you see when you climb up from Birmingham Road – only ageing Man U pilgrims and tourists like me pause to admire it.

Around a few market stalls offering clothes, potted plants and fresh veg, sellers or shoppers – I can't tell which are which – hang around chatting. The centre, in the permadrizzle, is hard to appreciate, but at its edges are patches of lawn and some fine buildings: the red-brick, neo-Georgian town hall and coroners' court by Alexander Harvey (who designed housing for Bournville model village) and his nephew and partner H. Graham Wicks; the turreted former police station next door; a handsome Eros who has already shot his arrow; the deco-influenced Fountain Arcade, dated 1925; the stately Saracens Head pub. A dead museum and art gallery was once a school of art that counted talented 1930s painter Percy Shakespeare among its alumni.

A 'sports bar' called the Old Glasshouse occupies a Victorian fire station. I see a lean, unkempt cat slink out of an alley across the road from the bar. It, too, looks of another era. Dudley is a patchwork of palimpsests: 1880s, 1930s, 1980s.

Overlooking the town is the limestone lump of Castle Hill, wooded and crowned with a ruined fortification. It's managed by a zoo, which would be a dead-cert destination for its twelve concrete animal enclosures by the Modernist Tecton Group, led by Russian-born Berthold Lubetkin, were it not for the caged animals. I spy Cecil B. DeMille crowds of children being siphoned into the zoo entrance. One day the hill and park will be returned to Dudley and the town will be connected up with nature, and not for twenty quid a head. Everyone will have a broad view of the West Midlands. Maybe the alley cat can sleep in the polar-bear pit.

A tramline is being built to connect to Wednesbury, whence to Birmingham, for jobs and shops and fun. I don't mean to be mean, but the rain – driving at times – and the unloved shabbiness of Dudley, casts me downward. The town looks islanded by retail parks and dual carriageways. Non-stop traffic grumbles past out-of-town motels, fast-food outlets, supermarkets and gyms. If most things are 'out of town' – an impression I can't shake off in parts of the Black Country – doesn't that make out of town, town?

There's a solution, a way out. Canals already do what light rail promises for the future. After a heavy shower that indicated the front had rained itself out, I set off to find an entry point. My route cuts through the leisure-oriented lowlands, and a reels-of-film sculpture dedicated to film director James Whale, placed there presumably because of the Showcase multiplex next door. The son of a blast furnaceman, Whale worked as a cobbler before studying at the art school in the dead museum, becoming a cartoonist and stage manager. Whale's 1931 *Frankenstein* established horror as a viable commercial genre, and was the first to depict the monster as a monobrowed blockhead with bolts through his neck. It made Boris Karloff a star, and he and Whale would collaborate on subsequent spinoffs.

I have no plan for my canal walk, but, knowing the M5 lies to the south-east, decide that will suffice as a destination. The noise levels dip as soon as I step on to the towpath and behind a wall of chaotic shrubbery. More than five hundred miles of canals criss-cross the West Midlands, built to link up industries and get goods to market. Dudley had coal and limestone mining, iron, steel, engineering, glass cutting and textiles. The town made cranes, chains, anchors (including the 16-ton centre anchor for RMS *Titanic*), nails, fire grates, anvils, vices. A lot of this has gone — elsewhere, out of fashion, to the dogs — but office workers and journalists should hesitate before they glibly pronounce on post-industrialism. As I walk along the canal I hear plenty of clangs and bangs and inhale regular drifts of noisome fumes.

I meet few co-walkers. One or two joggers. Only one holidaymaking narrowboat passes, navigating with care through reefs of duckweed, lily pad and water fern. Spying a snack bar behind a palisade fence, I make a detour and find myself inside a religious site: the Shri Venkateswara (Balaji) Temple was built in the nineties on the site of a disused farm and a former tip. The impressive granite gopura (pyramidal tower), adorned with stone carvings, takes inspiration from a mother-temple in Tirupathi, in south India. At the on-site canteen I enjoy a delicious dosa.

Sunshine and poppies emerge as I continue my walk. The other arresting landmark on the walk, forty minutes after the temple, is the underbelly of the M5, thundering and massive at ship's mast height above the quiet canal. Girders, anti-climb meshing, maintenance scaffolding, graffiti and warning signs: heavy traffic is thrilling when you're not trapped in it. I will revisit the M5 the following evening to have more fine Indian food, at the Vine in West Bromwich, one of the original desi pubs. But I have one more date to keep in Dudley.

I always expect to dislike theme parks, especially of the cleaned-up heritage-touting variety. But the Black Country Living Museum catches me in just the right mood: tired, a bit lonesome, or perhaps just fed up of the twenty-first century. Its displays range from 1712, and a Newcomen engine, to the interior of a semi-detached house decorated to represent 1968. The gas fire, plastic settee, floral wallpaper, Rothko-esque living-room carpet, drinks trolley and Dansette record player in a box belong to my childhood. Next door's interior is from the forties. The houses, built of cast iron, date from 1925, and were brought here from the Brewery Fields Estate. A mid-nineteenth-century leaning cottage was trans-located from Gornal Wood. Nearby is a replica of Lea Road Infant Welfare Centre, Wolverhampton. I browse the vintage chocolate bars and yellowing *Daily Herald*s in the corner shop. I have a pint of mild and a ham cob at the Bottle and Glass – originally sited beside the Stourbridge Canal – which has bay windows, bare benches and an open fire. It's an ersatz pub, with museum opening times, but the beer makes me nostalgic – but somewhat in the 'revolutionary' manner articulated by Walter Benjamin and Fredric Jameson. The museum's assemblage of periods and outlets feels political: a localist mini-universe, preserved to provoke.

Away from the residential and commercial, I pass a mine en-trance, chat to a cod-aluminium foundry worker and spend quarter of an hour learning about steel traps at a workshop relocated from Wednesfield. Four generations of Sidebothams made traps for killing rats, rabbits, bears, dingoes and lions. Stencils for the shipping crates show how global, and imperial, the commerce was: Natal, Bathurst, Buluwayo, Hobart, Stanleyville.

Labour without accidents, sweat, work, noise, fumes, injustice. Too clean to be true. The Living Museum's timeline is 1712–1968: the industrial revolution's early start and a pot-luck year for its end. I exit, stepping back into 2025, in a hazy, wondering dreamlike state, thinking someone should send Best, or Beckham, or Ronaldo, to fetch that ball.

———

                    where tourists seldom tread

Professor Kathryn Moore at Birmingham City University wants to turn the Black Country and the wider region around England's second city into a national park – but without changes in land ownership or the imposition of stringent conservation regulations. She believes it's time to get over our obsession with 'green and blue' – fields, fells, lakes, seasides – and treat areas holistically.

'This idea of a "national park" is not just about the natural environment. It's about the topography and the geology and everything in between, including what humans have done to the West Midlands over the millennia, including the industrial revolution. It's all about how identity and culture are shaped by landscape.'

The maps produced at the West Midlands National Park Lab remind us that, between residential, commercial and industrial zones are urban parks, waterways and a patchwork of environments – from heathland to pastoral settings to wooded areas, including Shakespeare's Forest of Arden. At the margins are areas evocative of the ancient shires absorbed by the metropolitan county of West Midlands in 1974. Beneath the tons of asphalt, concrete and steel are the contours of river valleys and hill ranges, overlooked when we speed through in a car.

'The whole area is a rolling upland plateau, watershed and river basin,' says Professor Moore. 'It was only when I began to draw the maps that I realised that there is an immense river valley between Birmingham and the fringes of Coventry, where the River Blythe runs before joining the Tame along with the tributaries of the Rea and Cole before flowing into the Trent, which goes to the North Sea. It's such a vast landscape that has been hidden away and largely ignored for so long you just don't notice it.'

I like the idea of national parks ceasing to be parcelled-off elsewheres. The Peak District, Brecon Beacons and Exmoor are not a short drive away. The people of South Wales, Derbyshire and Somerset will have to exert a little effort to visit the Black Country – where the blackness is now buried underfoot, and the countryside slowly gaining ground.

The playlist

'Deal With the Devil' by Judas Priest
'Inner City Life' by Goldie
'Far Far Away' by Slade
'Paranoid' by Black Sabbath
'Love Missile F1-11' by Sigue Sigue Sputnik
'To See the Walsall Aces' by Walsall Fans
'By Any Means' by Jorja Smith
'On With the Motley' by Frank Mullings and the British
    National Opera Company
'Sometimes It Snows in April' by Amar
'Ron Next Door' by Ron's Neighbours
'Black Country Woman' by Led Zeppelin
'Black Country Rock' by David Bowie
'Karma Chameleon' by Culture Club

7

Vagabonds and Chartists
Newport

And when I'm passing near St Paul's,
I see, beyond the dome and crowd,
Twm Barlum, that green pap in Gwent,
With its dark nipple in a cloud.

From 'The Mind's Liberty' by W. H. Davies

At low tide the Usk, spied from the train, is a forlorn ditch, a poor sort of border after the magnificence of the Severn Bridge and the Black Hills. Then I consider what the river has seen, and suffered, on its long journey from Y Mynydd Du at the western end of the Bannau Brycheiniog National Park. The Usk, the longest river entirely inside Wales, has the highest incidence of phosphates in the country due to agricultural run-off, industrial effluent and human and animal waste. No amount of spring water can dilute that surfeit of poison.

Newport, too, has been bullied, sullied, smoked, dirtied and dumped on over the centuries. It was once the seat of a Marcher lordship, from Proto-Indo-European *mereg* or Latin *margo*: margin, boundary, edge. A medieval ship was found buried in the west bank of the Usk in 2002, probably built in the Basque region and plying the lanes between Wales and Portugal. A castle was built by Hugh de Audley, 1st Earl of Gloucester, on top of an earlier Norman motte. Its remains are more or less discarded beside the main B4591 road and the railway bridge.

Above this rises the town, a mess of grandish Victorian and lumpen modern. My French-owned chain hotel on Upper Dock Street occupies the tallest building, known, laughably, as the Chartist Tower. Opposite is a humungous, vacant Debenhams store, which opened in 2015 with considerable pomp and much hubris, and closed just six years later. A needy poster, pasted all over the cliff-like walls, says, 'Bring This Space To Life'.

I admire the upper floors, parapets, cupolas and ostentatious chimney stacks of the Victorian retail and office buildings at the junction of Commercial Street, High Street and Skinner Street. At ground level is a sculpture dedicated to the Chartist Rising of 1839: *Unity, Prudence, Energy* by Christopher Kelly. A man and woman carry a maquette of Newport – they are bearing the conquered city, after a Roman tradition – accompanied by dancing children. A man with a sickle and a head-bowed figure in an overcoat stand back to back, between them a wheel and other symbols of industry. A sad-mouthed angel rises above recumbent or dead bodies. A bird perches on a pile of tomes. It's a busy allegory, and quite lost in the dead winter light and with plastic shopfronts on all sides.

From here, Commercial Street shoots south, dead straight, for seven hundred yards. I walk its length, pausing to photograph another curious statue – this one of, or inspired by, poet and vagabond W. H. Davies. Born in Newport in 1871, his father died when he was three, his mother remarried, and he was raised by a prim puritanical maternal grandmother and beer-swilling grandfather, a former mariner. In 1893, at the age of twenty-two, Davies set sail for New York. He travelled around America and Canada as a hobo, hopping on and off moving trains to get around – and I mean hopping, as he lost a leg while on his way to get rich in the Klondike. Dreams of gold turning to dust, he eventually returned to Britain.

The Autobiography of a Super-Tramp narrates his falling in love with freedom, with US railroads, with fellow panhandler Brum, and with cattlemen (as they were known before they were branded 'cowboys' by Hollywood). He labours on ranches, goes berry picking, overnights in boodle jails – where hobos could sleep for a small fee – and is invited to 'drink after drink with bewildering succession' by backwoods miners, come to town to squander their earnings. 'Teetotallers lack the sympathy and generosity of men that drink,' he writes. His exposure to the wilds makes him alert – and vulnerable – to the seasons. 'The greatest enemy to the man who has to carry on his body all his wardrobe, is rain'. Ultimately it turns him into a poet. Davies, not given to pontificating, sums up his tramping days and the words borne out of them briskly: 'Such has been my life, rolling unseen and unnoted, like a dark planet among the bright, and at last emitting a few rays of its own to show its whereabouts, which were kindly received by many and objected to by a few.'

Davies's poem 'Leisure' contains the famous line: 'What is this life if, full of care, we have no time to . . .' The answering statue, *Stand*

                                        where tourists seldom tread

and Stare, is a bronze sculpture evoking his freewheeling, independent spirit, loosely rooted to a tree of life, with two birds ready to fly with him when he next takes off. As I try to find an angle for my photograph, there's commotion behind me. A security guard has pounced on a woman, who has come off her bicycle. He removes a bag of shoplifted goods from her person and, when she appeals, returns her phone. Newport is full of people who look hard up, out of touch, stoned, lost. Doss-house hotels open on to shopping streets. I see people in dressing gowns in the afternoon. Davies would have felt at home.

I walk into an area called Pillgwenlly. The name is a compound of 'Pîl Gwynllyw' ('Gwynllyw's Pîl' in English). Gwynllyw was a Welsh king, warlord and livestock raider. It sounds, properly pronounced, a bit like 'gwinthloo'. Its corrupted English form is 'Woolos' and the echo is also there in Gwent. A 'pîl' is a localised topographical feature (found along the shore of the Bristol Channel, from Pembrokeshire and into Somerset) indicating a tidal inlet or narrow seawater creek, suitable as a harbour. Old maps show a pîl jutting in along the course of today's Lower Dock Street. Everyone calls the area plain Pill. It was one of Wales's earliest multicultural quarters. Six boarding houses, conveniently close to the docks, hosted Jamaican, Liberian and Sierra Leonan sailors. Some stayed.

I see Black faces, African food outlets and murals of local heroes. One shows a retired policeman, known simply as PC Val, who was a community police officer for more than thirty years. Another is of Pill's sometime carnival queen Alexia Cuthbert. There were race riots in the area after the First World War. The murals were vandalised in 2022.

At the end of the street is Newport Transporter Bridge, built in 1906 by Ferdinand Arnodin, the French engineer who pioneered these stupendous cableway structures. It is immense. I'd like to get right below it. But I'm tired after a long rail journey and lots of walking. Roads raging with cars block the way to the foot of the bridge. I turn and follow the Usk back to the Capitalist Tower, escorted by noisy seagulls, oozing, opalescent mudbanks, more bridges, submarine power lines. The HMS *Ajax* anchored here for the final time after being mauled by the mighty *Graf Spee* during the Battle of the River Plate. Today the river is empty as well as brown and sad and mucky-looking.

Newport's golden age, which was mainly black- and grey-hued, was the industrial period, when it rose to become one of the most important places in the nation for the exporting of coal and smelting of iron. As early as 1521 a writer described it as follows: 'The said town of Newport is a borough and a proper town and has a good haven coming into it, well occupied with small crays [merchant ships] where a very great ship may resort and have good harbour.' Newport was well placed to trade with Bristol and the inland port of Bridgwater. In the 1790s the Monmouthshire Canal was dug to bring the increasing amounts of coal, iron and limestone from Crumlin and Pontypool to the riverside. Docks were built from the 1840s and greatly expanded over the years. In 1914, Newport shipped more than six million tons of coal a year.

Granted city status in 2002, it is still a sort of industrial centre, now making tiny things such as semiconductors and microelectronics. A former coal magnate's mansion is occupied by Celtic Manor, the mega-sized golf hotel that looms over the M4. Here, the chipmaking managers come to drive and putt.

Newport Museum and Art Gallery is part of a new development, the Kingsway Centre. The museum section contains thousands of years of artefacts, from stone axes and an aurochs skeleton to pinned butterflies and stuffed birds to mangles and a Suffragette banner, and, as sometimes happens in such places, I am almost overwhelmed. I take refuge in the art on display, which includes *The Home Front* by Stanley Lewis (1905–2009), who was educated and later lectured at Newport College of Art. The painting is unfinished, the portraits of

 where tourists seldom tread

firemen, firewatchers, hospital doctors and nurses left uncoloured-in or as rough sketches, because Lewis was called up to do military service. The work was a propaganda commission, partly subverted by its proto-Pop Art elements.

The gallery proper, on a different floor, has mainly modern and contemporary pieces. As my gaze flits between portraits of the rural landscape and factory villages, I wonder if I now see a cluster of squashed terraces or a well-designed iron bridge through idealising lenses, as someone in 1924 might have viewed an agricultural scene from 1824, or 1724. Is lost-industrial the new fake-rural? But Terry Jones (1938–1992) – another Newport-educated painter and teacher – didn't let his work slip into idyll-ism. His *Death of the Town, Blaenavon* (undated) shows an unpeopled, smoke-less, traffic-less main road. Primary colours suggest shopfronts or paint jobs meant to cheer, but blue links the brooding hills, the rooftops and the window through which a sad-looking woman, seated in a chair, stares out. The central subject is a telegraph pole, cutting the painting in two as it might an artless amateur snap. In 2000, Blaenavon Industrial Landscape was inscribed as a World Heritage Site by UNESCO.

Finding the perfect pub, as imagined by Orwell, is a fool's errand. But the perfect pint is a matter of timing, luck, beer and intention. Ye Olde Murenger House isn't as old as it looks and feels – the building is early nineteenth century with much more recent mock-Tudor make-up on its facade – but inside it has the conspiratorial gloom of an era when inns were used for plotting insurrection. The barwoman calls me 'lovely' with every pint and payment. Four times in a too-short hour. I try not to think of Windsor Davies or sentimental Cliff in *Look Back in Anger*. But a simple endearment can banish evil. The Murenger hums with calm, mainly male conversation on this early evening at the end of February. Themes: London, rugby, women. I sit among but apart from the small groups, on a wooden bench at a table beside the frosted-glass windows, half reading a book about the

Newport Rising. A pint is a sacrament. My phone is off. Time to focus on the written word, while the beer slowly blurs and binds.

Chartism – the first mass movement driven by the working class – rose out of bitter disappointment with the 1832 Reform Act. The rotten boroughs were removed. Industrial towns were given MPs. But the right to vote depended on a substantial property qualification; only one fifth of adult males could vote, and women were barred. In 1838, the London Working Men's Association drew up the six demands of the People's Charter: a secret ballot, votes for all men over twenty-one, payment for MPs, equal-size constituencies, no property qualification for MPs and annual parliamentary elections. Skilled orators like Henry Vincent and John Frost (born in his father's Newport pub) educated and won over colliers and ironworkers. Vincent's arrest was followed by outbreaks of violence. Frost planned a march on Newport on 4 November 1839, where the Chartists planned to demand the release of Vincent. The authorities in Newport heard rumours the Chartists were armed and planning to seize the town. The mayor had 500 special constables sworn in and troops were mustered; thirty-two soldiers of the 45th Nottinghamshire Regiment of Foot were at the Westgate Hotel where the Chartist prisoners were being held.

At least four thousand (some sources say more like ten thousand) Chartists marched on Newport. A map in the museum – somewhere between the cider press and the Roman floor mosaics – shows three fronts converging from the Valleys, led by William Jones from Pontypool, Zephaniah Williams from Ebbw Vale and Frost from the Sirhowy Valley. Men walked in from Argoed, Crumlin, Merthyr and other towns. The soldiers were few but had superior firepower. Shots were fired by both sides in a fierce battle lasting just half an hour. Between ten and twenty-four Chartists were killed and upwards of fifty wounded.

The three leaders were arrested, tried and sentenced to be hanged and quartered; their sentences were reduced to transportation to Van

Diemen's Land. Frost returned in August 1856. He was greeted by a thousand well-wishers as he stepped off the Bristol packet. He spoke to the crowd from a window of the temperance hotel in Llanarth Street, saying that he still held the same opinions as seventeen years earlier and that he was determined to work for the radical reform of Parliament. He is Newport's great hero. The museum stands on John Frost Square. There used to be a Chartist mural on a walkway nearby, but it was destroyed by the council in 2013 to make way for the Friars Walk shopping centre – this despite a petition signed by over four thousand people damning the 'cultural vandalism'.

A shop-cum-meeting place at 170 Commercial Street called the Newport Rising Hub keeps the story alive, organising an annual festival every November and selling 'radical tea towels', tote bags, posters, T-shirts, graphic novels and sober history books published by Cardiff-based Six Points (named for the six points of the 1838 Charter). I bought *The Chartist Rambler*, by David Osmond, about the oft-overlooked preacher, bookseller and baker William Edwards, who was adored by the people of Monmouthshire and hugely influential in Newport's Chartist movement, but ended up being jailed for sedition and burnt in effigy by his former supporters. He was called a madman, a raver and a 'vagabondising, levelling, infidel, radical demagogue,' who sought to 'turn the world upside down'. The Hub, a flash of colour and insurgent enthusiasm in a strip of vacant shops, has most certainly brought its space to life.

I stopped to see the bullet holes in the porch of the Westgate Hotel, just a few doors along, still discernible almost two centuries on. The Newport uprising was the last armed confrontation inside Wales. On the ground were drops of blood from a recent skirmish.

Across the Usk lies Caerleon, home to Neolithic, Iron Age and Roman sites. The earliest legends of King Arthur place the seat of his kingdom not in Camelot but here. The landscape and its mythic–historic potency influenced author Arthur Machen (aka Arthur Llewellyn Jones), born in Caerleon in 1863. He worked as a journalist, magazine publisher, amateur historian and actor, but is best remembered as an author of fantasy and horror fiction, influencing a motley mix of artists from Arthur Conan Doyle to Jorge Luis Borges to the Fall's Mark E. Smith. Like other gifted fabulists of the uncanny, his fantastical writings hover at the ragged edges of history and reality.

In *Far Off Things* (1922) he claims only natives can relate to the countryside. 'As I think that the pure provincial can never understand the quiddity or essence of London, so I believe that for the born Londoner the country ever remains an incredible mystery. He knows that it is there – somewhere – but he has no true vision of it. In spite of himself he Londonises it, suburbanises it; he sticks a gas lamp or two in the lanes, dots some largish villas of red brick beside them, and extends the District or the Metropolitan to within easy distance of the dark wood.' Memory, assailing him while in the capital, flings Machen's thoughts homeward to 'deep silence, deep stillness everywhere; hills and dark wintry woods growing dim in the twilight, the mountain to the west a vague, huge mass against a faint afterlight of the dead day, grey and heavy clouds massed over all the sky.'

But in *Things Near and Far* (1923), London is granted its moment: 'And it is utterly true that he who cannot find wonder, mystery, awe, the sense of a new world and an undiscovered realm in the places by the Gray's Inn Road will never find those secrets elsewhere, not in the heart of Africa, not in the fabled hidden cities of Tibet.'

This line can be seen as the birthplace of British psycho-geography. Wherever we are, we can be anywhere and everywhere.

Arthur Machen and W. H. Davies met for lunch in Newport in 1937 to celebrate the former's seventy-fourth birthday. Drifter Davies and mesmeriser Machen, sharing stories of travels astral and real, on the banks of the primordial river.

                              where tourists seldom tread

A new charter

1. Replace the House of Lords with a house of the people composed of elected experts.
2. Introduce proportional representation.
3. Parties must put forward candidates with demonstrable ties to their constituencies.
4. Make the apparatus of government – including parliament – mobile; relocate the entire civil service outside of London.
5. Introduce a universal basic income; MPs will be paid the UBI and undertake no other paid roles during their term of office and for five further years thereafter.
6. Corruption or crime of any kind will lead to the ejection of representatives from their MP role as well as their party.
7. Voting will be compulsory.

8
Tin Cry
Redruth and Camborne

Archive
Library
Exhibitions
Come on in, the
café is open!

'The industrial revolution was born here,' says the plaque outside the old Barclays bank in Redruth. 'Gas lighting was invented in this town, the steam engine developed in the nearby mines.' Derbyshire, Lancashire, the West Midlands might quibble, but Cornwall deserves its chapter in the origin story.

Today the county is heavily sold to the British public as surfing, seaside, second homes, art, dining – anything but toil, filth, ideas and innovations. History is packaged as romantic fiction. Winston Graham (born Winston Grime in Manchester) used mining as the backdrop to his *Poldark* saga, but glinting seas and galloping horses stole the show in the small-screen adaptations. It is the lovely littoral people come for. When tourists head inland, they go to Jamaica Inn and the Eden Project – fictive history, neat and tidy nature. On the week I travelled down to Cornwall I received an email from a PR firm for a pricey hotel, or rather, 'an eco-inspired sanctuary nestled' at Mawgan Porth, launching a Restorative Sleep Break: 'The carefully curated package is designed to allow guests to re-balance and rest by drawing on ancient Ayurvedic principles and the healing power of nature.' Everything in Cornwall has been intensively *curated* for the consuming tourist.

Mining turned Redruth into an important, wealthy town. It has grand houses and old shops. A local community-centred campaign 'Looking Up' is about creativity and mental well-being, but is also an invitation to raise your gaze to handsome first-floor frontages. Both sides of a street called West End are taken up by a sprawling emporium that was once a draper's. The current tenants are a house-clearance store, a tattooist's and a gig venue. The shopfront has been preserved, with curved glass and elegant gold capitals against shiny black. A £6 million heritage-focused regeneration is afoot, with an upgrade of the old Butter Market as its centrepiece.

I walked around Redruth trying to imagine miners tramping around the alleyways, but it was daytime and dry and bright; historical fantasy is always easier when it's gloomy. Street art depicting 'Tinner's hounds' and a bronze miner with arms splayed like a scarecrow served as putative prompts, but mining was always hidden and apart, buried away, and this municipal memorialisation felt wanting. St Rumon's Gardens, inside the remnants of an ancient chapel, was like a tiny cloister: walls draped in moss and ferns bursting out of every broken stone. Across the road was Fairfield Park, with dull mown lawns, discarded beer cans, a low zipline to nowhere and blackbirds not in the mood for singing.

It began to rain. I walked over to Kresen Kernow, the county archive for Cornish history and language, installed in a former brewery. Marking the tenth anniversary of the Cornish being recognised as a national minority were displays of tapestries, photographs of Cornishmen in brass bands, hurling and 'wrasslin'', and lots of documents, including recipes for stargazy pie and hevva. The latter gets its name from the clifftop lookouts or 'huers' who helped fishermen find shoals of pilchards, calling out 'Hevva!' ('Here they are!') to alert the boats. Tradition says hevva cake – made with lard, fruit and sugar – was baked by the huers to welcome fishing crews back. The pilchards went into the pie.

Upstairs were treasures: tiny leatherbound books, a late-seventeenth-century manuscript of an account of the Cornish language (already dying out by then) by William Scawen. It includes the anonymous poem 'The Passion of Our Lord' (*Pascon agan Arluth*) – thought to be the oldest surviving complete text in Cornish – in the original and in Scawen's translation. There was an old map, and a ledger used for recording duties paid and shipments, containing columns of miners' names.

Cornish mining is said to date from as far back as 2000 BC. The Phoenicians sailed to Cornwall to trade for tin. Possibly. The Romans knew about it. It's not known where the Tin Islands (or Cassiterides) in classical accounts were precisely located. Maybe Camborne or Galicia, or Brittany. Somewhere in the Celtic fringe. In the western outposts, sources, and connections, are tenuous.

　　　　　　　　　　where tourists seldom tread

There's no Bronze Age without tin. No pewter, no solder. A soft silvery metal with a bluish tinge, it makes up two parts per million of the earth's crust, which makes it four hundred times more common than gold. When a cold tin bar is bent, the atoms cause a crackling sound. This is the 'tin cry', which, pushed, can lead to a breaking. Warm it and it's silent and pliable.

The borders of Cornwall were determined in 936 when King Hywel, of the ruling dynasty of Cornouaille, and Athelstan of Wessex agreed on a frontier at the Tamar, but the peninsula was of scant value to anyone till the mines began to give up their riches.

King John's 1201 Tinner's Charter marks the first serious attempt to regulate the industry. The payment of coinage (tax) at stannary towns like Penzance, Helston and Truro was obligatory. The Royal Duchy, created in 1337, had a stannary parliament which had a power 'equalling that of Westminster'. But while stannary law imbued the Cornish people with a spirit of difference and even independence, it was conceived to ensure the Crown extracted its portion of the county's wealth.

———

How like a thing of magic hast thou rose
Out of the Copper-caverns of the earth;
How like a thing that leaped into existence at a nod
Art thou, my native Camborne!

John Harris, miner and poet (1820–1884)

Camborne's terraces are grey and squat. Their facades, of snecked rubble, add character and look as you'd expect miners' houses should look. Civic palazzi, also in stone, hark to times of pride and prosperity. The old library, built by the locally renowned architect Silvanus Trevail, is a bold beauty. Outside stands a statue of the inventor Richard Trevithick, holding a model of a steam locomotive and a pair of dividers. A Wetherspoons occupies an opulent Italianate former

Market House. It faces off against two other pubs on the same corner: Tyacks Hotel, owned by the St Austell brewery, and the White Hart, which looks like the football pub and used to be 'notorious', according to the local press. The boozers are busy enough, I suppose, though some local lads prefer to buy their beers – tinnies, no doubt – at Poundland. The local bus is called the Tinner. Pied wagtails are called tinners because they nested in mine shafts.

The religious buildings are large; miners and their widows often sought help from above. Camborne's sole Grade I listed building is the parish church, dedicated to St Martin and St Meriadoc and said to have an impressive marble reredos. It was always locked when I tried the door, morning, afternoon and evening. Its graveyard is old, overgrown and lovely. Two of the Methodist temples still do their original job, while the third, an Edwardian Gothic pile on Trelowarren Street, is a branch of Costa. I had a coffee there. The inside was churchily peaceful, the only other customers half a dozen deaf people signing over their lattes. The Cornwall Deaf Community Centre is based in Camborne and is the only such meeting place in the county. The town has become a hub for the deaf and hard-of-hearing communities.

Most shops were on the same street: vapes, nails, crystals and incense at a store called Xanadu, Deano's kebab house, Lost in Music for DVDs of classic gigs, a tanning salon, pasty shops. A few years ago, I was asked to be a judge at the World Pasty Championships at the Eden Project; a dream assignment for me, though the day was almost spoiled when it ended with a bite of a pasty containing the world's hottest chilli pepper. In Camborne and Redruth, I ate three large pasties over three days. All were traditional peppery confections made with swede, potato and skirt steak, and uniformly delicious. After the last one, I felt puffy, peaky and heavy-limbed.

Camborne's heart lies underground. Just beyond the big Tesco – which stands on the former site of Holman No.1 Works, responsible for much mining engineering – was the great mine of Dulcoath. The sett was originally worked for alluvial tin in the 1580s. By the 1720s, copper was the focus. Richard Trevithick – father of the inventor – was chief engineer in the mid-eighteenth century, considered the 'best informed and most skilful Captain in all the Western Mines'. The copper was worked out by the opening decades of the nineteenth century and closure threatened, till mine captain Charles Thomas deduced that tin would be found deeper down. A mine that had started giving up metal ore at 300 feet was eventually drilled down to ten times that depth. On 20 September 1893, seven men died when a 600-foot-deep pile of waste rock fell on them at the 412 level – 412 fathoms, almost half a mile underground. When Dulcoath was stripped and mining operations ceased in 1920, there were seventy miles of underground tunnels – the rock had produced 350,000 tons of copper and 80,000 tons of tin. It's now owned by a Canadian firm which runs nearby South Crofty.

A mile and a half to the south of Camborne town centre, the King Edward Mining Museum occupies what was once one of the best-known mining colleges in the world. It was a working mine, with tin production offsetting most of the teaching costs.

Here I read how ever-improving steam engines – from Newcomen through Boulton & Watt to Trevithick's – allowed mining to become more efficient. Safety fuses designed by Camborne resident William Bickford saved lives. Engineering wizardry removed water, enabling deeper mining, and aided with the crushing of rocks. All around the area is the Great Flat Lode, an enormous, lens-shaped body of mineral-bearing rock that produced over ninety thousand tons of tin concentrate. In mining, 'flat' is relative. The ore is often hacked off vertical stopes but here they lie between 10 and 45 degrees. Ladders and, later, ingenious man engines were used to transport miners underground. Copper and tin were extensively mined, but there was also lead, nickel, zinc, arsenic and tungsten. Geological maps simplify the story, with primary colours and demarcated regions denoting rock types and ores.

The work of obtaining ore was hellish, men working with picks and shovels, bones and muscles. The tribute system of wages meant they earned a percentage of the production. Incomes fluctuated wildly. Women on the surface, known as bal maidens, 'dressed' the ore – breaking it up and separating what was saleable from the dross. They worked as waggoners and whim-horse attendants.

Pull and push migration impacted this corner of Cornwall profoundly. During a slump in the 1820s, skilled miners left the county to rehabilitate abandoned mines across South America, work lead deposits in Wisconsin and Illinois, and copper and lead deposits in Norway and Spain. They mined copper fields in South Australia and Michigan in the 1830s and 1840s. They took with them technology and expertise. Without the Cornish engine, deep-lode mining in California after the 1849 gold rush would have been considerably delayed. Cornishmen took football to Mexico; miners working for the Compañía Real del Monte y Pachuca founded the Pachuca Athletic Club in 1901. David Ager, a volunteer guide at the museum, told me, 'Around the world about seven million people have Cornish ancestry – a greater proportion of Cornish people left than left Ireland'. Many never came back. At the end of the nineteenth century, 90 per cent of the mines closed. Alluvial tin in Malaysia and mines in other British colonies provided cheaper metals.

The last room at the museum was filled with large, primitive-looking and ear-splitting machinery. David switched on a series of contraptions that separated the tin powder from rock and let me hold a reassuringly heavy ingot of tin rescued from the wreck of the SS *Cheerful*, which sank off St Ives in 1885. Some museums kill things, blunting our perception of history. This one shone a light on mining.

David gave me a map of the Great Flat Lode trail, a 7.5-mile path for walkers, cyclists and horse riders that takes in a dozen or so mining sites. It was an up-and-down walk, with a few short, steep climbs.

Miners would have tramped these paths before descending hundreds of fathoms inside the hills. The OS map showed lots of farms, their field edges dotted with shafts, chimneys, mines and disused quarries. The word 'wheal' – Cornish for 'workings' – recurred in place names.

Every mile or so I came to a ruined engine house. The lofty, slender buildings look like homes for skinny giants, especially where the chimney stands intact. Once they would have lain at the centre of thronging, pounding industrial sites, with counting houses and offices, and carts to shift the spoils and ore. Later tramways and railways were built, linking port, foundry and mine. They are now cloaked in ivy, providing roosts for corvids and surrounded by fields full of horses. At South Wheal Frances was the skeleton of an entire mining complex, as haunting as a ruined cathedral.

At Wheal Buller, beneath a television mast and a lonely house-less chimney, I was able to see the sea and the radar golf-ball at RAF Portreath, once used for stockpiling chemical weapons. A sharp drop and a zigzagging path took me to the summit of Carn Brea, occupied from the Neolithic era and the largest hill fort in Cornwall during the Iron Age. There's every chance mining was practised here four thousand years ago. I clambered over marshes and tugging bramble to reach the granite tors. Close by were a castle-folly and the Bassett Monument, a ninety-foot Celtic cross honouring Francis Basset, scion of the family that owned the mineral rights at Dulcoath and anti-slavery advocate. He was created a baronet for building defences to protect Plymouth from raids by Spanish and French forces in 1779.

From this vantage I could see the A30 and the Great Western Railway (which simultaneously developed mineral and tourist traffic around the turn of the twentieth century), as well as Redruth, Camborne and Pool, the settlement that lies between the two towns. Over South Crofty's headgear flapped the flag of St Piran. Synonymous with Cornwall and mining, it represents the white tin as veins against black rock.

Below the hill was Tregajorran, where Trevithick Jr was born in 1771. I arrived where I started, hot and tired. I had burned off perhaps two of the three pasties.

I drove home via the coast. It seemed rude to come all this way and ignore the beauty spots. Hell's Mouth was heavenly on a sunny morning. Emerald sea. Glowing gorse. I sat around, walked awhile, watched the fulmars. Three women with southern accents dashed past me with poles, talking non-stop. I was thrown a 'good morning' like an unearned tip. Looking inland I could see the TV mast, Carn Brea and the hills that held the tin. You could, walking the national trail, be blithely unaware of mines and work and the past. But if you stare hard you might spot the tallest of the chimneys, thin fingers pointing at the sky.

————

Cornwall is England's Costa Brava, its Koh Samui, its Rialto Bridge. It has turned over its energies to the mass production of leisure experiences for holidaying consumers, tourists content to leave Cornish history and culture hidden underground. Asa Briggs said Manchester was the 'shock city' of the industrial revolution. Cornwall is the shock county of the overtourism era. It moved from tin and copper mining to the extraction of the tourist coin in less than fifty years. What will be its next phase? On the back of the hyped pseudo-disruption precipitated by electric vehicle technologies, lithium deposits near St Austell and Redruth excite outside speculators as well as many locals, who lament the passing of 'proper jobs'. If the operators decide to go down the hard-rock route – rather than brine extraction – the expected boom might come with a terrible environmental price. Geothermal energy is another source of hope for those who would like to re-industrialise. Cornwall is also the UK's would-be Cape Canaveral, with a planned spaceport for air-launch take-offs and landings at Newquay Airport. The Lizard peninsula is a major radiocommunications and undersea cable hub.

Sooner than we might like to think, tourism could be supplanted by these thrusting, futuristic sectors. As heritage has found a place for mining, the future will one day look back at the twenty-first-century leisure industry through ambivalent spectacles — half rose-tinted, half dazzled-by-the-madness. People will reflect with confusion and perturbation on a time when the M5 and A30 hauled in Instagram diggers and TikTok panners. In a world doomed to be virtual, they will wonder at all the physical commotion of tourism. The suckers used to queue for fish and chips. They blushed on meeting a TV chef. They took their supermarket food and nimbyism on holiday. The metropolitan middle classes bought the cottages; everyone else moved out. Someone will make a miniseries about a dynasty torn apart by tourism.

9
Cider with Barbellion
Barnstaple

Barnstaple feels cut off. Dr Beeching hacked off the line to Taunton, and arriving by rail involves a V-shaped journey and a change of train at Exeter. The railway north through what looks on a map like a forty-mile wide field is called the Tarka Line, after the novel about an otter. The train that I take one sunny late afternoon is full of returning schoolkids, shirts unbuttoned, blazers awry. The hedged patchwork of pastoral land is the sort of superficial idyll you find in old children's stories. Devon is often described as England's loveliest county; it elides easily with historical fantasy. I spy palatial farmhouses at the top of ridges above sloping ex-meadows, cropped, ploughed (and probably chemicalled). Between one request stop and the next, clouds of hawthorn blossom drift in through the train windows. The old diesel, a three-carriage affair, goes chug-a-chuck-chuck. We pass a couple of tiny villages. There are no New Towns. No spent factories. No motorways. Nothing much, in fact. Does no one want to live in this green paradise? Or does Devon keep its head down so developers don't notice all this space and warm sky? The train is entirely white; the passengers who are not adolescents are of retirement age. After Eggesford, it's single track. The engine driver collects his token. As I arrive in Barnstaple, the smell of smeared muck overwhelms the carriage atmosphere. I think of Barbellion, not sure whether to hold his nose or inhale as deep as his battered lungs would allow.

This is the smartest town in this book and a tourist destination of sorts, though the vast majority of people who come swerve Barnstaple and head for the coast. It's one of the oldest settlements in the South-West. Nearby Pilton was made an ancient burh, or fortified town – against the Vikings – by Alfred the Great. Later the title was moved about a mile south to the banks of the River Taw. Barnstaple is thought to derive from the Old English *bearde*, or 'battle-axe', and *stapol*, meaning 'pillar' – the latter marking a ford. It was one of the richest towns in England; Barnstaple had a mint in the tenth century. A market and annual fair were in operation by 1274. The tax records of 1332 establish Barnstaple as the third-most prosperous borough in the county, after Exeter and Sutton Prior (Plymouth). In medieval England, a lot of wealth was concentrated along an east–west axis that ran from Kent to Devon; Barnstaple was its western extremity.

The bridge between the station and town is ancient and low and really too lovely for cars. A central thoroughfare is Boutport Street, packed with listed buildings. Barnstaple was a substantial port; a plaque on the riverside says five ships were sent to swell Drake's fleet for the battle against the Armada in 1588. Nearby is Queen Anne's Walk, a colonnaded building overlooking a paved square. A statue of the royal, with orb and sceptre, presides over garlanded heraldic escutcheons, one above each pillared bay, showing the arms of eleven leading Barnstaple families, the crest of the Borough of Barnstaple – a triple-towered castle – forming a twelfth. An exchange used to operate at this site, adjacent to the main quay. A lot of trade was with North America. Sailing from Devon, rather than Hampshire or East Anglia, reduced the duration of trans-Atlantic voyages by several days. Newfoundland cod, Irish wool, timber and tobacco were landed on the quayside, deals signed by touching the so-called Tome Stone, which still stands, protected behind iron railings. Across the road rises a grass-covered lump – a motte and bailey castle – in a car park behind a Marks & Spencer. From the summit you see Barnstaple is ringed by green hills.

As well as shipping, Barnstaple was known for the manufacture of woollen cloth, agriculture and, later, pottery. The town had its own customs house, which continued to grow until the mid-eighteenth century. When the port silted up, railways arrived to keep things on track. Ornate facades on shopfronts point to civic confidence and spare capital. Romantically ruinous mansions on Victoria Road suggest some people lost both of these. Half of the riverside town-houses, with their ornate balconies, look well-preserved; others are peeling, crumbling. It could be Richmond upon Thames, but without the easy commutes or London's overflowing money.

—

     where tourists seldom tread

In the shadowy heart of town is a cluster of Christian temples. The smallest, St Anne's, was a chantry chapel, where Masses were sung for the souls of the dead in the hope this might help them evade eternal torment. The ground floor was probably a charnel house, where old bones disturbed by later burials could be stored. The stone walls hold back earth much higher than the level of the row outside the church; a full four feet of death is kept at bay; digging dogs find human bones just six inches below the surface. For a time, the building was a grammar school, where John Gay of *Beggar's Opera* fame was educated. Now it's a cultural centre. Someone inside was playing Barry Manilow's 'Mandy' loudly. Later I passed beautiful almshouses, and one of the residents was listening to Billy Joel's 'Just the Way You Are'. A sax player near a hospice shop was blasting out 'Isn't She Lovely'. *MOR-tality: Now That's What We Call Barnstaple.*

On Butchers Row is a Pannier Market, a beautiful structure occupied by dreary-looking stalls, apathetically manned. Television always shows French and Italian markets bursting with fresh fruit and vegetables. This one sells nothing perishable; the atmosphere is stale and dusty. At the front of the market is a Guildhall. The Royal and Fortescue Hotel was, of old, a merchant's house and, somewhat later, a coaching inn called the Golden Lion; in the dining room a stunning Jacobean plasterwork ceiling depicts biblical scenes along with the arms of the company of Spanish merchants that commissioned the work – and used the house as a guild headquarters. I have dinner there.

Barnstaple is one of the most retired towns I have ever visited. Old couples sit eating small, simple meals, drinking water or half-lagers without speaking. I once judged shared silences harshly, but now think of it as wordless communing, a kind of romantic private religion. It's a great town for being old in, as it is at river level, generally flat, and with carefully laid cycle paths and parklands full of ancient trees. There are posh delis and bakeries, a trendy tiffin-themed curry restaurant, lots of coffee shops, with all three 'waves' represented.

Senior volunteers keep afloat the museum, housed inside a prominently positioned mansion once occupied by local publisher and philanthropist William Frederick Rock. The exhibits are a classic small-town clutter of whatever's at hand: fishing creels, old sweaters, coins, a Hotpoint top loader. When display items date from within your living memory, wistfulness vies with educational value and the realisation you, too, are a museum piece. A clever curator has added the names of donors to key artefacts. There's Phyllis White's Silk Screen, Ray Liverton's Gas Cooker, Beryl Foster's Christening Gown, Rev Squire's Xmas Decorations, Bishop Nympton's Parish Bier. A lot of material relates to Barnstaple Fair, said to be a thousand years old. I'm glad it's not happening during my visit. The idea of a timeworn fayre is no doubt greater than the reality. Local printer W. J. 'Buck' Taylor's Type Case and moveable letterpress type were probably used to produce campaign leaflets for the Common Wealth Party, co-founded by Barnstaple MP Richard Acland; the left-leaning socialist party had five MPs between 1942 and 1947 and played a key role in the establishment of a welfare state. Taylor was secretary until his death in 1992; the party was dissolved the following year.

People who live inland from tourist honeypots exude a resigned quasi-philosophical air. They have had to accept that tourism is the extraction of visitors' wealth, and that the latter has increased exponentially while their own has dwindled. The North Devon coast is popular with City workers and Greater Londoners, happy to pay double for lifestyle chimeras and local seafood. I took a ride on a bus to see Woolacombe, and walked the length of the wide, beautiful beach to Croyde. There I hopped on the bus back, which carried me via Saunton Sands, overlooked by thatched cottages, modernist villas and contemporary bunker-pads. Locals can but dream of such opulence, and must tolerate their views being obstructed.

I stayed at the merchant-class former Golden Lion but supped in the servants' Golden Lion Tap round the corner. There were benches outside

 where tourists seldom tread

and the sun was streaming down. I enjoyed hearing the Barumite accent, which suggested fishermen, farming and cider-drinking. I got a pint and returned to my bench and book – *The Journal of a Disappointed Man* (1919) by W. N. P. Barbellion, the Schopenhauer, Kierkegaard, Dostoevsky, Grossmith and Mole of Barnstaple – or, as he calls it, Downstable.

One source says he was born in 1889 at Joy Street; most say it was Cross Street. Both are apposite addresses. Bruce Frederick Cummings – as he was baptised – attended Rock Park School in Victoria Road and North Devon School at Trafalgar Lawn. Bright but reserved, even timid, he took a keen interest in natural history but followed the advice of others and the model of his father, an acerbic Tory columnist, taking up a career in journalism ('my Death Warrant') via a five-year apprenticeship at the *Devon and Exeter Daily Gazette*.

Later he managed to secure a stint at the British Museum (Natural History) but illness, his parents' deaths and a troubled relationship got in the way of any sustained career as a naturalist. The *Journal*, which he began to keep when he was thirteen, is a record of dashed dreams, ennui, bouts of sickness, notes for a novel never to be written, assorted vivisections, 'mental ebullition', loathing for Christians and humans in general ('I take a pride in my Simian ancestry') and self-disgust.

'I thoroughly believed that men and women and I were much better than we actually are. I have not come to the end of my disillusions even now. I still rub my eyes on occasion. I simply can't believe that we are such humbugs, hypocrites, self-deceivers. And strange to say it is the "good" people above all who most bitterly disappoint me. Give me a healthy liar, or a thief, or a vagabond and he arouses no expectations, and so I get no heart-burning. It is the good, the honest, the true, who cheat me of my boyhood's beliefs . . . I dissect everyone, even those I love.'

The pen name combines the surname of the proprietor of a chain of sweet shops with branches in South Kensington, Bond Street and elsewhere, and the initials for Wilhelm, Nero and Pilate, 'the world's three greatest failures'. American essayist Noel Perrin observed in an essay in his collection *A Reader's Delight* (1988), 'Besides its pleasing foreignness, Barbellion combines "barbarian" and "rebellion".' H. G. Wells (who some initially believed had written the *Journal*) provided the introduction to the first edition. Barbellion died seven months after the book was published to considerable acclaim. He was thirty.

Literary pilgrims should be pouring into Barnstaple, especially in winter. In an age of self-promotion, self-help, TikTok smiles and pouting narcissism, Barbellion is as curative as sea air. If this ancient burh turned optional stopover could write a journal, it would have to confess to some measure of disappointment. Barbellion, who writes that he hates the little town (though nowhere really pleases him), finds solace in beetling and beachcombing – and rigorous misanthropism. Nature, his journal asserts on every page, is also the self.

As sad music cheers sad people, the gloomy diary entries of Barnstaple's bard comfort the adrift, alienated reader far from home. Barbellion's barbed ruminations give his birthplace a literary depth. Morose existentialists need no longer flee to Copenhagen, Paris or Weimar to walk on the shady side of the street.

10

Short Flights from London
Hounslow, Croydon, Gillingham, Wokingham, Surbiton, Slough

Wokingham
Lloyds TSB

Town and Country. The Season. Home Counties. Fusty would-be national myths link London to its further fringes. The moronic gyre of the M25 is itself a literal spin-off from the capital's bullying centripetal influence on cities, towns, villages, fields, dreams, souls and bodies a hundred miles from Charing Cross's point zero. Metro-landish whimsy and Ballard-invoking interpretations by London's legions of urban explorers, fuguers and sorrowful flâneurs – many relocated from far-flung towns like the ones featured in this book – are meagre resistance against the Alpha+++ globalised bastion of obscurantist finance, property-idolatry and work–life imbalance. For the free-thinking, twenty-first-century citizen, London is largely no-go.

The towns at the edges afford visitors a glimpse of pasts and futures. Bypassed by the football and West End weekender coaches and Oxford Street-bound consumers, and disdained by inner-zoners, the weekday lives of these forgotten satellites are mysterious, their night-times haunted by shattered dreams, urban foxes, crimes and punishments.

————

Hounslow East, Hounslow Central, Hounslow West. Three stops on the tube where barely a soul alights. Everybody's bound for London, or for the aeropolis. The planes, seen descending far away to the east, are ghostly, silent. A string of incoming lights, like guided missiles. Close up, landing and taking off, through the perimeter fence, they are mundanely magnificent in their potency, their wired-in capacity for catastrophe. To the residents of Hounslow they are mostly invisible – no one can live looking up at the sky all the time – but they are always coming, and coming, coming again. A rumble and scream and they are gone. Contrails of toxic gases and, just occasionally, grenades of frozen shit; the flash of an expanding cruciform shadow on the pavement.

With 90,000 workers, Heathrow is the largest single-site employer in the UK. A quarter are BAME. Steady jobs. Travel without moving. As Gautam Malkani writes in *Londonstani,* his 2006 novel: 'Good desi boys who din't ever cause no trouble. But how many a them'll still be here in Hounslow in ten years' time, workin in Heathrow fuckin airport helpin goras catch planes to places so they could turn their own skin brown? No fuckin way I was gonna be hangin round with them saps no more, with those gimpy glasses I used to wear, my drain-pipe trousers an my batty books. Fuck that shit.'

In 1937, a wood-and-fabric Percival Vega Gull, bound for the Isle of Man, clipped a tree and crashed into 215 Hounslow Road, north Feltham. The pilot, his sole passenger and Elsie Abbey, who lived in the house, died. Air pollution is today's disaster, killing 200 Hounslowers every year.

I passed through – *used* – Hounslow scores of times between 2005 and 2012 when working mainly as a travel journalist. The easiest way to get from home to the airport was the bus from Kingston. Even when not going anywhere anytime soon, I'd get butterflies whenever I saw a 111, 281, 285 or X26. As if the bus might sprout wings and take off. When I did have to leave the country, I'd alight at Hounslow bus garage to walk the 100 yards to Hounslow East tube. I subconsciously tried not to look too much at the interchange's raw shabbiness, not to think much at all as I was processed towards the air-conditioned phased spaces of the airport terminals. Both were equally unwelcoming. Yet it was Hounslow, not Heathrow, that mirrored my mental state. I had chosen this work to get away from a chaotic personal life.

But after repeat visits, I couldn't blinker away the acutely contemporary settlement of multiply occupied dwellings, style-bereft mid-rise offices and blocks of flats, chicken, pizza and kebab outlets, chain stores, SIM-card sellers, bookies, money changers, pawn shops, mini-cabs, barbers, ethnic supermarkets, bus stops, bus lanes, bus station. Globalised, pan-ethnic, almost anonymous, but not quite. For there was something in the aesthetic and the anxious energy that prefaced what I'd find on arrival in the fraying edges of Lima, Chennai, Manila. Hounslow services London just as the distant outposts of Empire

   where tourists seldom tread

serviced it in the past. It is neighbourhood and serf-suburb, homely district and miniature developing nation, cowering in the shadow of the jet hub.

Leave the clogged and chaotic centre and Hounslow becomes one of the eeriest places in the UK. Residential areas back on to light industrial estates and warehouses. Traffic systems siphon cars and buses into the mega-cordon of the airport precinct. Tube stations lie stranded on islands. The skyline is a void. Beyond lie reservoirs and Windsor's greenery. Westward, where the planes ordinarily take off, has been spared the conurbations and terrible transit.

In the middle of this disaster zone is Hounslow Heath, where Cromwell stationed his forces and other armies came and went, practised and prayed. Flat and bald, it served as the baseline for the Ordnance Survey. One day, when flying is banned and before west London floods, the heath will segue into Heathrow and birders will flock at dawn and dusk to catch rare geese alighting on Lake Airstrip from the Terminal 3 hide.

———

Bowie in 1999: 'It represented everything I didn't want in my life, everything I wanted to get away from. I think it's the most derogatory thing I can say about somebody or something: "God, it's so fucking Croydon".' By that date, the tax-exiled duke was often being unoriginal in interviews. As Will Noble notes in *Croydonopolis: A Journey to the Greatest City That Never Was*, Sue Perkins, Harry Hill, Kenneth Williams, numerous fictional characters in novels, TV series and Hollywood scripts, and Henry VIII all found time to make disparaging remarks about London's most populous suburb.

Croydon is still a place London residents refer to dismissively if not with outright derision when they want to emphasise metropolitan credentials. I say 'still' as other more or less peripheral towns and boroughs – Peckham, Lewisham, Kingston, Clapton – have migrated from embarrassing to enlightened in recent times. Perhaps Croydon is drifting centre-wards too: films are made there, with the town standing in for New York and eastern Europe, and even as itself in Andrew Haigh's *All of Us Strangers*.

Croydon owns a deep past that might help it resist a frivolous putative future. Neolithic hut floors, hut circles and hearths have been identified. Ancient Greek coins and Teutonic pottery were unearthed. Named for crocuses, it prospered as a centre of saffron cultivation. It was a sizeable settlement at the time of the Domesday Book, its Surrey Street market up and running by the late thirteenth century. Then came a long ecclesiastical honeymoon when the Tudor Croydon Palace was the Archbishop of Canterbury's summer residence and operational headquarters for managing the episcopal estates of Surrey, Middlesex and Hertfordshire; monarchs dropped in. Today the building is a private girls' school. Six archbishops are buried in the graveyard of the Grade I listed parish church, Croydon Minster. Sheldon Street, Laud Street and Cranmer Road honour the prelates. A later summer residence was Addington Palace, a huge Palladian manor house that's now a wedding venue surrounded by a golf course.

Croydon was a spa town in the nineteenth century. In 1831, Decimus Burton designed a rustic thatched lodge and pleasure garden – with the precious well covered by a wigwam-like structure – off what is now Spa Hill. The Royal Beulah Spa and Gardens, which extended across twenty-five acres, was visited by Queen Victoria, Charles Dickens and William Makepeace Thackeray. During a tour in 1838, Johann Strauss I showcased the new sound of the waltz to a massive audience in the bespoke dance arena. The waters of the natural saline spring, tested by Michael Faraday, were said to be purer than those found at Bath and Wells, and saltier than Cheltenham's. The site hosted grand fetes and galas, balloon ascents, military bands, archery, a camera obscura and circus acts. One famous visiting tightrope walker and impresario, Pablo Fanque, is namechecked in the Beatles' 'Being for the Benefit of Mr Kite!' The spa's appeal faded when the Crystal

   where tourists seldom tread

Palace was re-erected nearby in 1854. Only the much-modified lodge, at the former entrance, has survived.

In December 1919, only months after reopening the skies to civil aircraft, the Air Ministry decided to close Hounslow airfield and move London's customs airport to the better facilities and location at Croydon. Two sites on either side of Plough Lane – a former RAF station located to the west, Waddon Aerodrome to the east – were made over to newly founded airlines, which used converted First World War bombers to connect London to the continent. Croydon to Paris–Le Bourget became the world's busiest air route. By the 1940s, the grass runways and lack of room for further expansion made the airport unsuitable for the new, larger airliners. In 1959, the landings ended and Croydon skies were returned to the corvids and pigeons.

Does anyone miss the glamour of aviation? Few would swap their town for Crawley near Gatwick. Croydonites are terrestrially well connected, with dozens of train stations in the borough and many intersecting lines, and the town sits at the heart of a tram service. East Croydon station is busier than Liverpool Lime Street and Edinburgh Waverley; South Croydon bus garage is a throbbing hub. The number 68, a 15-miler from Croydon to Chalk Farm, used to be one of London's great bus routes – I was a regular user in the mid-1980s – in a region lacking Tube lines.

A complicated iteration of Croydon's cosmopolitanism is its role in Britain's immigration story. Twenty-storey Lunar House and its sister tower, Apollo House, are the headquarters of the UK Visas and Immigration department. Nearby Electric House, an easier-on-the-eye Moderne edifice on a corner, used to be home to the Border Agency. This bureaucratic trio conspired to manufacture long queues of desperate asylum seekers, many from repressive, totalitarian nations. The buildings are interesting if you don't need to go inside them.

—

Ecclesiastical, healthful, airborne, Kafkaesque: Croydon keeps reinventing itself. Some £5.25 billion is being spent on projects such as Boxpark Croydon (a copycat of a Shoreditch scheme), the London Square commuter block, College Road (Europe's tallest modular tower), Carbuncle Cup-nominated Saffron Square and new restaurant and cultural 'quarters'. Perhaps the latter will get an Aladdin Sane statue, unveiled by native Bowie-phile Kate Moss, who has also made a point of dissociating herself from the town – which is itself so very fucking Croydon.

———

The river shimmers, shifts, suggests, rises and slips away. Dickens, in *The Uncommercial Traveller*, notes the effect this has on his mental state: 'There are small out of the way landing-places on the Thames and the Medway, where I do much of my summer idling. Running water is favourable to day-dreams. And a strong tidal river is the best of running water for mine.'

The intrusion of the Medway, a large, unruly estuary mirroring the larger Thames estuary to the north, seems excessive of nature. The name derives from Vaga and Med – meaning 'wandering' (related to 'vague' and 'vagabond') and 'middle', which, run together, are slippery as an eel.

History ebbs and flows. This is the last post before London on the road from the continent. The Britons followed a grass trackway to Canterbury. The route features in the Antonine Itinerary, the Romans' A-Z: a fast lane from their pontoon across the Thames to three Kentish ports. It was part of the Saxon Wæcelinga Stræt or Watling Street, the southern border of the Danelaw. Chaucer's pilgrims tramped along it. The Old Dover Road became the A2; an arrow of a thoroughfare compared to the snaky, hesitant M2.

A quarter of a million people live in the five Medway Towns. They have been gathering here for centuries for trade, for war, to ready

                    where tourists seldom tread

ships. Gillingham, with a population of 108,000, is the largest. The others are Chatham, Rainham, Strood and Rochester. The latter, with its cathedral, castle and Dickens connections, draws good numbers of visitors. Strood has a manor house where the Knights Templar rested. Rainham leans towards Kent but can't quite free itself. Chatham is shipbuilding and naval power; records of the royal fleet being moored here date from the mid-sixteenth century.

If the least lovely of the five towns, Gillingham is no no-place. A portion of the town – the manor of Grange – was a dependency of Hastings, one of the Cinque Ports that made up a powerful medieval maritime federation. Part of the royal dockyard extended here. It's the birthplace of the Elizabethan seafarer William Adams, who starred pseudonymously in James Clavell's bestselling 1975 novel, *Shogun*. He is often described as the first Englishman to have set foot in Japan.

History and localists love salience, but the towns have merged like water and silt, like the millions of tons of Portland cement made with the local mud. This is the Garden of England's car park, driveway, hardstanding. The Medway can be thought of as a linear suburb that exploded with the train. Life is built up, all link roads, bridges, tunnels, sheds and slipways. But these are conduits. And they throw shadows.

Confluences are innately creative. In the sixties, the five towns produced beat bands with trim, ambivalent names like the Strangers, the Strollers, the Offbeats, the Scapegoats, the Classmates. From the early eighties, dozens of new wave bands emerged, many fronted or fused by Billy Childish. Locally based musician, writer and anthropologist Chris de Coulon Berthoud, who's constructing a musical archive, says the term 'Medway scene' properly applies to 'the music of the Milk-shakes and the Prisoners, and the sound that emerged in the period after punk. A charity-shop-clad melding of punk and the beat and psych music of the 1960s on labels like (Childish's) Hangman Records, Empire Records, etc, led to there being a "Medway Scene" section in record shops across the world from Tokyo to Tallahassee. While many other places have had strongly identifiable musical styles attached to them (Bristol, Coventry, etc.), Medway, along with Liverpool, and Manchester, are the only places where the place name identifies the music so strongly.' Garrisons and ports are rough-edged but they're full of escapists and individualists. Young soldiers and sailors are a captive market and they ship in new ideas and sounds. In a lot of the music, there's a Medway angst, a Medway unwillingness to be fashionable, a Medway melancholy. Kevin Younger's the High Span evokes flux, wistfulness, loss, nostalgia, remoteness. In the future the only door is to the past.

There's a downbeat class-consciousness in Gillingham. In an amateur film made in 1982, when unemployment was a national crisis, Medway folk interviewed about their town rarely offered more than 'it's alright, innit?' The blurb for *Medway: A Novel* is 'Jamie Sinclair is a bipolar ex-chav, an impostor knocking at the door of the middle class. On a whim he decides to leave his toxic relationship and move back to his parents' house in Medway, to see if his hometown can fix him.' It sounds like irony by numbers. Penned by David Cramer Smith, the book is sold on a website called Medwayish, along with tea towels, mugs, prints, postcards. Alternative tourism, innit?

Medway has an art scene. The Stuckists, founded in 1999 by Charles Thomson and Billy Childish, describes itself as a radical, amateur, post-postmodernist, pro-paint, anti-gallery art movement 'opposed to the current pretensions of so-called Brit Art, Performance Art, Installation Art, Video Art, Conceptual Art, Minimal Art, Body Art, Digital Art and anything claiming to be art which incorporates dead animals or beds'.

If stuck in the past, or the Medway mud, it has won admirers and has spawned international spinoff scenes. Vague and vagabond, near but not too near the capital city, never fully mainstream.

———

                                   where tourists seldom tread

Living close to a Waitrose supermarket added £7,366.95 to the price of a Wokingham house in 2022, according to one source. According to another, the average price for properties within a half-a-mile walk from a Waitrose was £599,000 in comparison to £243,000 for homes which were within a ten- to twenty-mile radius of a branch of the store. What about fifty miles away? When do houses become free? If I owned a convenience store I would paint the frontage RYB Green #7BB135 to see what it did to the price of my maisonette above.

Wokingham has a Waitrose at the heart of its town centre – 'a regular haunt for Maidenhead MP and former prime minister Theresa May,' a local newspaper reports. On Google Maps, its only rivals are a masonic centre, a shrink, a cinema, a wine store and something called Giggling Squid. I don't know the mollusc, but I know Wokingham. My partner was raised there. We have used the town for the railway station, restaurants (Argentinian steak, posh Italian), barista coffee, and to source authentic Spanish deli produce like Padrón peppers and barquillos. The town does not stint on aspirational victuals. I sometimes wonder if the Spanish owner googled 'place in UK where people can afford authentic Spanish deli produce'.

Framing the retail are solid red-brick buildings – a grand, churchy town hall, tidy and elegant houses on Shute End, gracious Grade I listed almshouses – and a peppering of timber-framed Tudor properties. Things look settled, bedded down, steady – which can slip into stagnation. The parliamentary seat was Tory from 1885 till 2024; John 'Vulcan' Redwood sat in it from 1987 to the Tory meltdown. One midsummer evening, having a quiet pint at the Queen's Head on The Terrace – such a confident street name – I eavesdropped on two men who pretended to be interested in passing cars but were trapped inside a poignant short-story collection titled *What We Talk About When We Talk About Audis*. The sun was setting slowly, and in its reflective, dusty glare I might have been in Devon or Dorset. But step into a duller light and you see that this is a countrified market town that has been ganged up on by a commuter dormitory. The population is ever-increasing; a village has become a large town that wants, in spite of itself, to coalesce with Reading.

Wokingham's origins are Saxon. The name probably means 'Wocca's place', a tribal settlement. Before the Norman invasion, a chapel of ease was established in a clearing in the woods on the edge of Windsor Forest. The clearing became the town's oldest street, Le Rothe Strete – today's Rose Street. For a time, the town was mis-called Oakingham. Given a charter by Elizabeth I, it became known for its bell foundry, brickmaking and the manufacture of silk stockings. Nine Mile Ride, connecting Bracknell to Finchampstead, was built around 1702 so that Queen Anne could observe the hunt from her carriage. Running parallel to a Roman road, it was expanded by George III, who liked to ride to hounds in the royal forest. Today Nine Mile Ride is the B3430, just 6.7 miles long, and throbbing with traffic, but there are extant patches of woodland along its length. The smartest houses are to be found on unmetalled streets. Thrushes and blackbirds contend with the snarl of SUVs and the Robocop whine of EVs.

The road to becoming a commuter town was indirect. A line through Wokingham was first built to connect Reading with Redhill, on the Brighton line. It's a bucolic North Downs journey that usually ends, deflatingly, at Gatwick Airport. Later a line from Wokingham to London Waterloo opened, but it still takes at least seventy minutes to reach the capital (forty miles away). The texture and mood of a suburb derives a lot from the travelling time to work. Over an hour and a place can retain at least an attitude of countrification.

The Home Counties comprise anything from three to thirteen historic counties. While no one can agree which they are, most people have class-inflected ideas about them. My stream-of-prejudice word cloud includes: prosperity, subtopia, horses, cricket, Tudorbethan, the Beatles, bowlers, slammers, civil servants, lawyers. Notions about the Home Counties intersect with the deep English dichotomy of Town and Country, an inherited imaginary of aristocrats and other members

   where tourists seldom tread

of the ruling class travelling between London mansions and country piles. A few hundred people at any one time probably lived like that, but they disproportionately populate novels, costume dramas and the media. A semiotic slippage has occurred, and the Surrey commuter of 2025 is perceived to be eternally living in the fifties and a joyless emulator of the seasonally home-shifting nobles.

According to a 2019 YouGov poll, 29 per cent of 1,905 adults from across the UK believed London was a Home County. It's surely not, but the *Home Counties Magazine*, launched in 1899, was concerned only with describing them for Londoners. The latter continue to regard the outer green belt as a zone of recreation and leisure (while disdaining its way of life), while long-term residents of the Home Counties prize the difference and distance from the Smoke (while welcoming its inflated salaries).

It's a commonplace to call pleasant, safe towns that resist caricature dull or bland. Wokingham – which routinely tops admittedly unscientific surveys of happiest places to live, best towns in Berkshire, wealthiest street rankings, etc. – merits a visit because it is the ur-town of the Home Counties. Wokingham partly answers the questions: What do British people want? What does affluence look like? What is English success? Is this, then, the fabled, fortune-kissed 'South-East of England'? But all towns lie within a constellation of proximal forces, and when I drew around Wokingham on a map it looked like a spidery new Zodiac sign. In near orbit are Ascot Racecourse, Sandhurst, Wellington College, Farnborough Airport, Broadmoor and Waitrose's head office, while the Elizabeth line skimmed the edge of the borough, a whip, a lasso, a shackle.

———

I resided in Surbiton from 2007 to 2012, unhappily married but (or perhaps therefore) delighted to be a commuter. It was my equally unhappy ex-wife-to-be who suggested we relocate from grubby Herne

Hill to the riverbank idyll. She was from Argentina, and carried no parochial cultural baggage about The Suburbs – while for me, Surbiton, which looks like a portmanteau of 'suburb' and 'town', was a metonym for surrender and mediocrity. Whenever I had dealings with members of what passes for the London intelligentsia – usually plain snobs – they would, on hearing of my choice of base, deliver the expected: 'Surbiton, bah, boring, square, Surrey.' Some might mumble something about *The Good Life* (1975–8).

The latter was filmed in Northwood, north-west London, and set in a fictional Surbiton, and, thrillingly, my own life travelled through both. In 1987, on finishing university, I lived in Harrow-on-the-Hill and commuted for a time to Northwood and, subsequently, to Blackfriars. I hadn't studied Betjeman and was still too young and alive to concern myself with Metro-landish nostalgia, but I nonetheless enjoyed dressing up as a commuter. It was a defined role. It had a kind of heritage. I bought a blue-black Crombie coat, black leather gloves and a black umbrella. I loved to stand in a carriage on the Metropolitan line's 'fasts' and play the part. Sadly, the job was awful, and I had to give up the performative commuting. Twenty years on and I was at it again, now as a forty-something, stereotypically scruffy media employee, cramming myself on to non-stoppers from Surbiton to Waterloo.

It's fifteen miles down the A3 to London; the drive is a tedious affair, all bottlenecks, bus lanes and traffic lights. The non-stop trains take sixteen minutes. The reason for the high-speed line – for any line – is that Victorian coach operators of nearby Kingston upon Thames resisted competition from the iron horse. Consequently, the London and Southampton Railway bypassed the more important centre and stopped at an outlying township that had hitherto been named New Kingston and New Town, and was even known for a time as Kingston-upon-Railway before becoming Surbiton.

I delighted in the views, the speed, the cemeteries, Clapham Junction's multiplatform maw, Battersea Power Station. This time around,

London and work satisfied my needs at the arrival end of the line. But, my choice of dormitory was also stimulating and coming home had its highs.

The landmarks start as soon as you alight, for Surbiton station is a well-executed ode to reinforced concrete. Built in the 1930s by Southern Railway's architect James Robb Scott (1882–1965) – who was responsible for several eye-catching Modernist stations, as well as signal boxes and electrical control centres – in art deco style, its straight lines and whitewashed plainness suggest both an Odeon cinema and a mausoleum. Stepping away from this portal, we find ourselves on leafy lanes and stately avenues lined by demure Georgian townhouses, lofty Victorian terraces (the St Andrew's Square Conservation Area could be in South Kensington), thirties deco-influenced blocks, Flemish-style gables on the old post office, and to-be-expected mock-Tudor detached houses. Village-type pubs and restaurants punctuate the quietly elegant residential streets. This continues through the Seething Wells area – the name an unfortunate corruption of Siden Wells, which appears on maps from the eighteenth century. It was recorded on railway maps as a medicinal spring. At the other end of town, on the edge of Kingston, is the Hogsmill; upriver, at Tolworth, is the spot where Millais imagined the drowned Ophelia. Across the bridge is Home Park – the least thronging and most pastoral of the royal parks, with ancient meadows, floodplain ecosystems, a majestic herd of fallow deer and the Long Water – the original neighbour-impressing 'water feature', built by Charles II in 1660 as a wedding gift for bride-to-be Catherine of Braganza. Hampton Court is at the far end of the geometrical pool.

John Lennon, George Harrison and Ringo Starr lived south-west of Surbiton, close to Weybridge – richer, somewhat gated, more suited to super-successful artistes. This is not coincidental: Surbiton is neither London nor Surrey, neither ultra-middle class nor 'gritty'. It has an equilibrium, a yin-yang quality, and if it doesn't have the artificiality of a 'model village' it feels like a template for how a liveable town should be. I think of Surbiton as a sort of shock absorber between ideas and places. It is unpretentious, hard-working, self-made. Esher and Oxshott are about stockbroker money, football money, dodgy money. As the Queen of Suburbia said: 'This sort of thing simply does not go on in Surbiton.'

––––––––

The cultural establishment has been unkind to Slough. Betjeman's famous poem hollered: 'Come friendly bombs and fall on Slough! / It isn't fit for humans now, / There isn't grass to graze a cow. / Swarm over, Death!' The poet laureate later regretted penning it. Orwell's bitter, snobbish, repressed protagonist in *Keep the Aspidistra Flying*, Gordon Comstock, rues a trip to Slough, and the tea his girlfriend Rosemary insists on having there: 'They went to a large, dreary, draughty hotel near the station. Tea, with little wilting sandwiches and rock cakes like balls of putty, was two shillings a head.' A song by punk band Gallows inspired by Betjeman ranted, 'If this town had a name it would be defeat'.

David Brent also quotes the poem. Ricky Gervais used Slough to propel him to LA. The opening credits of *The Office* focus on Slough's grey architecture and roads. Its nightlife is derided in several episodes. Did it all begin with the town's name? It was spelled variously as Slo, Sloo, Le Slowe and plain Slow in pre-modern times, and the word features in *The Pilgrim's Progress* as a swampy medium of 'Despond' – despairing, giving up. Slough used to be in Bucks, but is now in Berks. No doubt the latter would like to pass it on, perhaps to London.

In June 1918, part of west Slough was bought by the government to establish a motor repair depot for army vehicles. The war ended while it was being built – shoddily – partly by PoWs. Subsequently, the site was opened with the aim of refitting military trucks, cars and motorcycles for civilian use. This failed and was replaced by a trading estate – the largest in Europe with a single owner, covering more than 180 hectares

                                    where tourists seldom tread

(450 acres). The customer directory today lists 216 companies, including car dealerships, fishing-tackle retailers, tyre suppliers, self-storage units, a nursery, DJ-ing gear rental, skin-care services and an antiques emporium; all human life. Mars's HQ is one of the big names; in 1932, the Mars Bar was invented in Slough. Sadly, Crossbow House, where the fictional paper company Wernham Hogg was based in *The Office*, was razed in 2013. A Premier Inn stands on the site. When I type a sentence about demolition it's often followed by that line: a Premier Inn stands on the site.

While Manchester embraced the massive Trafford Park industrial estate as part of its worker-bee DNA, Slough has always been uneasy about its commercial sprawl. After all, why can't every town look like Windsor? When Eton College resisted efforts to build a railway station, the project was shifted to Slough – which led to Slough station becoming, temporarily, the 'royal station'. The grand-looking Second Empire-style booking hall is Grade II listed. Of course, there is un-limited heritage and tourism fodder in the vicinity of Slough – on all sides are castles, country estates, Michelin-starred bistros and mil-dewed mansions where London's arty and political elites once chattered. Slough is a merciful release from all the National Trust prettiness and class voyeurism. I value the fact that you can see Slough's power station from Eton and Windsor. Some people would like to think the Home Counties are all pageant, toppers and race days. Slough is a hardcore commercial hub – a swamp of reality and reinforced concrete.

It's thought the name may have derived from the various sloughs in the area caused by rainwater flowing from the Chilterns to the Thames. Or it may refer to sloe bushes growing in the vicinity. Slough is also necrotic tissue, and I can't help feeling that connotations of decay and deadness holds the town back. It's time for Slough to slough off its sloughiness.

11
Ghost Story
Jaywick

OPEN
Welcome to
Jaywick
Martello Tower
Jaywick
Martello
Tower
MIND YOUR HEAD

P romotional flyers pasted along the front at Clacton-on-Sea promised a Les Miz night, Roy Hudd Tribute show and Chubby Brown. Later in the morning the D-Day eightieth anniversary commemorations would unfold with flags and pendants. The day before, Nigel Farage and his entourage had swung in to congratulate the town on its new parliamentary candidate. The gardens on the front were mown and weeded, the war memorial unblemished.

There's no getting around Clacton's poverty. For half a century or more, the old, the poor, the homeless have been relocated here. The centre at nine in the morning is like hundreds of other town centres, but there's a keener air of desperation. Factories, offices and workplaces are thin on the ground, just seventy miles from the heart of the capital and less than fifty from the commuter zone. Seaside towns were built for temporary distraction and recreation; some of their residents have been compelled to lives of enforced idleness, boredom and economic misery.

The walk to Jaywick is an hour of empty golden sand, busy golf links, low dunes and marsh. Time to dwell – and escape. There is a dishevelled and unloved air to some of the buildings; the sea calm and light green, shifting to bruise-blue under leaden clouds.

The Essex coast's extant Martello towers – six of an original eleven – arrest the gaze with their squatness and bulk. I'd never seen one previously and, like many people, am only familiar with the name from the opening scene of James Joyce's *Ulysses*. The tower close to central Clacton-on-Sea is a café. Another, at the edge of the town's golf course, has not been repurposed. The towers were misnamed after a fortification at Cape Mortella in Corsica, which British forces had struggled to capture in the early stages of the French Revolutionary Wars.

Jaywick comes like a Monsieur Hulot mirage. Grey swirling clouds and steady heat. On my left, beige beach and a narrow fringe of salt marsh. To my right, small and minimally detached houses. Almost all are single storey or else one and a half, with a room in the roof, little more than chalets. People say hello and are neighbourly. They look, to me, definitively Essexian – tanned, taut, steely, knowing. They speak coastal Cockney, unsoftened by decades far from Barking, Mile End, Hackney.

I try not to gawp. I have seen 'most deprived' headlines spewed up time and again. I know Trumpist Republican Nick Stella used an image of Jaywick to warn of American 'foreclosures, unemployment and economic recession'. I know of a benefits-themed reality show. I don't know if a 'poverty safari' is a thing; I scrutinise people and buildings irrespective of their socioeconomic status. But kindness isn't so hard. How bad can a place be? More interestingly, what good is there besides, what surprises, what subverts the unkind churnalism? Jaywick was identified as England's most-deprived neighbourhood in the government's Indices of Deprivation for 2010, 2015, 2019 and 2025. That itself is no reason to stay away.

Jaywick's coming into being was unlike other housing developments. Property developer Frank 'Foff' Stedman had clocked Clacton's popularity as a resort and believed he could sell parcels of land to Londoners. In 1928 he bought twenty-four acres of flood-prone fields and marshland. Residents were encouraged to buy small plots – twenty feet by fifty – for as little as £25 and self-build their holiday homes. Advertisements for off-plan houses from £52 describe the material as 'rough cast asbestos'; a pricier brick option was available.

The Plotlands model – also seen at Peacehaven in Sussex and Humberston in Lincolnshire – can be hitched to the utopianism of William Morris, who had argued for the virtues of self-sufficient communities for poor families away from large cities. But it's also a consequence of the unprofitability of agricultural land due to cheap imports and the peculiarly English fixation with owning a patch of land, however small and otiose.

The main buyers at Jaywick were traders and professionals from London's East End who could reach their beach retreat in just over an hour. Shops, cafés and entertainment venues sprang up. A promised lake and sports centre never materialised. One of the original estates, Brooklands, is arranged in the shape of a car radiator grille, with the roads named after various vehicle manufacturers; there are Hillman, Napier and Wolseley Avenues. Behind it is the smaller Grasslands and to the right, driving deeper inland, is the Village. Coaches regularly picked up holidaymakers throughout the 1930s from west Essex towns Ilford and Romford.

After the Blitz, many owners took up permanent residence in their seaside properties. Eighty years later, materials and decor and fixtures have changed but they are still weekend-sized and vulnerable to floods, time and family budgets. Or post-vulnerable in some cases.

I was aimed like a Napoleonic cannonball at a third Martello tower, the base of an Essex Council-funded community arts organisation. Director Charlotte said she wanted arts and culture to help locals learn about and express themselves. 'Wellness is part of it. But also, arts are seen as middle class. How do we make them accessible to everyone?' She stressed that the Jaywick community was cohesive and convivial. 'People have a bad perception but those who come are welcomed.'

The 'most deprived' headlines have driven residents closer together. They are producing a community manifesto. Past projects have included Arkade, which played on the role of amusement arcades and the fact Jaywick is particularly endangered by rising sea levels due to climate change; Days Like These, in which watercolour artists showed work to celebrate the natural beauty of a place routinely portrayed as a man-made horror; and Obsolete Studios, which revived the tradition of Victorian portrait photography, and captured Jaywick residents as individuals — something that never seems to happen in media representations.

On the first floor of the tower, poems written by locals were hung on washing lines, part of a writing project supervised by Essex University PhD student Lelia Ferro. The poems were good, very evidently worked at. Anna Mae, in 'Driving on the A133', raps towards pathos:

'Sirens blazing, blue lights flashing, drunkards fighting, eau de weed pervading, boom boxes blaring, foxes screaming way into the night, Seagulls screeching their morning calling, school kids running, mums beckoning, voices straining, muted threatening, coaches arriving, mobility scooters racing, cars parking, buckets and spades unloading, excited cries, tired of eye spying, children clambering eager to see the sea, new land dredged from marshes keeps on sinking, sea will continue claiming what is hers.'

The theme of the uncontrollable sea impinging on the land came up again and again in the poems, as did feminism, identity and prejudice.

'How to live in Essex, but not be Essex,' considers Viv Dawson in 'Duolinguist'. 'That was the question which plagued my childhood. / The roots which kept me safe in its rich and fertile soil / comprehensively tripped me up in concrete classrooms. / I straddled the county from its eastern shores / to the RP world beyond, purposely dropping, scattering and blatantly discarding / treacherous Ts, 'aitches, and glottal stops.'

Jaywick makes me question things. Its supposed otherness. My northern middle-class-ified university-educated white-collarness. Silos in general. On a sunny afternoon, it feels like a ghost town. Not quite there. As if the precariousness of its location blurs its edges and undermines its solidity.

Its deprivation is multifaceted and I am assured its shame and resilience are collective. I know I am there as a well-meaning voyeur, to some degree. Perhaps I am the ghost.

Under the warm grey sun the grey pebbledash is softened. The chalets are low and narrow. Minimal. Cosy? A palm tree. A stoved-in wall. A smashed window. A gnome garden. A pretty holiday cottage. A bunker. A bothie. Hello and good morning and dog talk and people limping and hurting and smiling. Salts of the salt marsh, these people. I feel I'm in a film about a lost time. Skunk whiff. Rich people might be alarmed by Jaywick if they came. They could be fearful. But outside the Sunspot Café this is just everything. Home.

                                    where tourists seldom tread

12
Memory Haven
Harwich

retain a single small, sharply drawn, personal recollection concerning Harwich: the boat train that operated from Liverpool Street station in the mid-eighties.

Harwich. Hoek. Berlin. Warszawa. Minsk. Mockba.

I arrived on the Hook of Holland–Harwich ferry once after visits to Poland and Czechoslovakia. At the time I was self-consciously fixated on Eastern European literature – Hašek, Kundera, Kafka, Miłosz – jazz, poster art and the mysteries of being behind the Iron Curtain. Bowie's *Low* and *'Heroes'* albums added to the cool coefficient. During the summer recess between university terms, doing dreary casual jobs in the basements of City banks, I'd pass through Liverpool Street in the early evening on my way home. I'd glance up at the mainline destinations before grumbling my way downstairs to catch the Tube to Manor House. Parkeston Quay was the final stop on this island – then Chagall, Švejk, Josef K, Świerzy, Sabina and Tereza, Stańko.

Sadly, I never used it to go east.

The unbearable heaviness of summer in London.

In the lounge at the Pier Hotel are vintage posters proclaiming 'Harwich for the Continent' and advertisements for holidays in Zeebrugge and Antwerp. In the era before car ferries and cheap flights there were boats to Esbjerg, Gothenburg, Hamburg, Helsingborg, Hirtshals and Oslo. A century ago, they transported entire trains to Europe in roll-on, roll-off fashion. Between 1924 and 1987, rail services from the Hook linked Harwich to Munich, Stockholm and, briefly, the Orient Express routes, as well as the Eastern Bloc.

The port and station now called Harwich International are no longer served by boat trains or any major trains at all. Only little shuttles between Harwich Town and Manningtree stop there these days. As Michael Offord, manager of the glorious Electric Palace Cinema, told me, 'Today, everything is geared to people not coming to Harwich.' In Essex, tourism usually means beaches and village greens, Roman sites and witch trials, stately homes and holiday parks. Tiny, truly on a limb, with lapping sea on both sides and two stops beyond the ferry port, Harwich Town is not even convenient enough to be bypassed.

A myth persists that an earlier, possibly Roman town, Orwell, was lost to the sea, vestiges of which have been very occasionally glimpsed (yet never formally logged) offshore on West Rocks. An early holder of the earldom of Norfolk built a church in 1177. A later one started a market in 1235. In 1318, the Franco-Yorkshireman Thomas de Brotherton, lord of the manor and 1st Earl of Norfolk – noble titles rarely make sense – granted Harwich a charter. At the mouth of the Stour and Orwell estuaries, it had obvious strategic value and soon became a busy fishing port, exporting wool and importing wine. A castle was built. From the Tudor period, Harwich grew in prominence. King Henry VIII visited in 1543. Under his coastal defence programme of Device Forts, three blockhouses were built to protect the town from seaborne attack.

Hawkins, Drake and Frobisher sailed from Harwich during the reign of Queen Elizabeth I. Privateer Christopher Newport, founder of Jamestown – the first permanent English settlement in the Americas – was christened at St Nicholas's church and married Katherine Proctor there on 19 October 1584. The wreck of his galleon, *Sea Venture*, off Bermuda inspired *The Tempest*; the ship proved to be 'no stronger than a nutshell and as leaky as an unstanched wench'. The sturdier *Mayflower* was built at Harwich and its captain, Christopher Jones, married two Harwich women: Sara Twitt, whose family lived at a property where the Alma Inn now stands, and Josian Gray. The latter had seafaring relatives and her late husband was a noted mariner. She inherited his house in Harwich, together with other land and property. Harwich was loyal to Queen Elizabeth I, sending three ships to join against the Spanish Armada in 1588. The town's increasing wealth from trading was bolstered further by the pillaging of Spanish ships.

Samuel Pepys, who was MP for Harwich in 1679 and again between 1685 and 1689, was Secretary of the Admiralty and had a prominent role at Trinity House. The organisation, which manages the UK's lighthouses, has its operational headquarters in the town. The dockside station is sealed off, but an array of buoys and lightships brought in for repairing and cleaning is visible through the chain-link fences. There's something enigmatic about the lower half of these vessels, which are underwater, far out to sea, for years at a time, bobbing and at times swinging wildly, yet fixed and life-saving in the worst of weathers. The multicoloured buoys and great mooring chains don't belong on a dry quayside. Turner made a red buoy an icon of Romanticism in his famous daubing of the painting *Helvoetsluys,* on Varnishing Day at the Royal Academy Summer Exhibition of 1832. He claimed he lashed himself to a steamer one wild night off Harwich to study a snowstorm. On the resulting painting, the ship, of which there is no record, was called *Ariel.* Like Prospero, Turner conjured with storms.

On exiting the railway station, visitors to Harwich are greeted by the High Lighthouse. I climbed the one hundred steps of the interior spiral staircase. In a cabinet on a landing were fading paperbacks by the Australian novelist Randolph Stow. He lived in Harwich from 1981 till his death in 2020. His last novel, *The Suburbs of Hell* (1984), is part morality tale and part murder mystery; the action unfolds in the eighties – digital alarm clocks, BBC radio, unemployment – but the setting, a 'blank-faced secretive old town' called Tornwich, has the texture of the distant past. Harwich feels like that, as if it has a phantasmal inner presence, such that, if you wandered into this or that unlit passage after dark, time might shift suddenly to the maritime era – the sort of place where you sometimes feel you are at sea.

I read the novel after returning home. Its shady, shadowy characters, superbly and ruthlessly rendered, would have made engaging drinking and dining companions in Harwich. I walked the same cobbled alleys and yards, quiet and tense; heard the same slightly alienating local speech patterns.

The Low Lighthouse, which sits prettily beside a row of beach huts, houses a Maritime Museum. When lined up, the two lighthouses' leading lights, which are 150 yards apart, promised safe entry into the estuary – except that silt and sand shift and drift. I peeked inside the Treadwheel Crane, a hamster's wheel for humans based on an ancient Roman contraption. I spent an hour admiring uniforms, model soldiers and machine guns at the circular Redoubt Fort, built on a tump south of the centre in 1808 to repel Napoleon. The fort's cannons were never fired in anger. The dank powder rooms were used as prisoner-of-war cells during the Second World War. Now they're visited by ghosthunters. To help affray costs, the site hosts sea shanty, beer and reenactment festivals. The Redoubt, which is continually being restored, is the largest ancient monument in Britain managed by a voluntary group – the Harwich Society, founded in 1969. It has more than 2,000 members – a significant proportion of the local population – with a hardcore of about fifty or sixty members who are very active.

I met several of them on my tour. Sue Daish, the town's council's first-ever high steward and a trustee of the society, unlocked doors with big old keys for me. Particularly evocative was Christopher Jones's jettied house at 21 King's Head Street, across from the Alma Inn. Upstairs the original wattle-and-daub walls are exposed, with scraps of horsehair visible amid the mud, or whatever was used; Sue called the material 'shit and stick'. Even more remarkable is a room at the rear of the guildhall, which occupies the site of an inn named 'The Bear' that was purchased by the council in 1673. It was used as a holding cell for prisoners waiting to be tried or sentenced. Etched into the wood panels on its walls are elaborate carvings of ships, gallows and symbols to ward off evil spirits, and a hot air balloon, all of which date from the late eighteenth century. One carving of a ship is believed to date from the time of the American War of Independence. Some experts believe it is the USS *Surprise*, which had been instructed to intercept the Harwich packet *Prince of Orange* in the English Channel, to seize secret documents. At the prow is a depiction of the US flag; as the first stars and stripes flag was only designed in 1776–7, it is most likely the earlier Continental Union Flag. A squiggle is believed to be a picture of a timber rattlesnake, the symbol of Virginia. Sue said, 'It's well known for never giving up. When Americans tourists see it, they say "'Don't tread on me" – apparently held to be an expression of patriotism, so I'm surprised I haven't heard Trump use it.'

The Electric Palace Cinema, built in 1911, is the oldest unaltered purpose-built cinema in Britain. It was almost demolished after being seriously damaged in the terrible North Sea flood of 1953 which killed eight people and left 3,500 homeless. Again, committed local volunteers saved it. Early projections would have been accompanied by music-hall performers and other acts. Fairground showman Charles Thurston – who had experience of travelling cinema, or Bioscope – financed its construction and the ornate, roll-up, roll-up frontage stands out. The opening film was the just-released *The Battle of Trafalgar*, produced by Thomas Edison. Nelson visited Harwich in August 1810 aboard the 32-gun frigate *Medusa* to check on the formation of the Sea Fencibles, a local defence force. He is said to have slipped off the ship to meet his lover Lady Hamilton at the Three Cups.

And why wouldn't he? Harwich's pubs are hideaways made for excesses of love and libation. Some ninety-four pubs have been named at forty-eight different sites. You often hear of such numbers in quite small towns. Our recent ancestors were sociable creatures, thirsty workers; home was not the high-walled castle it has become. Only around ten Harwich pubs remain, but they are lovely and most look as if they haven't been modernised. The Globe, opened in 1753, is a dimly lit conspiratorial drinking den under the brow of a jetty, with sash windows and external wiring. The British Flag, almost as old, has a Flemish-bond brick frontage and leaded windows; it was popular with Trinity House seamen. The Alma has a corridor bar where people would crowd in for a swift one or a bottle. Ex-pubs are sometimes evident because of old signage, as on the former Wellington.

Some of the old captains' houses are grand. Most residential proper-ties are small, no two alike, almost quaint, but they're not pimped up or even recently painted. It's as if residents here know their attractive harbour townlet could slip from its moorings and become a destina-tion. Let's keep things plain and simple, they have tacitly agreed. I'm not sure I've ever come across such a density of period architecture in so confined an area. Heritage in a city exists in pockets, providing a diversion from now. In the countryside it might be a mummified old hall or ruined abbey, with ice lollies and cream teas. Harwich is crammed with, and haunted by, its old, alluringly allusive places.

The town has a history of welcoming outsiders. Huguenots and Flem-ish Protestants found refuge here. A statue between the RNLI station and Ha'penny Pier, unveiled in 2022, commemorates the thousands of children who came in the Kindertransport. Many were accommo-dated at the nearby Dovercourt Bay holiday camp – which had a later life as the location for the eighties BBC sitcom *Hi-de-Hi*.

Harwich's close-knittedness stems from the peninsular setting, the camaraderie of shipbuilding, ferries and fishing; nearly full employ-ment in the past meant local people didn't have to travel far to work. They lived cheek by jowl and intermarried. Sue said, 'I know a man, aged fifty-plus, who has never travelled further than the traffic lights in Dovercourt, because he has never felt the need. Even though I have lived here on and off for fifty years, I still encounter people who turn out to be related to or used to be married to other people I know, and everyone seems to get along.

'I remember, when I was aged twenty or twenty-one, going to a sail-ing club Christmas dance in the mid 1970s and being shocked at how young people would attend alongside their siblings, parents, grand-parents, aunties, uncles and cousins and everyone enjoyed themselves.' I'd seen this kind of inter-generational bonding on the Greek island of Ikaria; it has been given as a cause of longevity, which is disputable, but it is bound to make for social cohesion and mutual well-being.

A Muniments of Harwich document contains records dating back six hundred years; thirty surnames ripple across the entries. The 1953 flood, 1987 hurricane (when lots of boats were wrecked) and pandemic have pushed people ever closer together. Harwich is a deep seaside community, a memory-haven, a ghost port, a kind of island, telling a story oceanically remote from Towie, 'Essex girl' and 'Mondeo man'.

The streets are quiet in the evening. Being at the end of the road, Harwich doesn't have through traffic. An earlier wooden Low Lighthouse is the subject of a painting by John Constable, with sailing ships in the distance; the serenity seems tenuous, with the sea wave-flecked and, further away, turning an almost lurid green under storm clouds. Now the same viewpoint encompasses Felixstowe, the UK's busiest cargo port, and its gargantuan vessels, the gantry cranes perpetually loading and offloading containers. When a sailing dinghy flutters past beneath a teetering Evergreen behemoth it's like a glider passing the Death Star. Maybe it was the wind direction, but I couldn't hear so much as a clang or a hum.

Sue mentioned how Harwich, in quite recent glory days, filled with Russians and Poles, shopping for jeans, and exchange students, and Swedes and Germans. It sent me back to the train I took from Warsaw, in the summer of 1986, and my fellow passengers: an African student from Marxist Benin studying in Moscow; a survivor of the Sobibor extermination camp in eastern Poland. How strange and terrible that Minsk and Moscow are more walled off today than in the chillest days of the Cold War.

My head was full of my and the town's memories as I walked back to the hotel. I heard a shanty emanating from the rear of the Alma, and wished I was someone else: an itinerant singer with a signature siren song; a trusted local, submerged in the audience; a Hemingway-sized toper, wading into the pub to buy rounds and whisper loudly about the sea.

13
Back to the River
Ipswich

P lace names are poems: Silent Street, where sound was dampened by straw out of respect for convalescing soldiers in the hospital; Smart Street, after a benevolent merchant, portman, library-builder and almshouse-endower. Star Lane, for Stella Maris, the guiding spirit at sea; Falcon Street and Dog's Head Street, lost pubs; Franciscan Way, leading to Grey Friars Road, St Peter's Street segueing into St Nicholas Street, evoke monkish times. Thirteen medieval churches rise above the compact old town, some in an advanced state of disrepair. Here and there, a renaissance; St Mary le Tower was recently redesignated as a minster, in recognition of its value to the community and its thousand years of existence. But that's not so long ago in these parts.

Jericho, Damascus, Thebes . . . Ipswich? As the name indicates, the town is of Anglo-Saxon foundation (it's been known as Gypeswych, Iepesuuicc, Ipswyche and other variations on 'Gip', meaning corner, and 'Wich', meaning landing place). An anonymous eighth- or ninth-century poem, 'The Ruin', records, probably in relation to Bath, or perhaps Chester, 'Their bulwarks were broken, their halls laid waste, the cities crumbled'. If older centres – London, Colchester, York – were abandoned when the Romans left, then Ipswich, founded in about 450, can – and does – claim to be the oldest 'English' town. At Rendelsham, fourteen miles north-east of Ipswich, illegal detectorists unearthed a major social and administrative centre. Four legit sweepers were called in to delve and dig. King Raedwald, the first Christian ruler of the East Angles, who died in 625, is probably buried at the site. The TV show about rivalrous detectorists was shot on location there.

I have to rummage in 2025 Ipswich to access its historical treasures, which lie scattered, disguised, buried, bullied. The town has one of the best-preserved medieval cores in the country, but post-1960 town planners have wrapped it in roads and houses and, latterly, retail and leisure big boxes – a barrier of chains. Modern apartment buildings wall in the River Orwell. Slowly, things are revealed by walking: the

Tooley's Court almshouses, lemon-hued half-timbered Curson Lodge, the gloriously pargeted Ancient House on the Buttermarket, the opulent town hall and even grander post office on the Cornhill, the main square. When I stand between the columns and arches of Lloyds Avenue I feel the prospect would not be out of place in Trieste or Venice, minus the overtourism and €10 cappuccinos. It's unseasonably warm in March; Ipswich is one of the country's driest, sunniest towns.

St Peter's church has a ceremonial side door dating from when Cardinal Wolsey planned a school for Ipswich. This most eminent Ipswichian was a butcher's son, possibly born in a tavern. His 550th birthday was celebrated in 2023. A local said the angle was 'local boy made good'. No one wanted to wait for the 600th. Perhaps *Wolf Hall* nudged things along, with the Cromwell story always shadowed by that of the beloved royal advisor, as moralising memory, as spectral murderee. Wolsey's fall from official grace led to the abandonment of the educational project he had in mind for his birthplace. Shakespeare and Fletcher refer to it in Act IV Scene 2 of *Henry VIII*, Queen Katherine's usher Griffith saying of Wolsey 'Those twins of learning that he raised in you, / Ipswich and Oxford! one of which fell with him'.

The town's museum is closed for a major refurb, which is a pity, as the Victorian interior looks splendid in photographs: glass cabinets for butterflies and a giraffe, intricate woodwork, wrought-iron balconies. I head instead to Tudor times, passing through expansive Christchurch Park – once the grounds of a priory – to visit its Mansion. Volunteer and Friend Erica shows me around. Only four families ever lived here – the Withypolls, Devereuxs, Fonnereaus, Cobbolds – each associated with their times' trades: Atlantic merchant-adventurers, titled nobles, Huguenot linen traders, brewing and banking. On the walls and up the staircases are portraits of whey-faced members of the gentry, pouting and powdered, their hairstyles frothing up and wilting as fashions change. The mansion's contents turn out to be a cryptic clutter-pile of artefacts, furniture and artworks, some pieces

                        where tourists seldom tread

sourced from old townhouses that were demolished, sometimes to make way for (long-gone) tramlines.

A standout exhibit is a patinaed oak overmantel rescued from a house on Fore Street that belonged to Thomas Eldred, who sailed with Thomas Cavendish in 1586 – on the second circumnavigation led by an English captain. On said mantel are depicted the flagship *Desire*, a globe and Aldred wielding a telescope. In a nearby corner hangs a portrait of Admiral Edward Vernon, who participated in the War of Jenkins' Ear and the capture of Portobelo; he was known for wearing garments of grogram cloth and is thought to have introduced rum-and-water toasts to the navy – or 'grog'. The floor is covered in Armada chests and other trunks and coffers. I spot Ipswich's coat of arms: three stern rudders, an innovation the town is reputed to have invented. Ipswich traded with northern Europe from Saxon times and grew to become a major Hanseatic League port, exporting wool and woollen cloth and importing wine from Bordeaux. Sixteenth-century agricultural writer, poet and farmer Thomas Tusser described it as 'a town of price, like Paradise'. Defoe remembered seeing 'perhaps two hundred sail of ships' lying in winter.

The mansion has significant collections of works by Thomas Gainsborough and John Constable. The former's *Holywells Park* – showing a deep-green idyllic landscaped panorama at eventide – broken up by translucent circular pools – has been called 'a turning point . . . probably the first landscape that is artistically independent and entirely his own'. The latter's *Golding Constable's Kitchen Garden* was painted in 1815, the year the artist's mother died after collapsing following a stroke in the garden, and when his father was ill. Long shadows and a very English summer storm sadden and threaten, respectively. He never sold the painting during his lifetime. The curators have blown up a section of the canvas so you can take a selfie 'in' a Constable. Close by was an exhibition of contemporary photography, *An Eye for Life*, featuring the work of Fleet Street lensman John Ferguson; his work ranges widely, from Bowie to warzones to

Pink in a taxi in Paris, but the images of black Ipswich evoke what he calls a town becoming 'increasingly progressive . . . some black people have never experienced racism till they leave here'.

The Ipswich section of Norman Scarfe's *Shell Guide to Suffolk*, published in 1960, opens with the line 'IPSWICH, the biggest port between Thames and Humber, a pleasant market town with prosperous traditional industries and the county town of East Suffolk'. None of this is true now, for various reasons, but the opening clause is the most arresting. Ipswich is still the busiest agricultural port in the UK, while nearby Felixstowe has supplanted it as a mega-port.

On the harbour front is Isaacs on the Quay, a pub carved out of an old maltings. Behind it, at 80 Fore Street, is – according to Historic England – 'the last surviving example of a C15–C17 Ipswich Merchants house with warehouses at the rear opening directly on the dock front, where merchandise was unshipped, stored and distributed wholesale or sold retail in the shop on the street front'. In the eighties, the local council considered filling the harbour in and building houses, but a festival in 1982 showed that the area could be a place of recreation as well as cultural preservation; the Ipswich Maritime Trust (IMT), still very active, grew out of this showdown.

The harbour is a melange of periods and styles. There's a looming, unused grain silo – once owned, the white-on-black painted sign says, by R. & W. Paul Ltd – that looks in need of a purpose. A similar building was torn down in 2006. The structure next door is plastered with 'Demolition in Progress' warnings and emits death rattles. There's a rusting frame of some other lost structure, and vivacious street art. The decay and ruins and graffiti work well together. An old warehouse, Waterfront House on Wherry Quay, has been preserved with its curious ironwork overhang. Newbuild, some of it sensitively aping the older buildings, promises harbourside living and workspaces. There's a posh hotel, several barista-run coffee shops, a growing university campus; when I looked up Suffolk and learned it was officially established in 2016, I supposed it was the UK's youngest university, but there have been ten more since then. The grandiose, colonnaded Victorian customs house aspires to preside over the whole, but is overlooked on all sides. In the large side window of a Londis store, the IMT has installed a pop-up mini-museum showing how the harbour grew and the New Cut was needed to enable vessels to turn. I look across to this channel and, scanning right of the masts in the yacht marina, see old signage on a red-brick gable for Fisons. Of all the firms associated with Ipswich – Ransomes, Cranes, Sims, Cobbold – Fisons is the one that rings a loud bell. Its chief advancement on foundation was manufacturing superphosphates from coprolites – fossilised dinosaur faeces. In 1842 a botany-loving vicar found a hoard of prehistoric turds in the villages around Trimley on the River Orwell. By adding sulphuric acid he established that fertiliser could be produced, which Fisons turned into a lucrative business. On the harbour front, Coprolite Street is all that remains of the manure-making heyday.

In Ronald Blythe's *Akenfield* (1969), I'd read how a trip to Felixstowe beach was the annual holiday of a Suffolk farmer at the turn of the twentieth century. A 1940s painting in the mansion, *The Felixstowe to Ipswich Coach*, by Russell Sidney Reeve, showed passengers returning home from a holiday, knitting, smoking, their legs kept from the chill with blankets, while a dog sleeps. I went in the opposite direction, taking the morning bus to Felixstowe to walk back to Ipswich along the Orwell.

Felixstowe has retained something of its Victorian elegance, with seafront villas above well-maintained gardens, and a long pier not overburdened by amusements. All are watched over by South Beach Mansion, where Empress Augusta Victoria – wife of Kaiser Wilhelm – and five of her sons stayed in 1891, leading to the town gaining fame as a spa town. Beside the Martello tower was a large café-restaurant with floor to ceiling windows, in which retired patrons were sweating in blinding sunshine and tea-steam.

The start of the walk was stuttering, with the way barred by the port. I waited at a security gate while a freight train screeched and whistled. The first hour was peri-industrial, and then suddenly I was plunged into spring-budding woods. On my right was the glory of Trimley Marshes, a Suffolk Wildlife Trust reserve protecting avocet, marsh harrier, curlew, greylag goose, Brent goose, little egret and even nightingale. I could hear geese and ducks gossiping.

The gantries were never out of sight – and never stopped moving, as the MSC *Katie*, recently arrived from Colombo, was loaded with containers.

The saltmarsh and mudflats – a 'managed realignment' – are folded into the Suffolk and Essex Coast and Heaths National Landscape. Lapwing and redshank populate the scrapes. Bitterns overwinter in the shelter of the reedbeds. At Levington Creek a brackish lagoon had formed following the 1953 floods, evolving into a sanctuary for estuarine birds. Children's voices rose from behind a bluff; a private school, I later found out, in the former home of Edward Vernon. Approaching Nacton, I came upon a cool but sun-blessed Caribbean-looking beach, where I ate my sandwich. I totted up my bird sightings: two kestrels, a shag, lots of waders and seabirds, sandpipers, an egret, passerines galore. The sky was filled with mewling and fluting and laughing. I am so used to being in western England – born there, dwelling there – amid fog and rain and cleft valley that the crisp and gentle east wind, travelling untroubled over flat land and water, clearing away any fuzziness, was a welcome weather holiday.

Ipswich announced itself with a big concrete box-girder bridge and busy suburbs. The town's smaller docks cut off the shore and I headed inland and up a hill, gaining a view of the derelict Cobbold Tolly Brewery standing haunted-house-like over Cliff Quay. I had walked from global scale to human scale, from computerisation and containment to marina and mouldering beer factory. Brewing, tanning, textiles, corsetry, shipbuilding and ship-loading: these

                              where tourists seldom tread

were the trades that drew in Suffolk's agricultural workers in the nineteenth century.

The Arcade Street Tavern occupies a Georgian townhouse on one side of an archway. The landlord, Ross, told me working from home was keeping people away; parties thrown on impulse were a rarity and, anyway, there was a generational shift, as under-thirties – at least, those who could afford to go out – preferred fruit smoothies. Their chief addiction was the smartphone. In the bathroom was a Tube map of lost, renamed and surviving pubs. More found poems; threnodies, epitaphs. Admiral's Hat. Admiral's Head. Blue Anchor. Britannia Inn. Ocean Queen. The Lost Pubs Project, which stretches back to the 1880s, lists 302 extinct pubs in this one town, and more than 45,000 in England. Ipswichians lament, in particular, the closure of the bar at the Great White Horse Hotel on Tavern Street, once a coaching house dating back to the early sixteenth century. In 1967 owners Trusthouse Forte wanted to demolish the building and replace it with offices and shops, but locals fought back and it was preserved. Nelson and George II stayed at least once, Dickens several times. In *The Pickwick Papers* he writes, 'Never was such labyrinths of uncarpeted passages, such clusters of mouldy, ill-lighted rooms, such huge numbers of small dens for eating or sleeping in, beneath any one roof, as are collected together between the four walls of the Great White Horse at Ipswich.'

Six Crown pubs have come and gone. In the extant one, all were watching the League Cup final. After Ipswich Town's humbling season it was an opportunity to vicariously sample the taste of victory. Portman Road, home of the Tractor Boys, is loved here but it is a lump of a building, all corrugated panels and vaulting trusses, an oafish member of the unbeautiful welcoming committee of architectural averageness. Bobby Robson, Alf Ramsey and rags-to-riches local legend Kevin Beattie are memorialised around the ground. Lisa, owner of Francophile bar and bistro the Crafty Fox, told me football was the thing that held the town together: 'Football is community. Ipswich is a large town that feels like a small town. Community matters and football is what people have in common. Even people you wouldn't normally expect to follow football follow Town.' The pragmatic rallying cry among the faithful is 'Follow the Town, up or down'. The Council's promo department called its campaign accompanying the 2024–5 season 'Added Time', as if expecting imminent relegation. Pasted in shop windows as part of a fan-led project were handsome posters for the season's matches – Ipswich's first in the Premier League since 2002 – inspired by vintage railway advertisements. The glory days were being given a retro makeover before they were even concluded.

I drank my way around twenty Ipswich pubs, some alone, some in the company of my nephew, Daniel, who was living in Suffolk. We got tipsy and reflective and remembered lost loved ones as families do. As I made my way back to my hotel on Neptune Quay, I realised I had forgotten to toast our reunion and the ending of our pub-crawl night with a shot of celebratory grog.

Suffolk farmers laid down their forks, fans and sickles in the 1870s during the great agricultural depression that followed the opening up of US prairies and steamship freighting, and again in the 1960s when widespread mechanisation decimated jobs – the 'second agricultural revolution' according to Ronald Blythe. Between these slumps fell two world wars, which also saw young country dwellers signing up to secure steady wages and full bellies. Following father into farming ceased to be the norm; young men denied being in 'reserved occupations'.

Which way should Ipswich look? To the river and the sea, or to farmland, fertiliser and fen? Which is the future, which the past?

History and the world flowed in through the Orwell. Between 1400 and the late twentieth century, UK trade tilted from northern Europe/France to the West/Atlantic and the Empire, and back to the EU: Ipswich, Bristol and Liverpool, Felixstowe. And now, no one knows.

There's a tension between the East Anglia of agriculture – *Akenfield* and Fisons – with its digging, downward force, and the outward pull of the river. Sea and land. Mud and coprolite. There is the prominence and weight of a past against an uncertain, but hopeful, future.

Post-war containerisation mirrors what happened in farming. Boxes and toxins. Cranes and factories. Family businesses transformed into groups, PLCs, floating initials. Mysteries became secrets. Grain vies with plastic unicorns. I wish containers were made of glass. I want to know what all the crap is that is offloaded on the wharves.

The town itself is chopped up badly. There is no natural flow between the ancient town centre and the harbourside. But one can easily imagine it being re-landscaped one day to create a seamless riverside town. Then again, the sea is rising, and Ipswich could one day be an island. Environmentalist Jules Pretty opens his 2021 book *This Luminous Coast* – about the author's reflective rambles along the East Anglian littoral – by telling us: 'This is a coast which is about to be lost. Not yet, but it will happen soon.' W. G. Sebald, contemplating low-lying lands devastated by storms and shifting trade patterns, writes that 'the east stands for lost causes'. But following the installation of the Trump/Vance/Witkoff Reich, the western skies look black.

Commercial interests ebb and flow. The Europe-facing ports might have their new moment sooner than anyone expected. Ipswich, the oldest town, could be great again. Is this a stream of consciousness speaking, or just this river on which Ipswich has partially turned its back?

14
To the Sky, to Infinity
Boston

have a soft spot in my secular soul for St Botolph, after whom Boston is named. When I was a theology student in the mid-1980s, I had a summer job as verger-cum-cleaner of St Botolph without Aldersgate in the City of London. It was a quiet church, well off the tourist trail. Unassuming from the outside, the nave had handsome colonnaded galleries and plaster vaulting that could uplift, even when I was mopping and dusting. Botolph is the patron saint of boundaries and travel. Three other churches dedicated to him once stood guard at London's gates.

His greatest house is in Boston, completed in the sixteenth century, and known as the Stump – despite being one of the tallest churches in the country. It was a beacon for returning sailors as well as those crossing the great ocean of the Fenlands. The name may refer to the fact it was not finished off with a spire, or to its resemblance to a lopped-off tree trunk. It might be a mocking nickname, coined by envious neighbours.

I paid a fee, was handed a key and climbed the 209 steps that spiral up the narrow shaft to the top. I could hear a billowing wind and the more comforting coo and burble of pigeons as I neared the uppermost gallery. Outside, the views were immense, west to the great fields of winter cereals and solar panels, north to Lincoln Cathedral and southeast to the Norfolk coast. It was mid-December, half past twelve, and the shadow of the Stump stretched out far below, more or less at the right time, like the gnomon of a giant sundial.

A bell behind my head bonged a quarter to. I descended like a nervous fireman, holding the rope all the way down.

Sunshine floods the inside of the lantern tower. Puritans replaced the original stained glass with clear to let in the 'cleanly' light of the Gospel. The tinted glass we see today is Victorian. Though its foundations lie in clay below the water table, often inundated by river and sea, the church is still almost perfectly perpendicular. It's a vaulting, expansive palace of arches, castellations, friezes and tracery, a Gothic hulk in the least 'gothick' of landscapes.

—

The Fens suggest an extension of the Low Countries, as if Doggerland slipped underwater only a century or two ago. The surrounding area is known as the Parts of Holland. Tulips are grown. The long-serving dykes, ditches and pumps, and even the modern Boston Tidal Barrier, would be familiar to a Netherlander. The Flemish bond, the curved gables and stepped frontages feel foreign, but not very. The outdoor sequences for the 1942 war film *One of Our Aircraft Is Missing*, set in Nazi-occupied Holland, were shot around Boston.

Old Boston looked east for trade. The Hanseatic League, which dominated the North and Baltic seas, had a local depot here. In the thirteenth century, the port of Boston was the second-most important maritime trading centre after London. Sheep fleeces, lead and salt were shipped to Europe. In came wine, pelts, spices and silk to be sold at the market. The earliest maps of Boston show the marketplace – one of the country's largest – at its current location. Once a year the London courts would close so that the monied could visit Boston for the May Fair.

But many Bostonians went west, joining the outflow of unhappy Christians who followed St Botolph's minister John Cotton and pilgrims' capo William Brewster (who was imprisoned in the Guild-hall) to New England. A twelfth of Boston's population would end up in Massachusetts. Architectural memories accompanied them. Yale University's Harkness Tower was inspired by the Boston Stump, as was New York's Riverside Church. Some skyscrapers are said to quote it.

In a far-off time when continental Europeans wanted to live in the UK – 2010–2015 – Boston attracted the largest contingent of Lithuanians and second-highest number of Polish immigrants in the country. Latvians and Romanians also made up sizeable communities and around a tenth of the town was of Eastern European origin. Some sixty-five languages were spoken in this town of 70,000 people; the Stump was suddenly a Tower of Babel. Following Brexit, many immigrants have gone home or elsewhere, but as I walk around the large square on market day, I hear Romanian, Polish and tongues I don't know but which come from the east. Communities have settled. Shop-fronts on the high street use the colours of foreign flags. One capacious caravan-type stall displays a huge array of cured meats and kielbasa.

The town could do with importing some buskers. The atmosphere is lively and upbeat, despite a cold breeze, but on Strait Bargate the worst violinist I've ever heard and a pretty awful synth player are providing an experimental soundtrack, bereft of melody, phrasing or even re-assuring repetition. Alleys peel off the marketplace in all directions. I dive down one, partly to escape the cacophony. I follow my nose, mapless, sometimes walking in circles. Several streets – Dolphin Lane, High Street, South Street, Wormgate – feel ancient, and all around Boston are historic buildings. When Nicholas Antram was revising the Lincolnshire volume of the Pevsner *Buildings of England* series in the mid-nineties, he said there was 'an urgent need for a detailed investiga-tion of the buildings in the town centre.' Boston had been ignored and overlooked, which had allowed developers to hold sway. Since then, Historic England has surveyed the town and noted its unique charac-ter. Boston's Guildhall is one of the oldest post-Roman brick buildings in England. No fewer than fourteen guilds – organisations concerned with religion as well as trade – powered its economy. It was one of only eleven Staple towns in the land in the fourteenth century, permitted to export wool – from a vast area of the Midlands – internationally. The funnel shape of the marketplace echoes those found in Halle, Aachen, Soest and Bonn. Towers and cloisters, warehouses and halls, mansions and a giant windmill are testament to Boston's two main golden ages as a medieval wool town and, following draining of the surrounding fens in the seventeenth and eighteenth centuries, as an agri-port.

A decade ago, Boston was deemed the 'most Brexit town', with 76 per cent of voters electing to leave the EU in the 2016 referendum. UKIP targeted the Boston and Skegness seat in the following year's general election, without much success, but still the right-wing press liked to keep up the pressure, referring to Boston as 'Little Poland' and 'Boston Lincolngrad.' In the 2024 general elections, Reform

UK's deputy leader, the Surrey-born, privately educated property dealer Richard Tice, won the seat.

In 2015, Boston joined the Hansa, a voluntary association of 200 cities across sixteen countries, founded to celebrate the original trading relationships and shared cultural heritage. Jane Keightley, an active member, says Boston's long history needs to be disseminated to remind people its roots are cosmopolitan: 'The town can be a bit of an island. We are out on a limb. A lack of education and the fact people don't travel means, to be honest, that they can be a bit racist and bigoted. We are trying to educate people that Boston was full of Lithuanians and Latvians back then.'

The Fens beguile. They look firm and flat but they are fluid. They invite the walker and the rider to make haste, but they hide traps and morasses. They flood, threatening farms and livestock, overflowing into rivers; the silting of the River Witham has played a determining role in Boston's fluctuating fortunes.

Prior to drainage, this was the territory of fen-slodgers, 'half amphibious beings who got their living by fishing and fowling'. They lived in reed-roofed dwellings, sloshing through the sludge in eel-skin garters (to ward off rheumatism), hacking out turves for fuel and snaring, shooting and vaulting dykes using long poles and walking on stilts. A race apart, some claimed the slodgers had webbed feet. When engineers came to control the watercourses and drain their homelands, they were too scattered to put up resistance.

Before he was a saint, Botolph was a Saxon noble from East Anglia. It's said he expelled devils from the swamps. It was probably a more mundane mission, draining the marshes and lighting the gases that were emitted – which resembled evil spirits.

In that plashy and indeterminate scape of half-land and half-water, the horizon can be a solace. Poet Paul Verlaine travelled to England in 1875 after being released from prison – he had been sent down for shooting his lover Arthur Rimbaud – and found himself at Stickney, teaching French and drawing. In search of more affluent pupils he moved to Boston, where he lodged with an Italian photographer who had a sideline – a museum of curiosities that included a whale skeleton. According to the poet's biographer, Bechhofer Roberts, the two bohemian expats 'emulated Jonah by placing a table and chairs inside the whale's belly and spending their leisure hours there over a glass of beer and a pipe'. When not out walking with his pupils, Verlaine worked on his poems. He missed Rimbaud desperately and wrote his very last letter to him while in Stickney. *Sagesse* (1880) contains this verse about the Fens:

Rows of hedges
Roll to infinity, sea
Clear in the clear mist
Which smells good, like young berries.

Debussy used the lines in one of his heartbreakingly beautiful *Trois Mélodies de Verlaine*.

to the sky, to infinity

15

Northbound

Doncaster

In that pleasant district of merry England which is watered by the river Don, there extended in ancient times a large forest, covering the greater part of the beautiful hills and valleys which lie between Sheffield and the pleasant town of Doncaster.

From *Ivanhoe* by Walter Scott

One definition of the North is 'point of no return'. From London, on horseback. In 1603 Sir Robert Carey, charged with delivering the news that Elizabeth had died to James at Holyrood, galloped the 170 miles from London to Doncaster in a single day. 'At Doncaster you were committed; there could be no turning back that day,' as historian Frank Musgrove puts it. Bolingbroke was proclaimed Henry IV at Doncaster. When preparing for the decisive battle at Flodden, the Earl of Surrey mobilised his forces at Doncaster. The northern powers met their foes to negotiate at Doncaster during the Pilgrimage of Grace. That great northern rising would never penetrate south of the Don.

England's envoys were only following their Roman forebears, whose route north to Hadrian's Wall was via Lincoln to Doncaster. Doncaster was a natural forward base for controlling the region, and for summits and, sometimes, skirmishes and battles. The Great North Road provides both entry point and focus for a day trip in ancient Donny.

The A18 aka Leger Way – named for Doncaster's famous flat race – is the inner ring road, noisy and fuming. Slicing through it, the A648, the Great North Road, becomes a boulevard as elegant as its name: Bennetthorpe. English street names are a last bulwark against the Americanisation of towns, the banal literalness of Screwfix and Specsavers. Walking into town I pass, on South Parade, smart early-nineteenth-century terraces – first in brick and then larger, stuccoed, more obviously Georgian townhouses. The road rises, the pavement broadens out generously. From the left-hand side, viewing the houses from a monument called the Hall Cross, hedgerows block off traffic. Anything that occludes cars – the second-ugliest thing in any town, parked or moving – is welcome.

Doncaster could be Bath. Extensive parks spread out on both sides of the road. At Regent Square, leafiness comes close in. I sit on a bench, and watch two cats luxuriating in the morning sunshine, beneath a blossoming cherry tree. Not all the properties are well kept.

The so-called Pillared House, where a plaque says the Prince of Wales stayed in 1806 when attending the races, is dilapidated. 'Boarded up by Adrian Welch' announces the sign on the windows. It's the name I see most frequently around town.

Opposite the terraces are: the Earl Hotel, a thirties building that has had its original art deco style not so much revived as blingingly reimagined; the Point, a thriving gallery, café and cultural space; and the Salutation, a lovely old boozer that still has its arch for the entrance of horse-drawn coaches. Doncaster now gathers pace, and this old main drag bristles with drinking holes. Pub names offer further resistance: the Tut N Shive, the Leopard, the Yorkshire Grey, the Angel and Royal; the Red Lion, where the name of the St Leger was decided; the Little Plough, which has an interior like a favourite grandma's parlour; the White Swan used to lay claim to having the 'world's tallest bar' – there are photographs online of averagely heighted people stretching up to collect their drinks. As elsewhere, locals lament the passing of Doncaster's glory days in the pubbing stakes, but I had a long discussion with a visitor from Selby on a day trip who told me, 'Donny is shtill a great shplace for a proper drink.' I would have loved, though, to reach up for another Old Horizontal at the high bar. Lost heritage of the castles and shambles kind moves me not at all, but pubs are living museums. On the edge of the town centre, the Rock-A-Hula Tiki Bar and Rodeos Wild West-themed bar are rearing up, cocktail shakers and cowboys come to supplant indigenous innkeepers.

Hall Gate becomes High Street. Across the ground are two undulating ribbons of tiles featuring timelines – one relating to Doncaster (floods, 1750; founding of Danecastre, 1152, Romans invade, 55 BC), the other to world events (Braille, 1837; Cubism, 1907; the Peruvian Chimu people, undated). The artwork is suggestive, unobtrusive, good fun.

Seriously standing above it is the Mansion House, one of two Grade I listed buildings, and the official base (though no longer residence) of the civic mayor. Free tours are organised every month. It has a grand

               where tourists seldom tread

staircase, meeting rooms, ballroom, former ladies' room for crocheting and tea, former men's drinking salon, vintage clocks, naval and air force mementos, and a handsome stained-glass window showing the coat of arms, which contains an owl, a raven, a griffin, a miner's safety lamp for the nine local collieries, an anchor for the former port at Bawtry Wharf on the River Idle, a lightning bolt signifying power generation and a British Rail Double Arrow. There are only four Mansion Houses in the UK; the others are in York, London and Edinburgh. Next door, on Priory Place – recalling the fourteenth-century Carmelite priory around which the medieval town grew – is the tourist information centre, where you can collect a free map and a guide to Doncaster's heritage buildings.

You see the Roman name Danum all over: Danum hotel; Danum plumbing and heating; Danum coffee, greenhouses, air conditioning, couplings, fulfilment. The Danum library, gallery and museum is a remarkable contemporary building, not only incorporating part of the Doncaster High School for Girls, but showcasing its 1906 brick and stone facade through tall windows. It is most striking after dark. The largest display space is dedicated to Doncaster's railway history.

Doncaster Works built two of the most celebrated British engines: *Flying Scotsman* and *Mallard*. These aren't on show, but York Railway Museum has loaned the Danum *Green Arrow* and *Atlantic 251* – two steam-puffing beasts forged by local hands. Rail enthusiasts, who had been stashing memorabilia in a clock tower at another school, donated a large collection of station and engine signage, scale models, guidebooks and other items, including a hot water bottle used by a driver and a Woodbine cigarettes dispenser. Known locally as the Plant, Doncaster Works produced the UK's first sleeping cars, dining cars and corridor coaches. More than four thousand people were employed there in the early twentieth century, and when production ceased in 1957, 2,228 new steam locomotives had rolled off the line; refurbishment continued for a few more years and ten thousand locos were overhauled at Doncaster Works. Some engines' names sound like sea vessels: *Flamboyant, Inflexible.* Others are cosier: *Bantam Cock, Daisy. Cock o' the North* recalls the Plant's glory days.

Locomotion is still integral to Doncaster life. Riding in on the Azuma you are reminded it's just two stops from Doncaster to Kings Cross (Grand Central trains go non-stop). Sixty-seven services on a weekday in each direction. This is 'supercommuter' territory. In the late eighties, I worked, briefly, as a civil servant and had a colleague who travelled daily from Doncaster to work at Earl's Court, eleven stops along the Piccadilly Line. I chatted to him briefly (he was always in a hurry) in the lift of our tower block and he assured me he had made the right choice, listing the benefits of local housing, family values, not living in London. He explained how he had a full breakfast every morning before catching up on sleep. He went straight to bed on arriving home in suburban Doncaster. We were chatting at around 6 p.m. He can't have been in his pyjamas before ten.

The Danum has beautiful library areas for adults and children, a great little restaurant, a museum and an art gallery that juxtaposes old masterish oils of race meetings and wigged grandees with contemporary work reflecting the most forward-looking attitudes to mental health and creativity-as-therapy.

The area around this impressive multi-use space is very much the New Doncaster. Next door are a sleek council HQ, a huge theatre, cinema, a large piazza with a multi-jet water feature, slick food outlets and a flash new technical college. Cuboids, chains, exposure, sharp angles. If you don't like it, cross the road for a fix of some seventies' retail 'late Modernism'. The decay is unspoiled, demolition a dead cert.

The Frenchgate shopping centre is easy to swerve. High Street runs past on one side. On the other runs Printing Office Street – an early instance of US-style literalism? – which is capped by a monument to Doncaster's miners. Called *A Rich Seam*, it was paid for with crowdfunding, created by Lawrence Edwards and depicts a life-size bronze miner standing between two twenty-ton lumps of York stone, into which are embedded thirty-nine bronze portraits of local miners, their family members, a pit nurse and a mines rescue worker. The main miner seems to have his eyes closed, listening to stories; some of the faces are downcast, all are serious. A flurry of mining activity at the end of the nineteenth century turned several villages into substantial colliery settlements – pit towns, some of them pressing in on Doncaster's hitherto green fringes. The furore must have been similar to when the shopping centre was dropped into the heart of the town, blitzing older structures: department stores, bus stops, tea shops.

On St Sepulchre Gate I see a tidily done relief of the Burtons name, high on the parapet of a building. The ground floor is shared by an optician's and a bank. The frontages are purple, red and snot green. Uglier even than parked cars. Nearby are markets for fish, meat, veg, clothes and takeaway food, with the indoor sections housed in the rear of the former Corn Exchange, a neoclassical Victorian building with a ribbed, panelled dome that nods to the Crystal Palace. The former Wool Market has been turned into an 'international food hall', closed during my visit. Immediately behind the smart redevelopment, multi-ethnic food and shopping have organically colonised Copley Road and Nether Hall Road. One supermarket claimed to be Bulgarian, Asian, English, Turkish, Polish and Romanian. There were several African stores, Middle Eastern food vendors and halal butchers. That evening I had dinner at La Boca, an Asian-run Argentinian steakhouse.

St George's church is Doncaster's other grade-I building. Known as the Minster, it's prominent and can be seen from afar, rising above the city. But it's been somewhat islanded by traffic and development. Designed by George Gilbert Scott, Pevsner said it was the 'proudest and most cathedral-like of . . . parish churches'. When I entered, the vicar was whispering a communion to a dozen congregants, mustered around the chancel. At the rear of the church, twice that number were waiting for a free meal. Doncaster has a large population of poor, poorly, pained and drink- and drug-dependent. I sat down while the service concluded. Dark and gloomy, and busy on the eye in the Gothic manner, with stained-glass windows whose light is rich and gorgeous for being subdued, the Minster's interior instructs the visitor to be patient and thoughtful. Jun'ichirō Tanizaki's *In Praise of Shadows* came to mind: 'Were it not for shadows there would be no beauty . . . [we] prefer a pensive lustre to a shallow brilliance, a murky light that, whether in a stone or an artefact, bespeaks a sheen of antiquity. Of course this "sheen of antiquity" of which we hear so much is in fact the glow of grime.'

After the bread and wine had been put away for the serving of soup, I walked out of town and over the railway line on the North Bridge. I looked back to the churches and then to the left, to HMP Doncaster. It, too, is stranded – by the River Don, Don Navigation and River Cheswold – and known to inmates and locals as Doncatraz. The road took me past the Danum Retail Park, where an ironic-civic planner had positioned a bench inside the tangle of low hedges, facing York Road, the name for this section of the A638. Rumbling waves of lorries, cars and vans came with each green light, while the footpath wavered between exhaust-scented pavement and parallel residential street. My phone was dying so I asked a man where the ridge began. He told me to look out for the Sun Inn.

I live right on the western border of the old West Riding of Yorkshire. The south and east are unfamiliar. Sunnier and drier, flatter and older. Doncaster is perhaps no longer the pleasantest town in the north, as it was for Walter Scott, but it has kind weather and warm, creamy stone instead of gritstone. It's a great British transit city. Doncaster wants its airport reopened – with its nuclear-bomber-, space-shuttle- and Antonov-friendly mega-runway. A local MP has proposed a huge orbital Superloop bus route connecting a string of towns and villages.

Through it all cuts the Roman Ridge, a branch off Ermine Street. When I get there, behind the Sun, there are light industrial units and

                               where tourists seldom tread

the hum and heave of the main road. It is unprepossessing, but a blue tit carolled a welcome to the footpath proper. Four magpies courted or quarrelled on a small playing field. A female blackbird landed to pick up leaf litter and fluff for her new spring nest.

I walked till I was well away from the last roundabout. There I found a well-placed bench and ate my pie, watching the traffic on the Great North Road. The Romans are said to have introduced the idea of topping pies, and here was I having a Topping's pie on the road by which their legionnaires, and recipes, arrived. A sort of Roman pie on a kind of Roman road. The only way was up.

16
Estates of Mind
Gateshead

North East
Or
Nowhere

The first time I alight at Newcastle Central station is at the age of fifty-eight. I call myself a northerner, and yet this north is a complete unknown. Chance or destiny? Lancashire lads in the eighties went to London for the Big City, Manchester or Liverpool for Our City, and Glasgow or Edinburgh for a More Northern City. Others – Bath, Bristol, Plymouth, Exeter – were pretty, small or irrelevant. The coal-mining, shipbuilding, steel- and glass-making North-East is the other half of my homeland, a canny challenge to the North-West's self-esteem. What kept us apart all these years? History, I suppose, and the green vagueness of Yorkshire.

Gateshead has been in the news since the beginning of the new millennium. The Baltic, Sage and the Millennium Bridge are big, eye-catching institutions and structures, shouting across the river at Newcastle – where the city council strongly opposed the culture-led regeneration of its lowly neighbour. This riverside is a work in progress. It draws shade where Newcastle gets sunshine. The navy still has a training centre on the water; the right bank is firmly on its recruitment map. Wasteland is sectioned off for a conference centre. Go east and you're soon among industrial units, new offices, razor wire and dead ends.

Mentioned by Bede, as you'd expect, Gateshead was *ad caput caprae* – at the goat's head – a headland grazed by goats or perhaps an allusion to a goat totem on the old Roman bridge. A faun could be a satyr-like creature or a symbol of the forest. This was the northern edge of the County Palatinate of Durham. Records of monastic life at Getehed date from the seventh century. A bishop ordered woodlands chopped down to build ships; the area became known as Felling. In 1080 a church was burned down with the Bishop of Durham inside. St Mary's, which stands near the site, is the oldest building on the quayside. On a brow, it once marked arrival and rest, gave travellers their bearings. Today it looks bewildered amid the brazen newbuild and is chained off when I pass.

How do you get to know a new place when you first arrive? Walking, talking, reading, looking – they all count. A circular bus is instructive and uniquely relaxing. The 51 and 52 (one route, two directions) is known as the East Gateshead Orbital. In just over an hour I'll be able to say I have been to all the places I can see on my map. There's Felling, Deckham, Wrekenton, Low Fell, High Fell, Sheriff Hill, Leam Lane, Windy Nook. There will be Fellingers who never made it to Sheriff Hill, for one reason or another. I can tell them about it.

On the top deck at the front, I get a rolling tour of social stratification and architectural eras and styles – terraced rows, Tyneside flats (houses with two doors), semi-detached red-bricks, older stone houses, prefabs. There are many front gardens and they are like whole-family confessions, curiously moving when seen from above. It's been a rare, welcome hot day in a non-starter summer, and the oncoming evening is almost sultry. Neighbours lean on fences talking. Two children splash as messily as possible in a small paddling pool. A man cuts his privets. A woman sucks on a hookah on a driveway filled with family members. We stop a lot. Teens split from groups and climb aboard the bus to go home, plugging their eyes straight into screens. Only I ride all the way, the tourist, scanning the houses, looking for what – clues? This is estate-land, a maze of streets crammed with houses laid out where slums were cleared.

From the bus it is chaotically human. Gateshead contains the evolutionary history of street patterns, from the straight rows north of Saltwell Park to labyrinths of crescents and cul-de-sacs obeying the rustic rubric of the garden suburb (I note street names like Gorsehill, Harebell Road, Celandine Way, Meadow Rise and lots of lots of Something Gardens) to council-decreed Lego-maze – full of right angles and hard edges, but disorientingly rigged with zigzags, doglegs and communal areas.

Some estates replaced earlier ones. A stone's throw away from Heworth interchange, where the bus pauses to synchronise with the timetable, was St Cuthbert's Village – a self-contained council estate built in the sixties of low- and medium-rise concrete blocks. It was opened by Harold Wilson in 1970, demolished in 1995. David Olusoga, who grew up there, has written with candour about being regularly bullied by racists and how living on an estate – having to declare in front of the class that his address was a 'walk' – 'an ersatz street, a "street in the sky"' – made everything worse. No one fell for the 'village' gimmick, even with St Cuthbert – Northumbria's beloved divine, sympathetic to the poor – tagged on. Olusoga writes that at least the Scottish term 'scheme' and US 'project' suggest 'civic action'.

'Estate' has semantic roots that link it to 'possession' and 'status'. Inherited estates rarely and barely change. Many council estates have been demolished and defiled, as well as denigrated in the press. Almost seven million council homes were built across the UK between 1919 and 1979, between the post-war Housing and Town Planning Act and the Thatcher manifesto that included the 'right to buy' clause, the most socially damaging transfer of public wealth in modern British political history. We ignore what is ubiquitous, and the media have tended to obsess over tower-block housing. Yet for millions of us, low-lying estates – council and private – are at the centre of childhood memories. What makes east Gateshead different is that it is almost all estates – private, council, ex-council. Lynsey Hanley has written, 'It is as though a wall exists between the city and the estate' and describes being raised on a council estate as akin to having a 'wall in the head'. Seen from outside, there are multiple layers of mystery. How much tolerance is needed for so many people to live in such close proximity? Does repetition erode individuality and/or self-worth? Does life on a close close doors, and imaginations? I can believe a grim memory of collective enclosure endures for some former residents. But Gateshead is complex, and some of the estates look spruce enough.

J. B. Priestley, passing through, asked, 'How is it that a town can contain one hundred and twenty-five thousand persons and yet look like a sprawling swollen industrial village?' Being a Yorkshireman, he didn't wait for his reader's reply. 'The answer is that this is a dormitory for the working class.' The most quoted lines in the Gateshead section of his *English Journey* are 'the whole town appeared to have been carefully planned by an enemy of the human race' and 'No true civilisation could have produced such a town'. Commentators have stressed that Priestley was in a foul mood due to too much travelling, a nasty cold and medicines that left him feeling seedy. It was a wet November and the author had spent unhappy times in Newcastle as a convalescing soldier after the First World War. Slagging off has long been the prerogative of the aloof metropolitan travel writer – and shit sticks.

At its industrial peak in the nineteenth century, Northumbria, though home to only 5.1 per cent of Britain's population, mined almost a fifth of the nation's coal, was responsible for more than a third of its coke, iron ore and pig iron, and built just over half of its merchant ships. The motto of the County Borough of Gateshead, *'Caput Inter Nubila Condit'* – 'Its head is in the clouds' – is a quote from Virgil's *Aeneid*. Chosen by a soot-humoured town clerk, it ironically captured Tyneside's smoky, filthy, sky-staining atmosphere. Priestley saw the dirt but knew the boom years were well over.

Yet I find chiaroscuro on the orbital bus. We pass Kells Lane. At no. 99 is Underhill, the first house in the world to be wired for domestic electric lighting. The large, imposing detached property – now a retirement home – was the residence of Sunderland-born scientist Sir Joseph Wilson Swan, inventor of the incandescent lamp. Dan Jackson writes, in *Northumbrians*, 'The insatiable, local demand for sources of power, led to the birth of the electricity industry on Tyneside.' The first street to be illuminated using electrical power was Mosley Street in Newcastle. This Enlightenment was literal: the Geordie lamp and friction match were other local inventions. *'Fiat Lux'* – let there be light – is inscribed on a bronze plaque honouring Swan on the former headquarters of the Newcastle upon Tyne Electricity Supply Company on Pilgrim Street.

Who needs Latin? I prefer sometime Poet Laureate contender U. A. Fanthorpe's melodious Geordie in her version of 'Caedmon's Hymn':

                              where tourists seldom tread

Forst ther wes nowt   nowt and neewhere
God felt the empty   space wi his finga
Let's hev sum   light sez God
Ootbye and inbye   so the light happened.

I pass another Enlightenment site at Windy Nook – the birthplace of Joseph Hopper, bibliophile and founder of the Durham Aged Mine-Workers' Homes Association, a staunch Primitive Methodist who preached his first sermon aged fifteen and read avidly on political economy, history and biography.

On several occasions the bus summits higher than mobile masts and affords the top-decker views of the sea in one direction and hillsides and clumps of trees in the other. Some cities go on and on. Here I feel like I'm on a built-up island with Northumberland as the green ocean.

At the beginning and end of its loop, the bus passes Coburg Street. No. 25 was used to shoot the sleazy neon-lit Las Vegas boarding house that features throughout *Get Carter*. The bus actually runs along Prince Consort Road, used in a shot when Thorpe (Bernard Hepton) is trying to escape Carter (Michael Caine). The then newly built St Cuthbert's Village, bridges and other locales in the wider North-East also feature, but the most keening lament heard here, and loudly online, is for Gateshead's Trinity Square car park – a symbol of graft and the backdrop to a murder in the film. Built by Owen Luder in 1967, it was almost universally admired by concrete-loving Modernists. It was torn down in 2010 to make way for a Tesco.

The bus passes close to Saltwell Park, where Gazza played football on Saturdays, joining matches between teams of older boys to test his mettle. I go back a couple of days after my bus ride to take a look around. There's some curious public art – lots of it nature-inspired and abstract – and an excellent café run by Anglo-Portuguese barista Daniel Francisco. He took advantage of lower rents (than in Newcastle) and the beautiful setting. The walk back to my hotel takes me through Bensham, along Coatsworth Road, a multicultural retail thoroughfare. There are grocery stores, shops, delis and services aimed at Turkish, Arabic and Caribbean residents, and the long-established Jewish community. Nearby Gateshead Talmudical College is the largest yeshiva (Rabbinical school) outside Israel and the US. Since Rabbi Shraga Feivel Zimmerman arrived from Brooklyn in 2008, the number of students has more than doubled to around 440. He calls Gateshead 'the Oxbridge of the UK Jewish community'.

Gateshead faces Newcastle across the Tyne, sharing the bracing bridges, musical accent, fierce local identity. On the posts of the High Level Bridge are short graffiti, like sentences in a flicker-book – one says 'North East or Nowhere'. Newcastle looks civic and cluttered, with churches and offices and a castle and its massive stadium. Gateshead is mainly residential, a melding of inner city and suburb. It has a town centre: the big Tesco, the bookies and boozers, the transport inter-change, the sense of non-place not quite offset by the curious street art – a shining, tilting halo of blown steel by Stephen Newby. Roads and rail dominate, and have budged most things out of their way: trains into and out of Newcastle use different bridges. Fast, four-lane A-roads including the A167 – laid out over the medieval Great North Road and still named 'High Street' – have left gaping canyons flooded with carbon monoxide and particulate matter. But off the highways and under the ironwork there is hope. Vane Gallery, housed in a long-dead pub called the Dun Cow on said High Street, is the place from which art trickles up to the grant-hogging showcase museums like the Baltic. Four walls of the ground floor have been hung for the town's first-ever Pride – events for which had been postponed by the July–August 2024 far-right, anti-immigration protests and riots.

'Gateshead can be like Brooklyn,' says director Paul Stone, who co-founded Vane and its umbrella non-profit community organisation Orbis in 1997. 'It's a place of potential. I've been through several cycles of funding and regeneration. Today I'm feeling optimistic. For the first time ever we're being listened to. Gateshead has challenges but I think

          where tourists seldom tread

grassroots arts projects are the way to ensure its revival has longevity.'

Art is a strange world, and he admits, 'Probably more people know us outside Gateshead than in Gateshead'. Orbis and Vane moved here in 2021, when the office block they occupied in central Newcastle was demolished to make room for an almost identical office block for the relocation of HMRC. Upstairs are 568 Records – a vinyl trove with a massive dance collection – tattooists, artists' studios and MakerSpace, an informal social and ideas club for tech and science people.

A smart wine bar and shop, three craft-beer bars, a doughnut shop and a 'horror café' have in recent years appeared at the southern end of the High Level Bridge – designed by Robert Stephenson – to encourage those who cross over to stay awhile. It feels quite European here, with piazzas under the railway bridges. The Central pub is wedge-shaped to fit in with the overhead railways.

Perhaps to get one over on Newcastle, Gateshead has disrupted shopping. When it opened in 1986 on a former power station's waterlogged ash dump, the Metrocentre was the largest indoor retail space in the UK – it was only knocked off the top spot when Westfield White City, the largest shopping centre in Europe, opened in 2008. It was a huge morale boost for the region, described by Newcastle author Alex Niven as 'the signature building of the age . . . so in tune with the spirit of its time and place that – to borrow a phrase of the philosopher Walter Benjamin – it was evidence of a collective dream'. Thatcher praised the 'will-power, perseverance and sheer guts to make it a reality of concrete and glass'. Local architect Ronald Chipchase, a Frank Lloyd Wright acolyte, designed the interior as a series of townscapes, with a Roman forum, antique village and Mediterranean village, with fountains with real fish, giant chessboards, synthetic trees, model hot-air balloons and a statue that shouted at passing shoppers. It was a fantastic theme park, albeit one in which people were enticed to spend and keep moving. Thinking again of Benjamin, the experience was as transformative for early visitors from Gateshead and Newcastle as the first glass-filled indoor arcades were for Parisians. Other towns looked to the North-East for a paradigm of how to spend Saturday afternoons, leisure time, and money.

Two years before the mega-mall was unveiled, its demise was being plotted at a house on Leam Lane Estate in Heworth – also on the 51/52 bus route – when seventy-two-year-old pensioner Jane Snowball made the first online purchase ever, of eggs, margarine and cornflakes, as part of a council initiative to help the elderly. Mrs Snowball used her television's remote control to make the order. A piece of cutting-edge computer technology called Videotex sent it down her phone line to the local supermarket; the goods were then packaged and delivered to her door. Greggs and Lloyds Pharmacy were the other participants. Globally, online shopping is worth around £5 trillion today.

The Angel bus – number 21 – connects all of the places mentioned above with the *Angel of the North*. Newcastle opposed this, too. So famous it sometimes inspires contempt, this retro-aeroplane-shaped, rust-coloured figure has been one of the most successful pieces of public art ever – if success is national fame. Most people drive past and miss the shrines at the statue's foot, where mourning families and loved ones have turned the secular site into a sacred and tender one. It faces south, ostensibly to welcome those arriving, but a northern prospect would be more fitting and hope-inducing. Perhaps the Angel betrays the fact its maker, Antony Gormley, is a Londoner. They could at least put Newby's *Halo* on its head, or play 'Angel Eyes' by Roxy Music through a speaker.

Still, everyone knows of the Angel, and its name has allowed the North-East to symbolically absorb the wider North. Dan Jackson calls the *Angel of the North* 'Gateshead's response in all its uncompromising virility to the priapic giant of the South at Cerne Abbas'. I'm not so sure. Angels are non-binary and lack genitals. Any come-on here is ambivalent, effected as it is by open wings made of cold, unbending steel.

17
Silver and Gold
Wick and Thurso

South Head

ath

'm catching the sleeper but won't get much sleep.

I live in Lancashire and the night train, mainly serving Londoners and Scots, stops at Preston at 12.30 a.m. on the way up and 4.30 a.m. on the return leg. I manage to doze for a couple of hours and wake to coffee and porridge somewhere north of Perth. The snow is up to the trackside. I spot a stag on a hillock, the great slab of the Cairngorms' central plateau, the platform sign for 'Dalwhinnie'. I hasten onward past Inverness on the Far North Line.

This 161-mile railway weaves through the Flow Country, the largest area of blanket bog on earth. Look on a map and you'll notice the line's sweeping meanders. While crossing wetland isn't easy, it's more straightforward than skirting the inlets and ups and downs of the coast. The train runs on an embankment and I can see glistening pools, rivulets and spongy peatland made up of sphagnum mosses, ling heather, asphodel and butterwort.

Formed over ten thousand years, the peat is up to 30 feet deep. In the seventies and eighties, government tax incentives encouraged forestry schemes. Swathes of bog that had been treeless since forever were drained, gouged with deep furrows, and planted with fast-growing conifers. The area became a battleground between pro-plantation developers and conservationists concerned at the destruction of such a rare, undisturbed habitat.

The area, recently designated a UNESCO World Heritage site, is now being allowed to recover, which is good for the planet – peat is a superb carbon store – and native fauna. Merlin, short-eared owls and golden eagles hunt over the mosses and pools. Divers, plover and greenshank feed and nest in the wetlands. Microhabitats support insects, spiders, amphibians, reptiles and small mammals like shrews.

North-east Scotland is flatter, sunnier, drier and less touristy than the fabled north-west, with its isles and lochs, Munros and Christmas trees. Whether you take the A9 or, like me, ride the Far North railway line, you gain an ever-growing sense of widening skies and horizons.

When I first travelled around Patagonia I spent a lot of time looking for analogues of the landscapes of my Lancashire home. Three decades later I find myself spotting little Patagonias in the moorlands and wastes of my homeland – Rochdale, South Wales, now here.

———

Herrings and whisky are two of my favourite things, separately and together. In mid-nineteenth century Wick, the combination caused social upheaval and moral outrage. The Rev. Charles Thomson observed, 'The herring fishing has increased wealth, but also wickedness. No care is taken of the 10,000 young strangers of both sexes, crowded together with the inhabitants during the six weeks of the fishing season . . . There is a great consumption of spirits, there being 22 public houses in Wick and 23 in Pulteneytown.' Wick, at the time, was the busiest herring port in Europe. As many as a thousand vessels were moored there. It's been estimated that in excess of 800 gallons of whisky – 5,000 bottles – were being consumed every week. Local men piled into the pubs, and when skippers arrived with their wages they would have a celebratory drink. Crews might be made up of eight men, buying round after round. Some went home with coppers.

What to do? The town's temperance-minded grandees arranged a referendum. Cannily, they enfranchised the wives. Following speeches, public meetings and newspaper columns by both 'wets' and 'drys', polling day arrived and a turnout of 77 per cent was recorded. Sixty-two per cent voted No Licence. Only bona fide travellers could henceforth legally purchase alcohol in Wick, and only as an accompaniment to a meal.

Prohibition was in force from 1922 to 1947, twelve years longer than in the US. Illicit alcohol was produced in at least two clandestine stills. Underground drinking dens, or shebeens, sprang up around the town, including one audaciously placed in a respectable restaurant, where a silver teapot was used to dispense whisky to knowing customers.

   where tourists seldom tread

The bars around Wick today still exude an illicit aura. They are painted in garish or hospital hues. Windows are small and infrequent. The famous red Tennent's 'T' smacks of the USSR or *1984*. None serve rollmops.

Wick is built from dark grey stone, sometimes plastered in light grey pebbledash known as harling. It looks tough, like a frontier town, crowding the slopes around the harbour built by Thomas Telford in the first decade of the nineteenth century. He designed Pulteney-town, arguably the first housing estate purpose-built to service an industry. North of the river, in Wick proper, the high street has been murdered. The herring were fished out long ago, and wind farms only employ a handful of hands. There is no cinema or supermarket. It could feel sad, but the surrounding countryside is dramatic and diverting; fulmars nest on the cliffs around the old castle, great slabs of rock double as a summer lido, headlands open up views of distant shores. A sign informs the wanderer: London 490 miles, Bergen 350 miles. Wick is Vik. The local DNA has been tested; it is proudly Nordic.

The local heritage museum, spread over several terraced houses, is an enthralling home for Wick's storied past, and all the artefacts that made life on the furthest edge liveable. It's a wonderfully varied collection, with reconstructions of every room in a home *c.*1900, plus lighthouse bulbs, wedding and funeral garments, military uniforms, boneshaker bicycles, replicas of a cooperage and 'smiddy' (blacksmith's), a fishing boat, and a superb and vast array of photographs from the herring heyday, including crisp images of the fishermen and gutter lassies who prepared the herrings or 'silver darlings', and the dockside heaving with hundreds of thousands of barrels full of salted fish.

I mentioned to Donald Henderson, the chair of the Wick Society, which runs the heritage centre, that the landscape reminded me of Patagonia. He nodded and mentioned, almost as an aside, that many people from Caithness emigrated to Patagonia to work on sheep farms. The following day a book called *From Caithness to Patagonia* by Ian Leith was left at reception in Mackays Hotel. Life imitating daydreams.

When the weather blows in, as it is wont to do, there is refuge in Mackays, a flat-iron corner on Ebeneezer Place – the shortest street in the world, it is claimed. It's one of those warm, welcoming, traditional hotels where a traveller can make a home from home. Its location, at a five-road crossing, is said to be mentioned in *Treasure Island*; Robert Louis Stevenson came here as a young man when his father was attempting to construct a breakwater. A crumbled wall-end records his failure.

Opened in 1826, shuttered during the prohibition years, sited in the heart of the old new town – whose bricks it has further darkened with a yeasty fungus – the Old Pulteney distillery has seen off all of Wick's booms and busts. In a crowded market, it has prospered as the 'maritime whisky', its promotional poetry promising a voyage 'from subtle coastal chords to more defined salty notes'. On the tour you pass through heat and cold, mizzle and damp, and wall-to-wall casks in the ancient warehouse, which inevitably recall the old fishy barrels. Herring gulls live here year round and have been christened by the distillers. Fraser and Smokey Joe cackled as I dipped and sipped and diluted, and scented and swilled the notes of sherry, bourbon, sea and sand, wind and memory.

———

I take the bus to Thurso. I only know two things about it. One, that it is the northernmost town in mainland Britain. Two, that it grew bigger and got richer thanks to the Dounreay nuclear testing and experimental site, which came on stream – or 'went critical', as the jargon goes – in the late 1950s.

It is an airier, slightly livelier town than Wick and has a nice beach. It's apparently a popular 'cold surf' hangout. Again, I find a welcoming hotel, the Pentland, and a great little museum. I learn a lovely

 where tourists seldom tread

third thing: that Thurso's etymology alludes to Thor, god of storms, sacred groves and trees – my favourite Marvel Comics character.

You can't come up here without going to Dunnet Head, Britain's most northerly point. I spend some time with Martin Murray, who is rebuilding an old grain mill at Castletown to make whisky, using the famous Caithness flagstone – as used at the Ground Zero memorial in New York – while conserving original features. He's not the only distiller betting on Far North branding. The Wolfburn and North Point Distilleries, which opened in 2013 and 2020 close to Thurso, and the even newer 8 Doors Distillery at John O'Groats, are turning the highest corner of the Highlands into a whisky hotspot. After I try a drop of the 8 Doors peated whisky, I meet up with American expat Jay Wilson, who created the John O'Groats Trail about a decade ago. We do the short hike along the coast to Duncansby Head, the north-easternmost point. It's all extremes on this corner.

Jay shows me some geos – deep gullies where the sea rushes in – and guides me across a patch of carpet bog. It rolls and shifts just like a soft rug. Flow Country: it's a perfect name. At the promontory, beneath the lighthouse, I look back and see, beyond a wall of impressive cliffs, the Noss Head lighthouse near Wick.

But which way am I to look – down or upward? Thurso is far north – as far from King's Cross as Budapest is from Paris. My gaze is drawn towards Stroma and the Orkneys. Why do travellers yearn to go to the ends of things?

I don't have an answer, but the urge is strongest in wide-open landscapes. Perhaps Thor came ashore and flattened Caithness and Sutherland by stamping his god-sized feet just to keep us wanting more.

18

New Wave, Auld Punk
East Kilbride and Paisley

What does a Scottish New Town sound like? Wind whipping across flagstones? Rain on precast concrete? Footsteps echoing around a concourse? Distorted, muff-pedalled, fuzz-wah-ing, reverb-drowned, semi-hollowbody Gretsch guitar?

Psychocandy (1985) was conceived in an East Kilbride bedroom by brothers William and Jim Reid, whose family had moved there in 1966. The Jesus and Mary Chain sounded like the Beach Boys minus the beach (and the jazz chords), fuzzboxing the world – because clarity was unbearable? The then-young New Town was an influence. On a Radio 4 documentary, Jim told David Scott that 'the isolation and the sense of not being part of . . . the music scene is kind of important to how we developed. It made us have an outsider's mentality, which continues, I suppose, to this day.' He said East Kilbride was a Shangri-La for those relocating from Glasgow. 'It was neat and tidy and clean, and we all had bathrooms and indoor toilets. As a kid, it seemed like the best place on earth to be.'

Scotland's first New Town, designated in 1947 and built from 1950, was an amalgamation of the low-density housing and zonal planning espoused by Garden City visionary Ebenezer Howard, Le Corbusier's 'automotive city', the pedestrian-centred ideals of Patrick Geddes and the anti-revivalist architectural fashions of the day. Eight miles south of Glasgow, it was a rejection of the city's uncontrolled sprawl and congested centre, which had evolved over centuries and been recently torn apart by the Luftwaffe and slum clearances.

Budgetary and other pressures soon increased the density of housing, but the overall design principles were laudable and futuristic – and the town has retained an airy, rational expansiveness. Footways, bridges and underpasses link residential quarters with shops, recreational parks and workplaces. The visitor can experience East Kilbride as a series of green spaces – at least till you get to the shops – by means of parks and tree-sheltered footpaths and alleys that break up the built-up. On exposed bluffs the westerly wind can be daunting, but there's always a nook to escape to, a sculpture or structure to hide behind.

Light industry is sited on the outskirts of the town, accessed via straight roads with lots and lots of roundabouts. Some of these are used for public art – cute bears, abstract spheres. A Banksy-style painting of William Reid adorns the passage off Murray Round-about. 'Isn't it pretty in Polo Mint City', sang Sharleen Spiteri.

The shopping centre was the focus of the original master plan, as in traditional towns. No one outside sci-fi imagined shopping would shift to the non-physical realm, that shoppers would choose van deliveries over family outings. Plans are afoot to demolish part of the EK Shopping Centre, the current name for four cojoined malls, which had forty-eight empty units at a recent count. A public con-sultation is looking into demolishing a third of East Kilbride town centre. Safe from the wrecking ball, surely, is the Dollan Baths (now Aqua Centre), which opened in 1968 and was the first Olympic-sized swimming pool built in Scotland. Designer Alexander Buchanan Campbell said he had been influenced by the architecture of the 1964 Summer Olympics in Tokyo and the work of Kenzō Tange. A cross between a ribcage and a giant crab, high on its hilltop, the building is extraordinary.

St Bride's Roman Catholic church is one of the most acclaimed mod-ern ecclesiastical buildings in Britain. It is pure mass, as solid and angular as religion is speculative and vague. Prayer-space as factory – designed by Isi Metzstein and Andy MacMillan of architecture firm Gillespie, Kidd & Coia – it was built using bricks repurposed from Victorian sewerage systems, a decision based on post-war material shortages. A 90-foot bell tower was added because a bishop thought the project lacked ecclesiastical character; it was felled in 1983 due to damage, which is a pity as it made the church even more eccentric and dramatic. You enter furtively, through a slit-door cut inside a curtain-like fold in the cliff-wall exterior. Inside it is uplifting in the manner

 where tourists seldom tread

of the Tate Modern Turbine Hall – the liberating emptiness of a high vault. Corbelling, staggering, setbacks and niches allude understatedly to medieval antecedents. A glint of blood-red glass in the side door, an asymmetrical altar with a backdrop suggesting flowing rosary beads, pared-down Stations of the Cross, warm wood, uncountable bricks: moments of modern religious art that stir me more than Renaissance masterpieces. I am barely conscious of two people seated on the far side, praying silently. If I believed, I would want this to be my parish church. The confessionals have stop and go lights.

There are lesser standouts. East Kilbride civic centre is a Bauhaus-esque chunk of concrete. A spiral ramp on the Plaza multistorey car park won a Civic Trust commendation. The boxy terraces and low-slung blocks of flats riff on Glasgow's tenements. The Ramada hotel channels Soviet functionalism. St Mark's Episcopal Church is a strik-ing A-frame, set off nicely by the over-looming oblong of a residential tower block. The star-shaped South Parish church is eye-catching, but condemned. Whimsical public sculptures by Jim Barclay and Stan Bonner survive, in patches, peeling; the Facebook page Lost East Kilbride is full of warm recollections of climbing on them. New Towns are getting on.

The town has not lost all connection with its past. At its edge is the National Museum of Rural Life, on the still-working Wester Kittochside farm but looking like an industrial unit. East Kilbride once was little more than a few primitive dwellings said to be dedicated to the Celtic goddess Brigid, reframed as St Bride of Kildare. Some research points to a conflation of the Virgin Mary and Saint Bridget. In the eighteenth century it was given the status of burgh of barony, allowing it to hold weekly markets and four annual fairs. The East Kilbride Open Cattle Show Society, whose roots date back to 1772, by the late 1940s had reportedly become 'the largest one-day cattle show in Scotland'.

The old part of town, known as the Village, still looks almost the part. A traditionally shaped Church of Scotland built from stone. A big pub on a small square. Kirk Wynd. Glebe Street. Cobbles and small shops. In 2018, the film *Nae Pasaran* had its local premiere at the Village Theatre. After the Chilean coup of 1973, workers at East Kilbride's Rolls-Royce plant downed tools, refusing to service and repair engines for the Chilean air force's Hawker Hunters. *Nae Pasaran* told their story, leading to three Scotsmen receiving the Order of Bernardo O'Higgins, Chile's highest honour. Currently, the theatre's roster lists the Springsteen Sessions, the Absolute Elvis Show, Nearly Elton and MacFloyd. Cover-band tribute gigs are the sound of the once pioneering, no longer new, part-condemned New Town. Fuzzboxes should be obligatory.

————

Someone on Reddit asks, 'Why is Paisley even still a place?' They go on to grouch about shops, praising East Kilbride in passing. Sixty comments follow. Your usual social media platform partisan pile-on – equal parts wit, bile and nonsense. At the end of it I knew Paisley was still a place.

As a northern Englander, I admit, I thought of Paisley as something imprecise – town, suburb, district – up there, probably near Glasgow, like Motherwell, Airdrie, Dumbarton. Towns that never garner attention, football teams that rarely win anything. Did I connect Paisley with the pattern? Not really. Did I know it was a textile powerhouse? No. Lancashire and West Yorkshire claim to own that story. If I ever thought about paisley, it was to do with hippies, Tie Rack, media types' shirts. I had no idea St Mirin came here from Bangor in Ireland and founded a monastery – as well as a football team.

This old town is far from being absorbed by the metropolis. Even on the fast non-stop train (nine minutes from Glasgow Central) you know you are crossing a proper green belt. On arrival, you see towers and domes above the trees. Paisley stands apart and it stands tall.

Big, bold buildings hint at booming textile times. The station – fourth busiest in the country – is Scots baronial. The town hall is a hefty neoclassical building, recently turned into a concert venue. The mighty abbey, built on the site of a twelfth-century Cluniac monastery, is a grand, solemn beauty. St Matthew's church, designed by local architect William Daniel McLennan, is a blend of perpendicular and art nouveau – somewhat influenced by Charles Rennie Mackintosh's Queen's Cross church in Glasgow, but more strident and startling.

On White Cart Water stand two monumental mills. The massive Anchor Mill building is now residential and sits beside a weir that looks like a wildish waterfall; Mile End Mill is a business centre which boasts a superb chimney, coffee shop and small textile museum. Paisley has gone big on repurposing. The dramatic Gothic hulk of the Coats building, built as a memorial church – and nicknamed the 'Baptist Cathedral of Europe' – is now an event space, used for weddings, proms and as a set for TV series.

The Coats family opened a cotton mill in the Paisley suburb of Ferguslie in 1826, and went on to build a global business. By the early twentieth century, J&P Coats was the third-largest firm in the world behind US Steel and Standard Oil. Their chief rivals were the Clarks, also of Paisley, who began as small-scale weavers and twine makers. When Napoleon's Berlin Decree of 1806 cut off Britain's supplies of flax and silk, Patrick Clark developed a fine 3-ply cotton thread to replace it. His brother James is credited with the invention of the wooden spool or bobbin. Paisley promotes itself as 'the town that thread built', but there were also hundreds of weavers, working mainly from home.

The Sma' Shot Cottages contain reconstructions of eighteenth- and nineteenth-century dwellings and workspaces containing looms. Their name alludes to a gossamer-thin length of thread used to bind the warp and weft threads; without it things fell apart. Weavers were forced to pay for this invisible thread out of their own pocket because, in the eyes of the middlemen, known as 'corks', it didn't add obvious value. The weavers protested, gathering to march whenever they heard the pounding beat of a Charleston drum. They eventually triumphed over the corks and a new table of prices was issued on 1 July 1856. Sma' Shot Day is celebrated every year.

During the Radical War of 1820, also known as the Scottish Insurrection, when weavers and artisans led strikes and protested at the introduction of new machinery, Paisley saw uprisings and cavalry charges. The factory system would, during the course of the nineteenth century, turn Paisley into Scotland's third-largest population centre. The town's reputation for working-class activism prompted Job Thornberry, the Radical MP in Disraeli's *Endymion* (1880), to advise, 'Keep your eye on Paisley.'

The Paisley pattern has its origins in Persia. The teardrop-shaped motif, known as *boteh* in Persian, is probably a stylised almond or cypress cone (the cypress was sacred to Zoroastrians). Kashmiri shawls containing the motif, shipped to Scotland by the British East India Company, were copied by Paisley weavers using jacquard looms, which replicated the complex patterns by means of punch cards. When paisley-patterned shawls were adopted by Queen Victoria and other British aristocrats, their appeal was assured at home and across the Empire.

Paisley Museum, currently undergoing a major refurbishment that will create a display space as good as any in Scotland, owns 1,200 shawls, as well as looms, pattern books and printing blocks. I was allowed to see the interior on a hard-hat tour and saw a paisley-emblazoned guitar carry-case and a Ken doll in a paisley top. The pattern shows up in street art, as the drifting feathers of a peacock or the imagined stage set for local lad Paolo Nutini – both on Brown's Lane. Jimi Hendrix and John Lennon are also on the walls, notably not showing off the local pattern (though both wore paisley shirts), as is Gerry Rafferty, born and raised here. 'Baker Street', so famous it is almost impossible to listen to rather than merely hear, is ostensibly about missing Paisley; the lyrics, if you can aurally edit out the sax

   where tourists seldom tread

for a moment, evoke the grimness of London for provincial dreamers. Rafferty was involved in legal wrangles over his music at the time and, coincidentally, reading Colin Wilson's *The Outsider*, which surveyed existentialist authors and their angst-ridden antiheroes. The relationship between alienation, capitalism and art was uppermost in Rafferty's mind.

Punk music found a generous home in Paisley in 1977, when Glasgow city councillors – led by Bill Aitken, the Tory head of licensing – expressed outrage following a particularly lively Stranglers concert at Glasgow City Halls. While an official ban was never passed, for several months punk bands were encouraged to play outside the city, at Paisley – venues like the Bungalow and the Silver Thread Hotel were happy to host the likes of Buzzcocks, the Saints, the Exploited, the Rezillos, Discharge and Paisley's very own Fegs (short for Ferguslie Park, a local council estate). Glasgow record shop Bruce's organised the 'punk Dunkirk', booking buses to transport gig-goers to Paisley. By the time Glasgow softened its position, Paisley was already established as a punk and hardcore haven.

Punk laid the ground for new wave, which in turn fed off California's Paisley Underground scene, named thus because Lina Sedillo, bass player with Los Angeles punk band Peer Group, alluded to her red paisley dress during rehearsals. Dozens of bands were influenced by the Paisley Underground, including Opal, which segued into Mazzy Star. The cover of their hugely acclaimed breakout album, *So Tonight That I Might See*, is a whirl of purple paisley patterns. Thus the famous motif, in the end, was woven into new wave music, psychedelia the common thread that links folk and post-punk.

Paisleyites call local friends and heroes 'buddies' – meaning bodies, and nothing to do with the 'buddy' of American English. A Buddie Walk of Fame, comprising ten paving stones spread around town, celebrates local legends, living and dead. They include *Porridge*'s Fulton Mackay; playwright, designer and painter John Byrne – whose

Slab Boys Trilogy, originally titled *Paisley Patterns*, is set in a carpet-making factory; Tom Conti; Nutini again, outside Castelvecchi, his parents' chip shop; Gerry Rafferty again, outside the Bungalow; David Tennant, near his school.

Buddie plaques should have been placed at Ferguslie Park, a poor and socially marginalised district north-west of the town near St Mirren's stadium. Byrne, Rafferty and Joe Egan, Rafferty's fellow singer and songwriter in Stealers Wheel, were raised here, as was Gordon Williams, author of the novel *From Scenes Like These*, which was nominated for the first-ever Booker Prize, in 1969. A blistering, brutally honest and funny portrayal of social deprivation, violence, sex and booze, it's as good as anything by Alan Sillitoe. Though set mainly in the Ayrshire countryside, it has the hard edges of an urban story. The novel was largely ignored until 2025, when it was reissued with a new introduction by James Robertson and glowing praise from 2020 Booker winner Douglas Stuart, among others. The fictional town referred to, Kilcaddie, sounds and smells and rains and fights like Paisley.

19
End of the Road
Barrow-in-Furness

Barrow

I n early August 1914, newlyweds D. H. and Frieda Lawrence were on a walking tour of the Lakeland fells with three friends when they 'came down to Barrow in Furness, and saw that war was declared. And we all went mad. I can remember soldiers kissing on Barrow station, and a woman shouting defiantly to her sweetheart "When you get at 'em, Clem, let 'em have it", as the train drew off – and in all the tram-cars "War". Messrs Vickers Maxim call in their workmen – and the great notices on Vickers' gateways – and the thousands of men streaming over the bridge.'

Lawrence, in this letter to Lady Cynthia Asquith, registers the shock of the transition from wildish Westmorland to industrial Lancashire, from 'the amazing, vivid, visionary beauty of everything' to the 'immense pain everywhere' occasioned by the outbreak of war. At the time Barrow was a huge machine-shop, a cacophonous, pulsating, smoking testament to all the things Lawrence feared and despised. The town was fixed in his mind as the place where any slender hope of a world at peace was decisively shredded.

Barrow-in-Furness stands a few miles south of the mouth of the River Duddon on the seaward side of the Furness Peninsula. It's thirty-five miles from the M6 by wiggling A-road – what has been called the longest cul-de-sac in Britain.

It was always a place set apart. For centuries, before trains and road tunnels made journeys easier, the Furness and Cartmel peninsulas were accessed from the sea or by walking across the sands of Morecambe Bay at low tide. Appended to the county of Cumbria in 1974, Barrow is historically part of Lonsdale in Lancashire; its reason for being is labour, not leisure.

The name Barrow comes from the Old Norse for 'bare island'; Furness means 'rump at the headland'. An Anglo-Saxon earl resided on Piel Island, later ceded to monks who built a harbour for shipping and storing grain, wine and wool. Their fortified warehouse grew into a castle, the fourteenth-century ruins of which are looked after by English Heritage. I hopped on the tiny ferry to visit, stopping at the Ship Inn for a pint. The landlord, Aaron Sanderson, is also the island's king.

The title is said to have originated with the landing of Yorkist pretender to the throne Lambert Simnel in 1487 and is most likely to have begun as a satirical homage. Tradition holds that a new landlord is formally crowned as King of Piel seated, wearing a helmet and holding a sword while alcohol is poured over their head. Graffiti on the throne, which is in the pub, references past coronations, as does an 1856 visitors' book. Knighthoods were also created, and in the early twentieth century Piel Island boasted a royal family, an entire cabinet including a prime minister, and a Lord Mayor. The only requirements of the king-cum-landlord are that they be 'a free drinker, a moderate smoker and an ardent lover of the opposite sex'.

A much larger island, Walney, forms a natural breakwater around Barrow – which is just as well, as it is said to be the windiest lowland spot in England. This protection and the Walney Channel – running from the River Duddon to Morecambe Bay – made conditions ideal for a shipyard. Shipbuilding, which began in earnest in the 1870s, was later taken over by Vickers. In 1901 the Royal Navy's first submarine, HMS *Holland 1* (aka *Torpedo Boat No 1*) was launched. Vickerstown Estate, a model village on an urban scale, was built between 1900 and 1906 to house employees. Dominion Street, Powerful Street and Vengeance Street recall Barrow-built warships.

The industrial past of Barrow-in-Furness is in evidence everywhere. Iron ore had been shipped through the port for decades, but the founding of the Haematite Iron and Steel Works in 1859 initiated a period of intense growth; Barrow would become the site of the largest steelworks in the world. During the 1880s salt was discovered by chance on Walney Island while boring for coal, and the Barrow Salt Works became a major concern.

—

   where tourists seldom tread

An 1866 trades directory calls Barrow a 'combination in appearance of Birkenhead and a gold finders' city on the edge of one of the western prairies of America'. Bolton-born engineer James Ramsden played a leading role in transforming Barrow into a fully fledged town. From 1846 he worked as a locomotive superintendent for the new Furness Railway Company, going on to become company secretary and managing director. Ramsden spearheaded the growth of the Barrow Shipbuilding Company, built new docks and massively expanded the iron and steel industries. He was also a notable benefactor, contributing to social and civic facilities within the town. He served five terms as Barrow's mayor.

Some called Ramsden's fast-rising town the 'English Chicago' (partly because of the fierce westerlies). The boom paid for stately Victorian and Edwardian buildings, including a Beaux Arts public library, an Italianate custom house, a red-brick and terracotta fire station and two Gothic Revival behemoths: the imposing town hall with its unexpected central tower (Pevsner: 'a monument to Barrow's prosperity') and the Duke of Edinburgh Hotel, where it's claimed Cary Grant and Charlie Chaplin were accommodated – though the latter was probably a clog-dancing child performer when he visited. Barrow's population grew from 150 in 1843 to 56,625 in 1901 – a Chicago-esque spurt for sure. Today there are 67,000 Barrovians. The local accent is hard to place, perhaps indicative of the mixture of peoples who migrated here to find work, and stayed.

In 2008, a survey commissioned by website locallife.co.uk identified Barrow as the 'most working-class town in the UK', on the dubious basis that it had a fish-and-chip shop, working men's club, bookmaker, greyhound track or trade-union office for every 2,917 of its residents. More pertinently, the town has nearly four times the national average of manufacturing jobs. Barrow is home to the Maritime-Submarine division of BAE Systems, the multinational arms maker. Like Vickers before it, the firm draws talent from all over the country. While salaries are at the higher end, the town centre, it has to be said, has benefitted little from the presence of an anchor-employer.

BAE builds and maintains the Royal Navy's Vanguard-class subs – the platform for the UK's Trident nuclear programme – as well as nuclear-powered Astute-class 'hunter-killer' submarines such as HMS *Anson*, designs for which were found in the gents at the local Wetherspoons in April 2023. The Devonshire Dock Hall dominates the sprawling site, which is to the south-west of the town centre. It's a gargantuan, window-less groundscraper visible from Morecambe promenade – fifteen miles away as the crow flies – and from passing ferries to Ireland. One evening I walked its perimeter, surveying the razor wire, CCTV cameras and signs advising me to 'Beware Aggressive Seagulls' – on a factory that produces underwater tubes, at £3 billion a pop, to annihilate Chinese and Russian cities. Inevitably, security guards were following me and two vans pulled in at speed – their drivers were probably bored – to ask why I was taking photographs. I mentioned D. H. Lawrence and told them I was pleased to have found the old Vickers gates still in place. They told me I had broken no law but that 'they get twitchy', before driving off to be bored again. Who 'they' were was not clarified.

When Paul Theroux visited the Cumbrian coast in 1982, while writing *The Kingdom by the Sea*, he was aghast at the size and inscrutability of the Sellafield energy plant, twenty-four miles north of Barrow. I've been there and can relate to his impression. But the activities in the Dock Hall are equally opaque, and its nuclear goals uniquely belli-cose. In March 2025, Keir Starmer visited Barrow to lay the keel of the Dreadnought submarine, 'the next generation of the UK's nuclear de-terrent'. He announced that the king had agreed to confer the 'Royal' title on the port. When in Royal Barrow, you can't but wonder at the effect this mega-structure has on residents' inner lives.

Less ominously, the town is a wind-energy superpower. One of the UK's earliest offshore wind farms opened off Barrow in July 2006. Now there are five, including the 56-square-mile Walney extension, for a time the biggest of its type in the world.

                    where tourists seldom tread

Lancashire is littered with post-industrial graveyards. This isn't one of them.

Early on a Sunday morning I walk up to Furness Abbey, along the leafy avenues where the town's founding industrialists once resided. Their mansions are now mainly care homes or else draughty piles where the elderly live at home. I see nurses making their rounds.

The abbey, once the grandest in the North-West, has enough vestigial walls and foundations to feed the imagination. Wordsworth wrote two sonnets praising the 'sacred Ruin' and its ivy-swathed loveliness, taking the opportunity in both to attack William Cavendish, 7th Duke of Devonshire, founder and developer of the Furness Railway, docks, steelworks and jute works. 'Simple-hearted' railway labourers, says Wordsworth, resting from their labours beside the abbey ruins, experience awe – unlike the 'Profane Despoilers', their bosses.

Wordsworth's Duddon sonnets, based on walks beside the river that flows along the Cumberland/Lancashire border, provided the subtext for a five-sonnet sequence by Portuguese poet Fernando Pessoa. He never visited but probably became familiar with the town's name from Barrow-built ships at anchor in Lisbon.

Pessoa, who used seventy-five pseudonyms during his short career, adopted the name Álvaro de Campos to write the sonnets. A modern riposte to Wordsworth's riverine ruminations, 'Barrow-on-Furness' [*sic*] finds its narrator, a much-travelled Portuguese engineer, seated on a drum in the docks, melancholy and unmoored. He is equally alienated by the place, by nature and by his own thoughts. The fifth sonnet concludes: 'The metaphysics of sensations – let us put / An end to this and to everything else. Ah, / What human yearning to be river or wharf!' Wordsworth wanted the natural world to flood his soul and body; Pessoa/Campos wants his thoughts to flow out into things.

Standing on the shore at Earnse Bay on Walney, the western skies offer a different order of escape to that promised by the Lake District

National Park. Light, air, rain, wind are all different here. Barrow-in-Furness, on the margins of the map, is a peaceful kind of armaments town – at least until the next time we all go mad and Clem takes the train again.

20
Alternative Ulsters
Armagh and Enniskillen

THE TOASTERY
VINCENT'S

waited too long to go to Northern Ireland. It's only a small sea between Lancashire and Ulster, but crossing it never occurred to my parents, or friends, or – to be honest – me in later life. It wasn't an obvious holiday option. I lacked blood ties, though I recall a Killilea and a McVey in the extended family – and the Irish seemed to be all about family. The Troubles, which dominated the news when I was young, were too real and close and ugly to ever be a mere frisson. Tim Parry, the twelve-year-old who died in the Warrington bombings of 1993, was a pupil at my school a few years behind me.

All of this played into my staying away, and no doubt to my making trips instead, as an adult, to Galway and Cork, Dublin and the Dingle, and to the Fleadh festivals of Cavan and Sligo – the Ireland of Bloomsday, green hills, fiddles and bodhrans, lonely islands and the 'Wild Atlantic Way'.

At last, in 2023–4 I made crossings of the northern roads of the Irish Sea. I entered through Belfast, saw the walls, the flags, the old inns, and then took off for towns whose names were once at the top of the news, but whose histories were usually reduced to a few decades in the second half of the twentieth century. Sometimes the road trip felt like a homecoming. The weather and the skies, humour and prejudices and the contours of townscapes were familiar. I sensed deeper currents. The Liverpudlians and South Lancastrians I had grown up with were connected to Ulster and beyond by faith, migration and ancestry. But Northern Ireland is crammed with its own history and is, in some respects, like an outpost of Empire: slavery, lordly land-grabbing, flags, the Royal family. You can't understand anything about Britain if you ignore its closest 'foreign' country.

———

Widow's Friends lay forgotten in flower beds outside a smart red-brick house at the top of Abbey Street. Bramleys were piled high outside a door for anyone to pick up. Kerry Pippin trees softened the edges of the business-minded, functional City Hotel.

I had missed Armagh's food festival by one day, but not the apple harvest. I had had no idea this was the centre of 'orchard county'. Then again, I didn't know the city was the mother-metropolis of Irish Catholicism and the Church of Ireland – Canterbury, Westminster and Liverpool all at once. That it was a Celtic mythology vortex. That it hosted a Georgian architecture festival every November.

Anyone who grew up between the sixties and nineties is familiar with Armagh from bloody headlines. South Armagh in particular was portrayed as a Provisional IRA redoubt, as if nothing else ever happened there.

Would-be dark tourists should start with etymology. The deep, underpinning Celtic sources of modern tensions are there in the name. Armagh alludes to the Ard Macha, a hill in the town associated with the goddess Macha. Like other sovereignty goddesses who personified territory and granted it to Irish kings through marriage or sex, Macha is associated with the land, fertility, kingship, war and horses. Her name probably derives from the Proto-Celtic word for 'plain', where food is grown and battles unfold. But the 'Ard', the 'high place', is safer, stronger.

On a tilting pedestal at the foot of Scotch Street stands a stainless-steel muscular figure caught in the act of balancing. The name of it is *For the Love of Emer* and it was made by Northern Irish artist Martin Heron.

Local Blue Badge guide Donna Fox tells me the story behind the statue. Irish people recount myths with disturbing casualness. She talks of sovereigns and banquets and wild dogs as if these are common currency. I imagine Iceland is a bit like this: sagas for breakfast. When she mentions Cú Chulainn, all I can think of is, I wonder how that's spelled, and a Pogues song.

The story is worth spelling out. While watching a hurling match, the king of Ulster – who ruled at Navan Fort – is so impressed by the sporting prowess of his young nephew Setanta that he invites him to a feast at the house of the blacksmith Culann. Setanta, who goes along as soon as the match is over, finds the door to the banqueting hall guarded by Culann's loyal hound. When the dog attacks him, Setanta kills it using his hurley. To appease the devastated Culann, Setanta promises to rear another dog for him and, in the meantime, to act as a canine stand-in – thus becoming Cú Chulainn: Culann's Hound.

Cú Chulainn is a beautiful man and a womaniser. Ireland's fathers worry he will come along and steal their daughters. When finally he sets his heart on a woman called Emer, Cú Chulainn has to prove himself in battle. Heron's statue focuses not on the dog-slaying nor on Cú Chulainn's many deeds as a warrior but on his proving himself by balancing. This he learned from a druidess who was able to balance her breast on the tip of a five-barbed spear.

The Celtic myth-vortex drew St Patrick in the fifth century. No one knows precisely where Ireland's patron saint originated, but he was British. He was abducted as a child and taken to Ireland; he returned there as an adult with a mission to convert his barbarous enslavers. The Ard Macha was the ideal location for a church (in the same way that former mosques were often the sites chosen for the building of Spanish churches). Armagh became a scholastic centre, home to the most important monastery in Ireland. The Book of Armagh, less famous than the Book of Kells, is a ninth-century illuminated manuscript that contains the earliest example of Patrick's *Confessio*. It's kept at Trinity College in Dublin, but Armagh remains the capital of the two churches. The Church of Ireland cathedral is thought to stand on the second site chosen by Patrick. An earlier site on Scotch Street, known as Patrick's Fold, is now occupied by a retirement home.

St Patrick decreed that Armagh Cathedral would have primacy, thus making the town the equivalent of Canterbury. The church has been burned to the ground – by Vikings and lightning strikes – and rebuilt as many as seventeen times over the centuries, and is now largely a nineteenth-century Gothic structure. It has many notable features. A granite figure called the Tandragee Idol dates from the Iron Age. A weather-worn Celtic cross that once stood outside is from the eleventh century. The nave is crooked, echoing Christ's bowed head on the cross. The stained glass is gorgeous. But I was most absorbed by the list of abbots, bishops and archbishops, which runs continuously from 444 (Patrick) to today. The names start off as Old Irish (Ailill, Carlaen, Nuadha), turn Norse (de Jorse, Fitzralph), become principally English (Kite, Lancaster) with the Reformation and Plantation of Ulster, visit Rome (Spinelli de Palatio), dip some toes in Scotland (Stuart, Gregg, Armstrong) and then revert to Irish-born clerics, mainly (McCann, McDowell). Among them stands out the name of James Ussher, the prolific Dublin-born scholar who came up with the date of 22 October 4004 BC for the Creation – or, to be more precise, 'the entrance of the night preceding the 23rd day of October . . . the year before Christ 4004' – so, about 6 p.m. on the 22nd. I remember seeing his chronology in an old brownish family bible when I was little. It was the most amazing fact I had ever come across. Then I spotted that Noah had died aged 950, having built an ark when he was a spritely 600.

A Church of Ireland Archbishop, Richard Robinson, built much of the Armagh we see today. When he arrived in 1765, Robinson found a slumbrous, self-hating town. The cathedral was run-down, there were no public buildings, and one commentator, Arthur Young, described it as 'a nest of mud cabins'. Robinson built a 'Primatial Palace' which John Wesley described as 'neat and handsome, but not magnificent'. He repaired the cathedral and added a spire, and founded Northern Ireland's first public library, widely regarded as one of the finest Georgian buildings in the city. He also rebuilt the Royal School and founded an observatory as part of his ambition to establish 'a second university in the Province of Ulster', and secured the Mall, a green lung with a cricket pitch that runs along the north-east edge of the town.

 where tourists seldom tread

The cathedral is russet-coloured. Like an apple. Outside is a series of lovely green spaces: a monastic herb garden, with dwarf box hedging; an orchard garden of bush-trained fruit trees and espaliered trees on the walls; a more formal parterre garden; and a contemplative garden, divided into 'rooms' for reflection and meditation. The High King of Ireland, Brian Boru, was buried here in 1014, and a large bronze mask of his face made by Mayo sculptor Rory Breslin occupies a central position in the herb garden. His face is shown sliced up, to show that light streams even through violent death.

Armagh is the only city in the world with two cathedrals honouring one saint – Patrick, of course. The Church of Ireland cathedral owns the bulk of stories and legends. The Roman Catholic cathedral has bulk, pure and simple. To get to it, I descend into a built-up area to climb up towards a daunting, domineering structure. Built between 1840 and 1904 – following numerous delays and modifications – it's a statement church, and the statement, shouted loudly, is: there has been no Catholic mother church since the Reformation, so here you go, have this one.

A statue of St Patrick stands on one side of the main door. On the other is St Malachy, Bishop of Armagh in the twelfth century, holding a cross and an apple; he is said to have planted apple trees for times of famine. The Roman cathedral is on Sandy Hill, and when it's not facing down congregants it is facing across to the Church of Ireland cathedral on the more central Sally Hill. Around and between the big churches run Upper English Street, Scotch Street, Upper Irish Street; on the latter I pause at a mural depicting Cú Chulainn and the Goddess Macha surrounded by many of the elements that make up this town's historical collage – St Patrick, Gaelic sports, the Book of Armagh, Armagh railway station, Jonathan Swift (the library has his annotated copy of *Gulliver's Travels*), a Claddagh ring, and, at the feet of the Romantic legends, the two cathedrals.

I slept fitfully in Armagh. It wasn't due to the overload of myth and information, nor the stouts and whiskies I consumed with a large plate of fish and chips in the City Hotel's ersatz pub. Noisy neighbours in my hotel were celebrating something but it had turned sour. I thought I heard someone shout, 'I don't want it!' A man sobbed as he made his way down the corridor. More bothersome were the conspiring voices of women, which seemed to be discussing passionately, all through the night, in accents heavy as peat. I know, it's a crude simile, but the scenes beyond the door suggested a Frank O'Connor story, set in old peasant country, but with subliminal intimations that give the plot universal value. I imagined a divorce was in the offing and that it might all turn physical.

When insomnia beat me into submission I listened to the radio. I thought it would be wasteful not to use the lost sleep-time researching my location. Maybe my choice wasn't the wisest: an old BBC broadcast featuring Fergal Keane and Peter Taylor comparing their experiences of reporting the Troubles. Both were anxious to assert the era was far from over, notwithstanding the Good Friday Agreement, and that understanding the conflict meant studying centuries of history across the island of Ireland. They stressed the feebleness of the myth, maintained by some people in the Republic of Ireland then and now, that the problem is all up there – up here. Up here, where I was, tossing, turning, fretting.

———

The fifty or so miles I drove to get to Enniskillen seemed like many more, the roads increasingly rural, farm traffic slowing me down. Or perhaps I was groggy after the unquiet night. I parked at a hotel outside town that looked like a golf club crossed with a motel but had river views. There was plenty of water in the sky, with great sheets of Atlantic rain flapping under low clouds. I walked into town along the cycle track beside a main road. The emergency services had sealed off a road at the entrance to town and fire engines were busy putting out a major fire; a derelict hotel had gone up in flames.

The steep streets were waterfalls. I hid in a coffee shop and read about what lay beneath and around me. Enniskillen occupies an island at the

                    where tourists seldom tread

confluence of Lower and Upper Lough Erne. North and south lie countless islands, and an amphibious ecology of rushes and reeds, waterfowl and waders, and fishers who dangle spoon-shaped lures to catch pike. On White Island in Lower Lough Erne are seven figures that suggest the deadly sins. In the graveyard at Caldragh on Boa Island is a two-faced pagan deity, probably Badhbh (the hooded crow), the banshee-like goddess of war and death after whom the island is named. Seamus Heaney's poem 'January God' suggests further dualisms: 'God-eyed, sex-mouthed, its brain / A watery wound . . . I faltered near his power.'

Enniskillen is the Island of Kathleen, Queen of the Formorians, supernatural raiders from the sea. It was founded in 1612 by a charter issued by the earthly invader, James VI and I, the Scot who hated witches almost as much as he hated Irish Gaels. He sent thousands of planters (Scottish and English Protestant settlers) to pacify, anglicise and carve up Ulster. Cambridge-educated Captain William Cole was awarded a grant of land, upon which he built a church, a school, a jail and court and houses for burgesses. He constructed bridges and refurbished and added a tower to Enniskillen Castle – which had been the medieval seat of the Maguire (Mag Uidhir) chieftains of Fermanagh. A market house and diamond – a common feature of Plantation towns – were placed at the centre.

Alleys and cross-streets were added over the centuries. Enniskillen's streets, like those in Spain, have their previous names displayed on ceramic plaques. Queen Street was formerly Barracks Street and Brewery Lane. Belmore Street was Gaol Street. Hospital Lane became Preaching Lane, which later became Wesley Street. An alley beside St Michael's was Bank Lane as well as Peg o' the Bull Lane, after one Peggy who sold bullseyes from a confectionery stall. Eden Street was Pudding Lane, after the offal from slaughterhouses. The main street was once Drawbridge. The modern signage, by artist Eleanor Wheeler, conjures ghosts and old ways. Another scheme, 'Walking on Words', features cryptic messages embossed on twenty-one granite blocks in the pavement. Tis Poteen I Adore. Rousseaux moustier. The Gin Palace. The very soil of Eden. An t-im.

It's not all words. Wall murals celebrate local themes, wildlife and famous former inhabitants – including Oscar Wilde, who attended the Portora Royal School. A separate installation, made up of 150 gold-leaf swallows adorning buildings, nods to Wilde's 'The Happy Prince'. The story opens with a high tower allegedly inspired by Enniskillen's Cole's Monument – dedicated to General Sir Galbraith Lowry Cole, a descendant of the above-mentioned Cole – which young Oscar could see from his dormitory window at the school. An oversized chess set – with thirty-two pieces and sixty-four cubes spread around bars and cafés – pays homage to keen chess-player Samuel Beckett, another Portora alumnus; he made the school's bullying headmaster cry by telling him to 'hit one of your own size'. *Murphy* was influenced by chess; it informs the subtext and title of *Endgame*.

Enniskillen hosted the annual Happy Days Beckett Festival from 2012 to 2023. Wandering around the old market square, I was tracked by the beady eyes of a living local legend, actor Adrian Dunbar. When asked to direct Beckett's *Catastrophe* for the 2014 festival, he wrote in the *Guardian*, 'I have often wondered . . . what effect his formative years at Portora and his engagement with Enniskillen and Fermanagh had on him. As a child growing up there I was for the most part very happy. I was brought up in what was left of the old streets on the island. In the 1960s, in a gross act of social engineering, some civil servants decided to move the people off the island, destroying Georgian housing, and replace them with roads and car parks. In Beckett's time, however, the town and its people were connected entirely to the lough, their homes and streets ran directly down to the shore.'

Perhaps signs, plaques and street art help commuting Enniskilleners recall the insular town of yore. There's a powerful appetite here for the past. Frank Roofe, who has been helping diaspora Irish to trace their genealogies for decades, says, 'Many families crept back slowly over time into their former ancestral home areas. Those who didn't make

 where tourists seldom tread

it back remember their Townland names which are still used today. When we are successful in locating their old family homestead here in Ireland, the tears of joy flow freely.' The Townlands are Ireland's secret map: ancient territories that underlie modern boroughs, named for marshes, churches, oak woods, forts. Carrickyheenan. Knockalough. Woaghternerry. County Fermanagh comprises 2,305 Townlands, Northern Ireland almost ten thousand.

The solid, stately Enniskillen Workhouse ('gabled roofs and elevated chimney shafts give it a pleasant, pleasing and picturesque appearance', said its architect, George Wilkinson), which opened in 1844, has been preserved as a reminder of the famine period and its aftermath, doubling as heritage centre and business hub. 'With the building, its stories, its voices, and its people, we see beauty and sorrow walk hand in hand,' says historian Catherine Scott, who had the site listed in 2009 when she heard it was scheduled for demolition. Yet another community project is creating a 'memory map' of the lives of the young men from Enniskillen who died in the First World War; the backstreet tenements where they lived, known as the 'Dardanelles', were demolished in 1970. Frank is deeply involved. 'Although I was born in London, I was brought to Enniskillen when I was just over one year old. My father was from the old streets. My grandmother was dying so we came home to look after her and never went back. I was brought up in Strand Street which was a major part of the "Old Dardanelles". Although inhabited mostly by poor people, it had a heart that beat unity, love, and caring for each other. That feeling remains today and can be seen in our reminiscence talks which we hold on different town subjects and old Enniskillen photographs.'

When the rain turned biblical, I dived into St Macartin's Cathedral, which stands at the high street's summit, where William Cole built his church. The name of its patron, Macartin, or more commonly Macartan, means 'son of the rowan tree'; he was a convert who became

St Patrick's 'strong man', quite literally at times, carrying his frail master across rivers and marshlands. Someone was practising on the organ and as I was alone it was affecting. But the church was not a restful place. Regimental flags were hanging from every beam, most of the crosses on show were the coloured ones of Union Jacks. On a back wall a black stone plaque was etched in gold with the names of twenty-five soldiers, members of the 4th (County Fermanagh) Battalion, Ulster Defence Regiment. I found it deeply saddening – all the deaths had taken place between 1971 and 1988, comfortably inside the span of my youth and early manhood.

This Church of Ireland cathedral doesn't have to face off a rival across a valley. On the opposite side of the street stands St Michael's, a large French Gothic Revival Catholic church. A serpent above the door eats sinners. Inside are gentle-on-the-eye naturalistic paintings of the Life of Christ by Michael Healy, known more for his work in stained glass, and Charles Russell. The spires seemed to almost lean in towards one another.

The rest of the high street is shops, banks, cafés and plenty of bars. Of the latter, Blakes of the Hollow stands out for its bright red paintwork and Victorian interior decor, with beautiful tiles on the floor (replicas of those in St Michael's) and tiny wood-panelled snugs – including one where women used to drink separately. The tourist trade was boosted for a while by a *Game of Thrones* door inside, one of ten made using wood salvaged from two trees from an avenue of beeches in County Antrim known as Dark Hedges (the Kingsroad in the franchise), which fell during 2016's Storm Gertrude. Ordinary pub doors have their own magic. John McGahern said: 'If Irish pubs were churches, Blake's (of) the Hollow would be the cathedral of them all.'

Near the top of town, looming over the Diamond, is the impressive Renaissance-style town hall; the Continuity IRA exploded a bomb here in 2003. At the foot of town is the run-down, largely unused Clinton Peace Centre, on the site of the 1987 Remembrance Day IRA

          where tourists seldom tread

bombing – hard by the town's cenotaph – that caused twelve deaths. The Erne curls into town a few paces away from here. By the East Bridge you remember, again, it's an island town. Venice, Tenochtitlan, Atlantis . . . Enniskillen.

I slept well on the lough-side. In the morning the view towards the river was calming. The rains had blown through, leaving behind a drifting mist that looked like it had recently awoken. The water was silver and flat, disturbed by neat vees where ducks or geese sailed past. At the outer edges of the built-over town, the quag and bog, the low green hills beyond and the great invisible lakes held a quiet allure.

21
Castaways
Douglas and Ramsey

No man is an island except . . . a quip too yawningly obvious to finish, allegedly made famous by Ken Dodd, and if that's true it's very apt as Liverpool has historic links with the oft-overlooked island. A lot of the overlooking takes place from the ferry; far more people go by sea from the Mersey to Belfast than to the Isle of Man, but there it is, low on the starboard, mysterious, quiet and unassuming. Why do English people, Scots, Irish and Welsh, islanders all, rudely ignore this significant lump of sea-girdled rock? Perhaps because the two things that are routinely reported about it are the TT race (and its high body count) and the fact that the island is a 'financial services' centre – that is, a haven for tax-dodgers. In 1989, Dodd was taken to court for false accounting and cheating, including taking £777,453 in banknotes by air to the Isle of Man. He was cleared. 'I told the Inland Revenue I didn't owe them a penny because I lived near the seaside,' he said. A widespread perception that the Isle of Man was once a popular holiday destination but has become old-fashioned and passé is a third factor. Irony, hype, the media or middle-class fads haven't come to the rescue. Until now.

Arrive on the ferry and Douglas's sweeping front takes time to take in. The island has a population of 84,000 – about the same as High Wycombe, Stockton-on-Tees or Weston-super-Mare – and a third live here and in neighbouring Onchan. But, as well as a seaside resort that faces the rising sun and bossy, bullying England, it is a capital city with a miniature downtown and 'national' cultural institutions; behind Douglas are not only suburbs but a country – though some prefer to say 'Crown dependency' – and mountain massifs heavy with history.

Walking along Loch Promenade, seaside Victorian/Edwardian is the overriding theme. Plaster-clad terraces. Tall, slender hotels with solid-sounding names like Granville, Marina, Cunard House, Admiral House. Some look forgotten, a few almost seamy. Others – the Halvard, the Gresham – have been painted and glammed-up. There are lots. Seaside resorts sometimes emit their own distinctive note of desperation.

Look how many people used to come! Where have they gone? Probably to sunnier, cheaper islands: Kos, Ibiza, Koh Samui, Tenerife.

Dodgy fonts abound, and the accent is on value: ('The original Quidds inn – Affordable Beer Started Here'). Oddities break up the wedding-cake architecture. There's a statue of the Bee Gees, exuding 'Stayin' Alive' attitude as they stride, upright, hair a-waft, towards a building site. They're slightly larger than life. Earworms wriggle as you study the fair likenesses. 'Tragedy'! 'Jive Talkin''! 'I've Gotta Get a Message to You'! Bob Stanley called his biography of the brothers *Children of the World*, after their 1976 album. They were international superstars: rootless, globetrotting, glamorous. From Douglas to Manchester to Queensland to Miami to anywhere. But, Stanley writes, 'They would make [the Isle of Man] their playground, a sandpit they could return to when times were rough, a place entirely other to the pop world.' Robin Gibb, the one with the flaky, vulnerable voice, named his last album after one of their Douglas addresses: *50 St Catherine's Drive*. A little man bent over a stick walks past, a local; he ignores the trio, or can't muster the energy to raise his head. He must be about the same age as the sole surviving Bee Gee, Barry.

At the corner with Howard Street is a striking brutalist Methodist church, with a grey slab facade decked out with a skinny green cross, topped by an aggressively angular roof. Part-way along is a classic broad-fronted grand hotel, the Sefton, somewhat subverted by the name of its 'theatre bar': Sir Norman's. At the entrance is a seated statue of Norman Wisdom, who lived on the Isle of Man for almost three decades and is buried in Bride at the island's northern tip. Beside rises the festively stuccoed and columned facade of the Gaiety Theatre and Opera House, rebuilt in 1899 to the designs of Frank Matcham (of London Palladium and Blackpool Tower Ballroom fame). A glitzy cocktail-and-music bar bears his name.

It isn't all fun and frolics. Turn to the sea and there in the bay on tiny St Mary's Isle is the castellated Tower of Refuge, built in 1832 'for the else forlorn' – in Wordsworth's words – by Douglas native Sir William Hillary, founder of the Royal National Lifeboat Institution. People who live on large islands forget the fact. I doubt the Manx do; the sea is always near, usually in view. Over several days, I note that there's always a big boat at the southern end of the prom, arriving, leaving, loading, unloading. It reminds you of connection, and of escape.

Douglas isn't the Isle of Man any more than Liverpool or Blackpool is England. The town's Manx Museum struggles to squeeze all the island's history into a single site. It's often remarked that from the highest point, Snaefell, you can see seven kingdoms: the Isle of Man, England, Ireland, Scotland, Wales, Neptune and Heaven. The Isle of Man, or *Ellan Vannin,* is a microcosm of its neighbours, a Venn diagram and site of conflict. There were Celtic and Norse kings of Mann, with names like Tutagual, Diwg and Ragnall, from the fifth through to the thirteenth century, at which point the island became a suzerainty of Norway. The Archdiocese of Nidaros, a metropolitan see in present-day Trondheim, included the diocese of Sodor, comprised of the Hebrides, the Islands of the Firth of Clyde and Isle of Man. (Following a visit to the Isle of Man, the Rev. Wilbert Awdry adopted the name for the island on which Thomas the Tank Engine and his friends lived.) The Manx, like north-tilting Shetlanders and Orcadians, are probably pensive on aurora nights.

After a brief summer of full independence, the island fell under English rule, and from 1405 to 1765 many of the kings, later lords, of Mann were members of the Stanley family – who, as Earls of Derby, were landed aristocracy, hobnobbing with royals, parliamentarians and bishops. As is the way with noble landlords, the Stanleys were infrequent visitors, but James Stanley, the 7th Earl and a prominent Royalist, took refuge on the island during the English Civil Wars. He added to the fortifications at Peel Castle, which, sitting on its own island (once associated with Arthurian Avalon), served as a safe house.

The regalities (feudal rights) of the Isle of Man were purchased by the British Crown in 1765, an event known here as Yn Chialg Vooar – 'The Great Swindle'. In the nineteenth century, Douglas became the capital and home to the Tynwald, or parliament. Its name derives from the Old Norse *Þingvǫllr*, meaning 'the meeting place of the assembly'. The Manx Tynwald claims to be more than a thousand years old, making it the 'oldest continuous parliament' on the planet, but there is no record of the first meeting. The Tynwald only elected its own members from 1866, and a Crown dependency is not a fully independent entity, even if Charles is Lord of Mann rather than king, and the island has passed its own laws pertaining to issues such as corporal punishment, tax and assisted dying.

The room at the museum dedicated to seaside tourism is meant as a cheeky, cheesy finale after the politics and history. It's filled with romantic posters, vintage advertisements and pictures of beauty queens and the steamships that gave birth to the resort once dubbed the 'Naples of the North'. Pier-end ditties are piped into the room: 'No I don't want to go to Idaho, I don't want to go to Tennessee, take me with a smile to Mona's Isle . . . I want to be a tripper and eat a juicy kipper, in the dear old Isle of Man.' It's so effortfully innocent, so self-consciously jolly and down to earth, that it prompts incredulity.

A lot of today's tourism business revolves around antiquated transport systems. The old trains and trams routinely fill with tourists 'of a certain age', keen to be shaken and shuddered up and down the Manx mountains.

I rode in a wooden carriage to Port Erin. It was a morning of heavy and relentless rain and, with billowing steam mingling with the deluge, and mist rising off the slopes, the views of green fields, woods and, somewhere down below, the sea, were somewhat obscured. I shared the carriage with strangers, who coughed and giggled at double entendres, as if a vintage comedy virus was in circulation. Opened in 1873, the Isle of Man Steam Railway is the longest narrow-gauge line in Britain still using original locomotives and coaches, and while it's a cold, noisy affair, locals still use it to get from A to B. It's not as frequent as the bus, but it isn't much slower. Port Erin sits above a pretty little bay, but the weather drove me to seek shelter, tea and a calorific lunch in the ultra-trad chippy.

North of Douglas is the mile-long Douglas Bay Horse Tramway, which runs from Villa Marina to Derby Castle, where the Manx Electric Railway takes passengers on to Laxey, to then ride on the Snaefell Mountain Railway up to the island's highest point. Before neutering became the norm, a colony of feral Manx cats thrived at the horse-tram stables. They were often observed tackling herring gulls, their longer back legs enabling them to jump fast and far to catch their prey. Manx activist and fabulist Sophia Morrison recounts how the Manx cat lost its tail when it got trapped in the door of the ark. They were popular ships' cats because of a common naval belief that a cat could bring on a storm using magic stored in its tail. No tail, no shipwreck.

The Isle of Man's early-twentieth-century holidaymaking zenith co-incided, not incidentally, with an apogee of artistic and literary creativity. As well as Morrison, there was T. E. Brown, who wrote Anglo-Manx poetry, and Hall Caine, the remarkable Manx novelist and dramatist who was a friend of Bram Stoker and the Pre-Raphaelites.

During 2025–6, a room at the Manx Museum was occupied by the temporary show *Knox: Order and Beauty*, showcasing the work of Archibald Knox, born in the outskirts of Douglas in 1864. A promi-nent member of this group of 'tenacious patriots', Knox was a pioneer of modern design. The museum had pulled off the coup of mounting the largest show of his work to date, with more than two hundred pieces on display. His best-known work was for the department store Liberty, including 'Cymric' silverware and 'Tudric' pewterware in-spired by Celtic crosses. But he also crafted silver clocks and cigarette boxes, tea caddies and textiles, ink wells and tableware, typography and gravestones. Knox was a skilled painter. His landscapes and seascapes render the Isle of Man as stormy and grey, capturing the vulnerability of a small island, and the drama of its skies. He is quoted as saying, 'Hush, look at that cloud!' Great churning nimbuses roll over washed-out ground, edging the earth out of the canvas. From rounded bare hills and flat-topped moors he teases abstract forms.

Knox worked as a teacher, illustrator and during the war a censor at a Manx internment camp. Reflecting on this time in later life, he said: 'We became post-impressionists, cubists, unnamed venturists . . . twenty-five years before such experiments were known in London'. He also said, 'Never be ordinary. Better be nothing than that.'

————

By road or by heritage electric railway the distance from Douglas to Ramsey is only around fifteen miles but it is a meandering, mountain-scaling journey. For those delivering post or running errands by horseback or on foot it must have been a challenge (though that doesn't deter hardy modern-day hikers). The Isle of Man's longest river, the Sulby, plummets from the unpeopled uplands, carving out a long, beautiful glen.

Vikings, as well as Scots, entered the Isle of Man at the mouth of the Sulby. Ramsey's name derives from the Old Norse for 'wild garlic river'. The small working port breaks up a shoreline of sand and pebble beaches backed by apartment buildings and grand-seeming hotels. Timber and aggregate are massed up on the wharves. A bulk carrier, *Snaefell River*, is moored beneath a single tall crane. To the south is the long, ruinous Queen's Pier, once a landing stage. Victoria never disembarked but the pier recalls her visit. Above town is the Albert Tower. The consort made landfall.

I climb a hill to see the tower close-up. I have been told Ramsey, backed by hills, is protected by a rain shadow, but it is pelting down, with a cold draught blowing in from somewhere – the walk, through

   where tourists seldom tread

Elfin Glen, is a drenching, desultory affair. Even workmen, charged with improving the road surface on a hairpin corner for the TT, are hiding in their vans and lorries.

When I am back on the low shore, the sun comes out and the wind stops completely. Eider ducks are mewling in a small group at the end of the southern harbour wall, as if swapping the latest gossip. I can hear the surf clawing at stones; Manx has a word for this, *soodraght* (SOO-drakh). Ramsey was once a very popular seaside resort, with steam packet ships to Kirkcudbright and Garlieston in Dumfries and Galloway, to Liverpool and Whitehaven (I can see the Cumbrian fells). The peach-hued Belvedere Court hotel promises 'Victorian Grandeur', announcing itself as 'Famous throughout the World and Ramsey'. A swing bridge connects the northern beach to Ramsey town centre, a likeable mishmash of centenarian buildings housing pubs, food and drink outlets, antique and bric-a-brac shops – and a very eighties strip mall with a Tesco, dry cleaner's, model shop and tattooist's.

On the edge of town I find myself at Grove House, now a museum. It was the holiday home of the island's second-most famous Gibb family. Duncan Gibb was a shipping agent from Greenoch. The parents of his wife, Janet Blake, were from Liverpool and Bristol, port people. The house reaches out to foreign climes. A tiger skin on the floor of the drawing room. A leopard skin in the bedroom. Mahogany furniture from a primeval forest. Curtains from India. A japanned backgammon set. When the men sailed away, or died out, a matriarchy took over. I had lunch at the far grander Milntown Estate – quinoa salad, when I'd half expected teacakes or scones. Both country piles have beautiful gardens. Washed by the Gulf Stream, the Isle of Man is ideal for growing things.

If ports are quiet and useless at low tide, it's when their poetic coefficient increases. Ramsey's U-shaped harbour becomes a seaweed-spattered, glistening artwork. Gulls and corvids pick in the pools and potter on the mudflats. Large boats sink on to pilings, smaller ones lean over to sleep. Rotting old wooden structures, recently submerged, stand at their full height. A thin snaking trail of water waits for the return of the sea. The Trafalgar pub, on West Quay, is a seaman's boozer, the windows small enough to forget the dawn's miserable catch, the last terrible tempest. I drink an Odin's mild in the corner. Locals look bristlingly familiar with one another, conspiratorial, as if they know something I never will. John Donne and Ken Dodd aside, the Isle of Man is adept at making a mainlander feel apart.

I drive up to Maughold with Ruth Keggin Gell. The village, which grew around a pre-Norse religious community, is named after a pirate-turned-bishop who became the Isle of Man's patron saint. Its cemetery, sheltering beneath a thousand-year-old church, itself shielded by a tump covered in glowing gorse, is famous.

Ruth is the island's Manx Language Development Officer – though she prefers the job title 'Yn Greinneyder' or 'The Encourager'. She began learning Manx after university and now, aged thirty-six, is fluent, using the language to teach others and to perform folk music.

'Although I use it for work, I prefer speaking Manx to English. It sounds corny but I feel nicer. It feels like my soul language. I have a bigger vocabulary in English but I find I'm happier and more myself in Manx. I wonder if that's because I came to it through music and song.' She says the latest census records 2,223 Manx speakers (none of them as a first language, as the last native speaker died in 1974), and that naysaying is dying out. Tourists, apparently, are called 'skibbyltee boghtey' in Manx, which Ruth translates as 'poor acrobats'. Others render it as 'poor nimble folk', pitying rather than derogatory.

The novelist Hall Caine is buried at Maughold, with a grave-stone by Knox. But Ruth wants to show me an array of forty-five medieval stones brought here from across the parish, protected under a purpose-built shelter or cross-house. Deciphering is a slow, pleasurable process. One fragment contains an alpha and omega; another features a hunting scene; yet another a distinctive boar figure. The

    where tourists seldom tread

eighth-century Blackman's Cross is inscribed with Anglican runes and trefoil knots. It bears the name of Blagkmon, who may have been the grandson of King Ida of Northumbria, who took refuge with his family on the Isle of Man. Guriat's Cross has the name of a Welsh prince written in Hiberno-Saxon. The Hedin Cross depicts a Viking ship, the only such representation on the island.

It's an entrancing place and a node for so much of Man's strange history, which, with the passing of the heyday of seaside holidays, need no longer be occluded.

22
Radical Angles
Nelson and Colne

I could forgive England all the vulgarity and all the depressing disappointment of London for the magnificent spirit of these north country working people. As long as that is the stuff of which they are made, then indeed Britons never, never shall be slaves.

From *Letters from London* by C. L. R. James

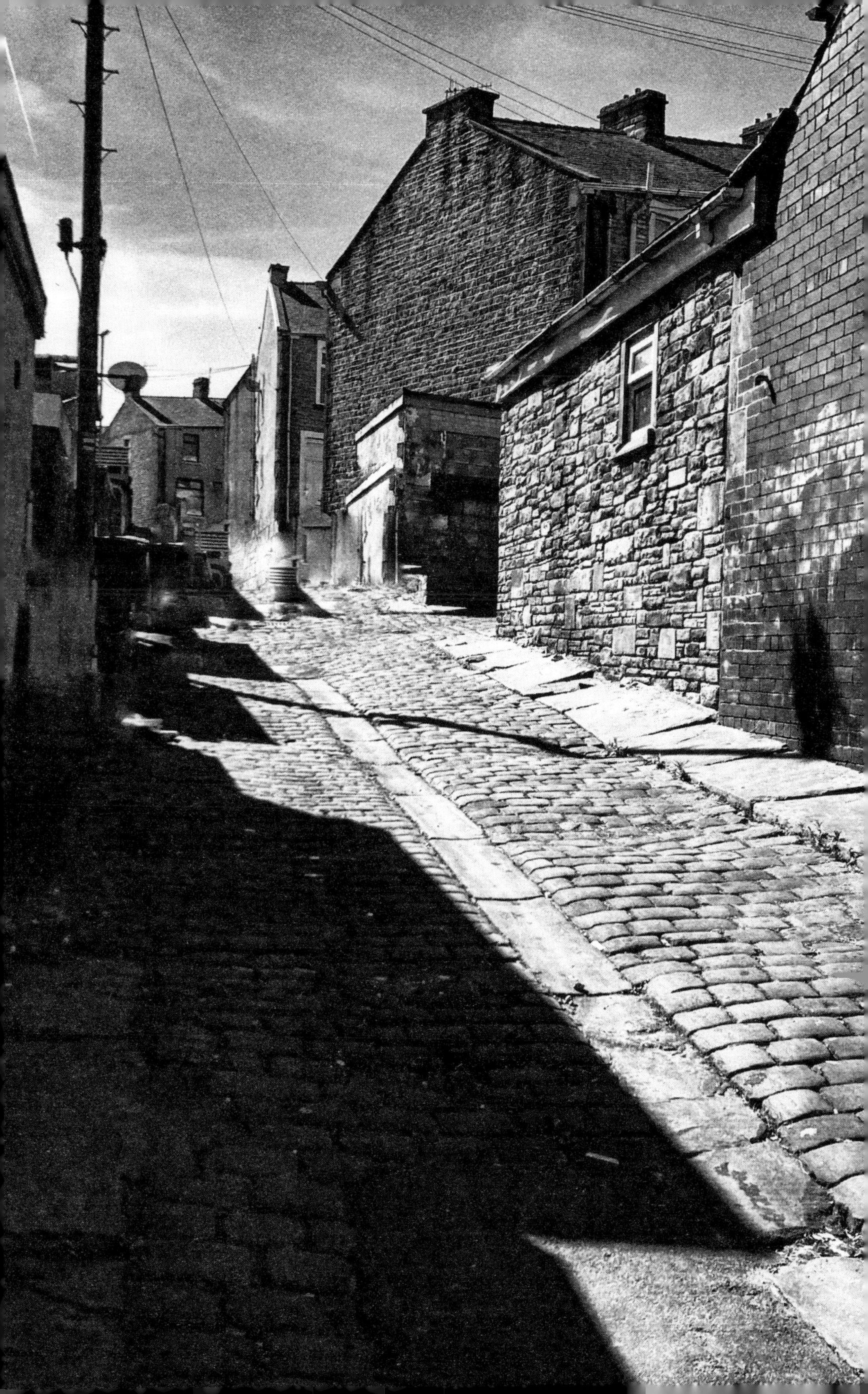

Lancashire's name freights (forges, fires) connotations and contradictions unlike other counties. The compound effect of the region's pioneering industrial history, the presence of two large, globally renowned cities, and the densely populated, urbanised settlements in the east, south and along the coast, make it different from all the rest. Yorkshire, its supposed rival, is huge, green, ancient, tourist-filled. Cheshire is more pastoral, per capita wealthier and not very northern. The Irish Sea and the Pennines exert particular and powerful pressures – historical, cultural, spiritual, meteorological – on Lancashire.

The governance of the shire was carved up in 1974, reducing the official council-run area to a much smaller size, with Liverpool and Manchester excised, which complicates storytelling and messes with memories. A pre-reorganisation population of 5.1 million (the largest county outside London) was reduced to 1.5 million. Lancaster became the only city (joined by Preston in 2002), Blackpool the most populous urban area. Some Merseysiders and Mancunians continue to invoke old Lancashire; others have let it slip away northward, and into history.

That I was born in Lancashire in 1966 adds a twisted umbilical connection. That I now live here again after a gap of almost four decades means I am conflicted by homecoming anxieties, nostalgic rediscoveries and a small but significant geographical shift; I was born in the Lancastrian south-west and now live in the north-east. These feel as different as their English namesakes.

———

I arrived by towpath. It was the start of a short midwinter day, crisp and blue-skied. A flat walk appealed. I was dropped off on a bridge outside Accrington, from where I followed the Leeds and Liverpool Canal through the built-up, beaten-up dale formed by the River Calder and its tributary, Pendle Water. The canal runs parallel to the river and the M65, a strange motorway that begins confidently at the

M6 and seems to be aiming for Yorkshire's West Riding but suddenly dies close to where I'm headed, at a roundabout and a large car park. Lorry-hum accompanied me for all of my walk-in. Only Pendle Hill stands between the Ribble Valley and this one, but they are separated by mountains of aspiration. The latter is agricultural, affluent, white. Here is the opposite.

No town is born totally *ex nihilo*, but Nelson comes close. An early description is 'a peat covered and rain sodden wilderness'. An 1844 map shows a cotton factory, two chapels, a pub, a post office. Most locals resided in outlying villages. A *Preston Guardian* article of 12 February 1881 reports, 'Nelson is undoubtedly a modern town. Fifty years ago, it was entirely unknown, and no mention of it appears in any books dealing with the ancient history of the County.'

The canal, opened in 1816, enabled the fledgling settlement to ship its wares. When the railway came in 1849, it was known as Marsden – but there was already a Marsden in Yorkshire. The train guard would shout 'Nelson!' as the train came to a halt by the Lord Nelson inn. The name stuck. Locals boast, half-heartedly, theirs is the only town named after a pub. It's a pity the pub didn't have a sparkier Lancashire name, like Hark to Bounty, Tut and Shive, or Jolly Hatters.

Two thousand terraced houses sprang up around the station – built from stone, many are still there, laid out on a gridiron plan. Mid-nineteenth-century Nelson had nine small general stores, two drapers, two druggists, one tailor and one stationer. There were a saddler's shop and two smithies. By 1876, to these were added butchers, cab-inet makers, cloggers, drapers, glass and china dealers, greengrocers, ironmongers and tobacconists – plus corner shops and fish-and-chips shops; after 1861, twenty-one branches of the Cooperative Society. There were more than a dozen each of pubs and churches or chapels. I reel the list off as it is fairly typical of nineteenth-century British towns and because I haven't done so in the book's preceding postcards. What towns – and townspeople – miss isn't only what we remember from our own lifetimes.

Twenty-odd cotton mills, with 21,000 looms, employed around 10,000 workers. Nine-tenths of Nelson's buildings and population were dedicated to textiles. Local mills specialised in fine cloths such as Venetians and Florentines, which allowed the town to ride out swings in demand for the cheaper cloths produced further down the valley. Pendle Borough has more than ninety mill buildings, most of which stand empty. I'd seen the sad husk of Whitefield Mill from the canalside. All that remains of Riverside Mill is a chimney. Lomeshaye Bridge Mill and Spring Bank Mill survive as mixed-use spaces. Brierfield Mill has been converted into posh flats. A forty-foot-high shuttle on the high street is meant to celebrate, or at least remind people, of the weaving days; it's an ineffectual monument, conveying nothing of the power, graft, suffering or pride of textile workers.

There were smaller concerns dedicated to brewing, quarrying, coal mining, corn milling, soap manufacture, brick and pipe making and engineering – but it's Nelson's contribution to confectionery that gives historians something to suck on. The Victory V lozenge – originally made with liquorice, linseed, acacia gum and chlorodyne (containing chloroform, the opiate laudanum and cannabis) – was invented by two local men, Thomas Fryer and Dr Edward Smith. Admiral Nelson's flagship adorned some early tins along with red-cheeked sailors; others featured sledding children, nurses and a hammer smacking an anvil to show the sweets were 'forged for strength'. The lozenges were intended to ease sore throats, chills and coughs and provide oral heat 'for cold journeys', and no doubt gave the impression of freeing textile workers' pipes of dangerous microfibres. By the 1920s they were a mainstream treat and popular with schoolboys, offering a sanctioned taste of forbidden adult medicine. A more mass-market mouth-pleaser was developed by an Austrian confectioner employed at Fryer's in the 1860s. He was asked to make a mould for jelly bears, but the resulting sweets looked like newborn infants. They were duly rebranded, the *Burnley Express* carrying cheery adverts for 'Victory' Unclaimed Babies. At the time it wasn't unusual to find babies left on church steps. The Victory Factory, closed in 1987 and demolished the following year, stood at what is now Victory Close, opposite Pendle Wavelengths swimming pool.

Nelson has always been a town of immigrants. The first weavers came in from surrounding villages. In the late nineteenth century tin miners from Cornwall and lead miners from Yorkshire came to work in East Lancashire mills and mines. In the 1960s, a second wave of immigrants arrived from the Indian subcontinent, especially Pakistan. Mills were keen to take on skilled workers who could replace ageing operatives – though the textile industry was already in its death throes. Today, around 50 per cent of Nelson's population is of Asian heritage. This nudges it a little above the Pendle borough average, and is a handy stat for London-based hacks parachuted north to file their annual 'divided town' story for publications on either side of the political spectrum. 'Whites at the top of the valley, Asians at the bottom. Is Nelson another town ready to blow?' hollered the *Independent* in 2001. 'The fish-eaters and the fasters' was the somewhat cryptic headline in the *New Statesman* in 2017. The *Byline Times* reported in 2024 a new division opening up between Muslims who approved of Nelson's large number of mosques – sixteen at the last count – and those who felt they reflected a 'lack of unity and tribal rivalry' in the community.

Nelson is a poor town. Its centre looks stripped back and under-used. Half the units in the small shopping centre are vacant. The Lord Nelson looks shut – shuttered? – at lunchtime. A small market has been set up around the base of the shuttle, the Mancunian stallholders sitting tapping away at their phones beside racks of cheap saris, garish synthetic-fibre towels and Disney-themed blankets. The only non-food store doing lively trade is the Suraj Bazaar in the former Burton's building, which sells smarter saris and hijabs. I watch as a white couple quarrel over a can of beer. The man barks into a phone. An old bloke asks me if I am from the council. I was taking photographs; nobody does that in Nelson. We chat for a while about Victory Vs, ghosts, the mills. He's originally from Wiltshire. 'No one talks to anyone any more,' he complains.

This is not my first time here. One Friday evening, driving north, I took a wrong turn at Burnley and found myself driving through Nelson. A heavy shower had not quite finished but people were beginning to emerge, summoned by the Maghrib call to prayer. The satnav guided me through terraced estates, their walls grey with damp, their pavements glossy. Hundreds of boys and girls in plain robes and white thobes were going to the madrasahs. The scene was striking and a little bit surreal.

The first Asian millworkers were men, and they integrated easily enough. Faith and family changed the way many lived. But the winding-up of textile and factory jobs means there's now no obvious common ground for people from different cultures to meet. Nelson is more biracial than multiracial. It's not a particularly complex community. But it's left to schools, youth clubs, library, community arts organisations like In Situ, Super Slow Way and Mid Pennine Arts and innovative companies like publisher Pendle Press to form connections and encourage conversations.

Sport can help. Burnley is a bridge-building powerhouse at this end of the valley (Blackburn rules the other end), while Nelson FC is a minnow of a team – despite once playing in the Second Division and beating Real Madrid 4–2 in Spain. The Seedhill Cricket Ground attracts small crowds these days but it, too, has played its part breaking down race barriers. Trinidadian all-rounder Learie Constantine, in England for the 1928 West Indies cricket tour, signed a three-year professional contract to play at Nelson. Despite initial doubts about the town, he ended up staying until 1949. His large terraced house at 3 Meredith Street is above the town centre and has a blue plaque; when I visited it was unoccupied. Facing down a sometimes-hostile environment, he won over the locals and was adopted as 'Our Connie'. In 1930 Constantine joined the League of Coloured Peoples, a British civil rights organisation; during the Second World War he worked for the Ministry of Labour and National Service with responsibility for West Indians employed in English factories.

In 1943 he was given four days' leave to captain the West Indies team against England at Lord's. Prior to his arrival he was assured by the Imperial Hotel in London's Russell Square there was no objection to his colour. When he arrived at the hotel it was made clear that he and his family were not welcome. Constantine brought a successful action against the Imperial for breach of contract. His 1954 book *The Colour Bar* addressed the pervasive racial discrimination suffered by black people. Constantine became a popular broadcaster and was awarded the MBE in 1945. He was called to the Trinidad bar in 1955 and served as Trinidad and Tobago's High Commissioner from 1961 to 1964. He was knighted in 1962 and made Britain's first black peer in 1969, as Baron Constantine of Maraval and Nelson. He died in London in 1971. Of the town he said, 'I am a better person: I am better materially, I am better socially. I have grown more tolerant, I have grown less self-ish. I am a better citizen for the time I have been in Nelson.'

The Trinidadian Marxist journalist and historian C. L. R. James lodged with Constantine in 1932, helping him write his autobiography, *Cricket and I* (1933). James befriended local baker Harry Spencer. On hill walks taken on Sundays they discussed social and political issues. Harry funded trips to Paris for James to undertake research on the slave revolt in Haiti for his seminal book *The Black Jacobins* – it carries the dedication 'To my good friends Harry and Elizabeth Spencer of Nelson, Lancashire, England.'

James was politically at home in Nelson. The parliamentary consti-tuency of Clitheroe, which included Nelson and Colne, was held by Liberal Ughtred Kay-Shuttleworth through five elections from 1885. In a 1902 by-election, cotton worker and trade unionist David

Shackleton won the seat, becoming Labour's third MP. Left-wing political groups and weaving unions were strong. The latter were particularly militant during the lockouts of 1911–12 and 1928 (prompted by weavers insisting on a closed-shop recruitment policy), and volatile protests during the latter led to a local newspaper branding the town 'Little Moscow'. But socialism rather than communism was the main creed, and another nickname, 'Red Nelson', is probably more fitting. The First World War saw the emergence of a sizeable pacifist movement, too, leading to schisms between conscientious objectors and those who believed in the national war aims.

The building that best embodies local radical history is Unity Hall on Vernon Street. In 1906 the Independent Labour Party (ILP) collected money through penny subscriptions and bazaars to provide a building for working people in Nelson. It would be 'a place for us', in the words of a fundraising leaflet, providing a library, entertainment, lectures, meetings and baths. The fund topped £3,000, a large sum for mostly low-paid weavers to raise. Two years later, the opening of what was then known as the Socialist Institute was preceded by 500 people marching through the town behind the Brierfield Brass Band. Ribbons were snipped by Blackburn MP and the first Labour chancellor of the exchequer, Philip Snowden, and his human-rights-activist wife Ethel. One foundation stone, in memory of William Morris and Edward Fay, was laid by Katherine Bruce Glasier, a prominent ILP figure, known as 'the grandmother of the Labour Party'. The other, in memory of Caroline Martyn and Enid Stacy, was laid by Selina Cooper, who had moved to Nelson from Cornwall with her family in 1875 following her father's death. She started working in the mills aged ten as a half-timer, and went full time from the age of thirteen. Cooper played a leading role in politicising and organising local women textile workers. She joined the suffragists and the anti-war movement during the First World War, was part of a delegation of women to Nazi Germany to campaign for the release of women prisoners, became an elected member of Nelson's Board of Guardians, a justice of the peace and a key figure in the Independent Labour Party. Cooper lived at 59 St Mary Street, which has a plaque (though not an official English Heritage one).

The streets of stone terraces are attractive, many framing bracing views of Pendle Hill's south-eastern face and the steep slope – beloved of fell runners – that plummets from the summit, called the Big End. To enable millworkers to access the countryside, Nelson socialists founded the Clarion House at nearby Roughlee. It's a living, breathing community nexus and poignant memorial to al fresco idealism. During the late nineteenth and early twentieth centuries, Clarion Houses popped up in many rural areas, providing nature-loving factory and mill workers with a place to rest and enjoy refreshments. The clubhouses sprang from the Clarion movement, a loosely affiliated socialist organisation based around a Manchester newspaper of the same name.

Open to the public on Sundays (though there are special events and craft lessons and other activities for local groups midweek) and run by a small team of dedicated volunteers, the last Clarion House sits in an idyllic spot with a garden that faces east along a wide valley. Tea is served in pint mugs and copies of the *Morning Star* are spread around the long benches. On the walls are posters from the Spanish Civil War and photographs of Nelson and Colne MP and vocal opponent of capital punishment Sydney Silverman. There's a beautiful stained-glass window, and a banner emblazoned with 'Workers of the World Unite'. The place has become a focal point and meeting place for the Pendle Radicals (named for the hill as much as the borough), a group of history-aware hikers who devise trails and organise talks to celebrate the lives of the above-mentioned left-leaning legends. When I moved to the area in 2021, they were my welcoming committee, embracing incomers and strangers like members of a family or a non-religious fellowship.

———

  where tourists seldom tread

Streets are always steeper in memory. Colne is like a childhood dream, with the vaulting angles of an Italian hilltop village, making the climber pause to look back and around, slyly catching breath. Chimneys used to challenge the hills but now there are wide open spaces where textile mills have been flattened. Primet Foundry, listed, is a rare survivor and an impressive example of a combined loom manufactory, foundry and textile mill.

My bronchi boosted by a Victory V, I stride up and down Colne's cobbled streets. I am trying to decide which is the steepest. Sutherland Street leaves me winded. As I stroll slowly along Albert Road – the start of the high street that runs along the top of the slopes – I can see that Colne is whiter, less mosque-y and wealthier than Nelson. There are posh cakes at Blondie Brownie, pizzas and foot-tall burgers at Olives Café & Grill 'Bistro & Mediterranean'. At Tubbs bar, beer drinkers are sunning themselves on the outdoor terrace. Banny's British Kitchen does haddock and chips with raita and plant-based chicken tikka kebabs.

Wallace Henry Hartley, bandmaster on the *Titanic*, was born here in 1878. His birthplace was 92 Greenfield Hill; a later family home at 90 Albert Road has a blue plaque. He learned violin and, eventually, fiddled his way to a job on the White Star Line. One of several disputed legends initiated by people who were rescued – and couldn't have known – is that Hartley led the band in playing 'Nearer, My God, to Thee' as the ship sank. Hartley reportedly said he would like the hymn for his funeral. His body was found two weeks after the sinking, his violin case strapped to his back. A funeral was held at the Bethel Independent Methodist Church, where he had sung in the choir led by his father. Thousands attended. He's buried at Keighley Road cemetery and a monument stands off Albert Road. Inevitably, the local Wetherspoons is named after him. Hartley's violin was sold at auction in 2013 for £1.1 million – the highest sum paid for *Titanic* memorabilia until three pocket watches set new records in 2024 and 2025.

As well as salty sublime, Colne does cobblestoned ridiculous. The cod stage-musical scenes for the song 'Every Sperm Is Sacred' in Monty Python's *The Meaning of Life* were shot at the corner of Bankfield Street and Hargreaves Street. Here wedge-shaped terraced houses open on to pavements that must be lethal when it's icy. The band English Teacher's 'The World's Biggest Paving Slab' honours a larger-than-average paving stone outside Colne town hall laid in the 1890s – when, of course, they built things to last. The promo video references the Python film somewhat tangentially, and the Pendle witches; it features Colne streets and shops, including Cemetery Chippy, as well as the Atom, a panopticon above nearby Wycoller village.

Colne is where industrial Lancashire runs out of steam, and not only because of the razings and the realities of the service-sector economy. Look on a map and you will see that here grey turns to green. If you walk directly north you'll not hit an urban area until Edinburgh. The Pennine Way wiggles past nearby. Colne people also enjoy views of the Big End. Skipton is close, reached on low roads through the Aire Gap or via the mile-long narrowboat portal of the Foulridge Tunnel on the Leeds and Liverpool Canal.

Consequently, Colne makes you want to get out to the local wilds. Thomas Arthur Leonard, who resided on Keighley Road, worked as a local pastor. He began encouraging members of his church's social guild to take 'recreative and educational' holidays, rather than join the Wakes Weeks mass exoduses to seaside resorts like Blackpool. In the June of 1891 he organised a holiday for thirty-two members of the Dockray Square Congregational Church in Colne. The four-day trip to Ambleside in the Lake District was a spartan affair, with no alcohol allowed and group singing obligatory. He later wrote, 'In those days we were content with very primitive arrangements, so long as they gave us the joy and freedom of the open fells.' Leonard established the Co-operative Holidays Association in 1897, opening residential centres in rural settings, and ran it till 1912. One of his stated reasons

                              where tourists seldom tread

for leaving was that it had tilted towards organising trips for the middle classes rather than workers. He later established the Holiday Fellowship, and was involved in setting up the Youth Hostels Association. He was elected Chairman of the National Council of Ramblers' Federations, an office he held until 1935 when the National Council was re-constituted as the Ramblers' Association and he was elected its first president. Leonard added a fourth to the three Rs – rambling – and has been called the 'godfather of the adventure holiday'.

———

Until I found myself living close to it, mill-town Lancashire was a vague schoolbook memory. Its Pennine reality – looms and spindles required flowing streams – was unfamiliar to someone raised on the West Lancashire plain.

There's something almost mythic about the large red-brick mills, with their cliff-high walls, tall, skinny, sometimes ornate chimneys and prison-like geometric windows, testament to countless working lives, to camaraderie, to the mysteries of mass production. They seem less slick, more trustworthy, than today's glass-and-steel towers with their work-live-play ruse. When they were new, people gawped in awe or horror at mills. Karl Friedrich Schinkel, visiting in 1826, called them 'the miracles of the new age'. Though now they are old, and unused, skeletal and cold, they still command respect.

Dark secrets loiter in their shadows. Nelson and Colne were integral to the North-West textile-producing region that historian Douglas Farnie called 'Cottonia'. They were connected, via Liverpool and Lancaster, to the slave ports of West Africa, the plantations of Alabama and South Carolina, the monopolies of South Asia. When prices (though not wages) went up in Nelson and Colne, the lash was used more keenly elsewhere. Capitalism was cultivated, spun and finished in these Lancashire towns.

Still, the old mills provoke misplaced, confused nostalgia. They prompt idealised fantasies of children playing in car-free, cobbled streets, polished doorsteps and people dropping in unannounced. Where have the noise and danger, drudgery and dictatorial managers, gone? In 2022, the Pendle Radicals devised a twenty-five-mile Two Toms walking trail to honour the lives and work of Thomas A. Leonard and Tom Stephenson, another great local champion of the outdoors and access for all. We found ourselves tramping up and down Colne's paved inclines, admiring the clear-running river, photographing the extant mills. It's quite something that these streets have become leisure spaces, urban equivalents of the sharp-angled haunches of the surrounding hills.

23
First Canal, First Railway, First Home, Last Walk
St Helens

n the beginning: fields and farms, tumps and coppices, marshes and mosses. My surname's all over the map. Simonswood Moss. Reed's Moss. Moss Wood. Clare's Moss Plantation. Moss Bank. Mossborough Moss. William Camden, travelling across Lancashire in 1582, grumbled about 'certaine moist places and unwholesome called Mosses'.

Their origin lies in the melting of glaciers, which left an extensive deposit of till covering the lowlands. They were drained for agriculture and destroyed by industry. George Stephenson, laying the world's first intercity railway line in the late 1820s, dumped piles of sandy spoil on Highfield Moss. It has survived and is now a Site of Special Scientific Interest. Solitary and mining bees nest in the sand.

Across the road is the empty space where the two oblong towers of Parkside Colliery stood. It was the last deep pit in the Lancashire Coalfield. My dad's last workplace.

From the ice age to the machine age to the dole age – to the age of extinction.

I've never had a town to call my own. I was born and raised through to teenhood in a village. I spent the next three decades living in cities. But a town, St Helens, owns part of me.

It was the place to go to shop, eat, drink, see a band, stand in corners in pubs and discos (this was 'tapping off' circa 1982), buy records, catch up with family, talk things over, go to Saints matches, visit uncles and aunts, play pitch and putt, walk in the park, attend registry-office weddings. The place to *be*. The urban space closest to home. A child's capital city. Superstores, markets, big churches, the pictures, a theatre, bookshop, foreign food. A first encounter with all that.

The village, Burtonwood, was small, safe, as familiar as my bedroom wallpaper or pet sheepdog, sometimes sleepy. St Helens was busy, awake, full of strangers.

–

St Helens is named for Elyn – patron saint of roadbuilders and protectress of travellers. In 1552, a chapel of ease stood at the junction of four ancient manors: Eccleston, Windle, Parr and Sutton. The main parish church occupies the site today.

My dad knew all St Helen's villages, instinctively sensed where the borders between them lay. Pocket Nook, Clinkham Wood, Thatto Heath, Nutgrove, Lea Green, Marshall's Cross, Laffak, Islands Brow, Peasley Cross, Haresfinch, Clock Face, Parr Stocks, Fingerpost, Rainhill, Haydock, Crank, Billinge, Blackbrook.

I was young. I was driven around. I didn't learn the names or shape of the town till now. I didn't learn the history.

Local lads and leading academics T. C. Barker and J. R. Harris recount, in their 500-page tome *A Merseyside Town in the Industrial Revolution: St Helens 1750–1900*, how St Helens gave birth to 'the first English canal' – and how, due to a series of chain reactions, especially fitting in a town that would turn to foundries and chemicals, the waterway gave birth to St Helens.

Packhorses and donkey-drawn carts were slow and expensive. Navigations were built where watercourses could be widened. In 1754, a survey was commissioned to explore the possibility of building a waterway to ship coal from St Helens to the Mersey and on to the Cheshire salt works.

The financier-in-chief, St Helens-born John Ashton, owned salt works near Hale on the Mersey. Four Liverpool merchants backed the project, notably John Blackburne, owner of a large salt works in the city. The surveyor and chief engineer Henry Berry, from Parr in St Helens, had overseen the construction of the Salthouse, George's and Kings docks.

The problem was that the Sankey, flowing to the east of St Helens, was a brook. It was narrow and in wet weather overflowed its banks. But Berry knew that if he recommended a true 'cut' – i.e. canal – the project would likely be voted down in Parliament. In March 1754, a

                    where tourists seldom tread

projected cut between Salford and Leigh had been thrown out by the Commons.

South Lancashire folk are crafty. Berry didn't even tell his paymasters about his plan to construct a bona fide canal until after the ground was broken. The brook would serve principally as a source of water but the canal would run along its own ten-mile course, from Parr to the Mersey, with two branches at the St Helens end: Penny Bridge at Blackbrook and Gerard's Bridge.

The Sankey Canal opened in 1757, four years before the Bridgewater Canal. It was later extended to Fiddler's Ferry, to cut out a winding section of the Mersey, and then to Widnes. At the northern end it was extended to Ravenhead, close to the centre of St Helens, and to Sutton, which would become part of the town. Provided with convenient canal-side docks and access to lucrative markets, wealthy Liverpool families sank dozens of new pits around St Helens. As Barker and Harris put it, 'For the next seventy-five years, the economic life of the St Helens district was dominated by the waterway . . . this was indeed the Canal Age.'

I didn't hear about the Sankey Canal as a child. The last boats motored along it in 1959, seven years before I was born. I can't recall teachers ever telling us about this industrial watershed.

The canal led to the exponential expansion of the coalfield. St Helens soon had its first mining magnates: Sarah Clayton, 'Queen of Parr'; Thomas Case; Charles Dagnall. The abundant coal seams – and local sources of sand and fireclay – inspired Scottish merchant John Mackay to build a massive glassworks at Ravenhead. William Pilkington would soon get in on the act. Drawn by the glow of furnaces, Michael Hughes, an agent of Anglesey's Parys Mine Company, brought copper to the town. The Greenall family opened breweries and pubs to quench the thirst of all the new workers. Thomas Beecham came from Oxford, via Wigan, touting his laxatives and slogans: 'A never-failing remedy for deafness', 'Worth a guinea a box', 'Beecham's Pills save doctor's bills'. James Muspratt and Josiah Gamble built alkali works. Trains steamed into and out of St Helens, to Liverpool and Manchester, to the Runcorn Gap. Mersey flats chugged up and down the Sankey. The town became an industrial and transport nexus. Commodities were shipped all over the UK and the British Empire. In 1865, the trade in chemicals with the US was sufficient for Washington DC to appoint a consular agent to the town.

Reading Barker and Harris's book is, for a twenty-first-century Sintelenser, like reading the Old Testament or a book about ancient magic. The sheer industry of the place and its people has a fabulous quality. Public spirit played a pentecostal role. The town's pollution was an environmental Sodom and Gomorrah; one brook was 'an open sepulchre of pestiferous odours'. Churches set their face against brothels and boozers. The panoplies of trades and leisure activities and civic buildings and manufactures and immigrants drawn to the boom-town make for breathless lists, and, in retrospect, moving litanies.

'Architecturally there is nothing to be said for St Helens,' writes Nikolaus Pevsner, sniffily, in his 1969 guide to South Lancashire. What he means, of course, is that there is little that is old, nothing that is aristocratic. For that reason, local people reserve a special fond-ness for the Friends Meeting House at the eastern end of Church Street. It's a simple, squat seventeenth-century stone house, rebuilt in the eighteenth (Pevsner: 'The rebuilding cannot have amounted to much'). This moody little cottage – the oldest building in the town centre, probably the oldest meeting house still in use in Lancashire – is utterly unlike the rest of the town. Not being a Quaker, I never went inside. I thought it was abandoned and haunted.

The oldest man-made structure in St Helens is Windleshaw Chantry, built in 1415 by Sir Thomas Gerard, following his return from the Battle of Agincourt. The Bishop of Coventry and Lichfield gave permission for Masses to be given there. All that remains are a few sections of wall and a skeletal tower, standing at the edge of the town's main cemetery, a mile from the centre. The late local historian Ted Forsyth spotted evidence of gravestones buried deep underground just over a decade ago; hundreds have been unearthed and a volunteer group is continuing Ted's work. A talismanic tomb is that of Jean-Baptiste François Graux de la Bruyere, the immigrant from Picardy credited with bringing glassmaking to the town. The inscription on his gravestone reads: 'Here lie the remains of Jn° Bap^t Fran^c Graux de la Bruyere', 'He was the first Who brought to Perfection A Work of very considerable Magnitude And Importance To the Commercial Interest of the British Nation The Cast Plate Glass Manufactory'.

St Helens has lots of Protestant and Catholic churches – the boom years led to intense Irish immigration – and several merit an upward glance. Gothic St Mary Lowe House, with its copper dome and tall west tower, has a certain grim magnificence that increases as the weather deteriorates. Red-brick St Mark's stands tall on North Road. Of the modern additions, St Patrick's in Clinkham Wood, deconsecrated and due to be reborn as a special education centre, and Ormskirk Street United Reformed Church look like prayer centres that would feel homely to factory workers.

The town was always torn between glass and coal; you needed fire to make glass but a well-flung rock could shatter it. Colliers were initially seen as outsiders, marginalised for their dark, underground habits, and only redefined as stalwarts and honest men in the last century. Glassmaking superpower Pilkington – in the era when it belonged to the town rather than to a Japanese conglomerate – invested heavily in architectural one-upmanship. Reflection Court on Canal Street, built as an administrative headquarters in the thirties, has a streamlined, ship-like brick facade, influenced by the architecture of the Dutch modernist Willem Marinus Dudok.

At the firm's Alexandra Park site on Prescot Road is a far bolder statement. By 1950, Pilkington was one of the biggest producers of flat glass in the world. On the strength of this success, it commissioned the architect Edwin Maxwell Fry, who had worked with the Bauhaus founder Walter Gropius and with Le Corbusier, to build a head office with an artificial lake on a sixteen-acre site just outside St Helens town centre. The thirteen-storey tower block and surrounding structures, built between 1959 and 1963, made ample use of Pilkington's gleaming hi-tech window glass. Historic England lists the building as 'one of the earliest and best-surviving examples of a greenfield headquarters complex'.

Thomas Beecham spent £30,000 (more than £4 million today) on the red-brick, sandstone and terracotta headquarters for his pharmaceutical company that stands on Westfield Street; its raffish clock tower is a beloved landmark.

The Gamble Institute and town hall on Victoria Square are still handsome.

These may be scant pickings for a Pevsnerian snob, but the removal of the familiar is the real story. St Helens has lost, as well as factories and coal mines, the shops, pubs and social spaces that made work bearable. It has lost streets and markets, hotels and clubs, cinemas and libraries. Names as well as physical structures have disappeared. Along with the anchor industries, the tethering sites have gone.

The returning native must, then, conjure a ghost town. Walking through empty shopping centres, past shuttered fronts, I visit the skateboard shop where I was bought a Tony Alva board, ideal for Californian bowls (less so for gravelly Lancashire back alleys); Stolen from Ivor, which stocked Bowie keks, wing-collared shirts and studs with chains to wear on your tie knot; the jeans stall on the market; Woolworths for toffees. Pick and nick. I look at the plain frontage of Helena House, the secretive entrance of the Fleece Hotel, the open door on the Charcoal Grill. I can see Our Price and Martins, where I bought Buzzcocks' 'Orgasm Addict' and Bowie's *David Live*, the latter

     where tourists seldom tread

on a mid-morning mission, wagging it to walk from our village, five miles away, with best mate Mike, and then on to school.

The Sefton Arms delivers two scenes: one, in the mid-eighties, sitting with dad and Uncle Bernard looking across the room at a bare wall against which were leaning four or five old men, all drinking pints of dark beer, perhaps with whiskies on the side. I am now probably only a couple of years younger than they were. A second memory, from the 2010s, having a Christmas drink with Mike and, in the loo, I tipsily chat to an old bloke and he tells me he knew my dad, who was dead by then. The man spoke fondly and respectfully of him. The memories are bittersweet, or bitter-mild.

At the Albert I see Gnarl play and snog a lovely local goth. At the Swan, on Corporation Street beside the bus station, I get very drunk with Mike one long summer day. Hysteria, sadness and something like desperation lurks in that image. By then the pub was already where we lunged for youthful memories.

The Swan was scheduled for demolition at the end of 2024. You have to write quickly when it comes to British towns. Their buildings drop faster than you can type. Today is 6 May 2025; in eleven days the bus station will be closed to be razed. The buses were: the 329 to Southport and home; the 10 to Liverpool and the university; 141 to Earlestown via Burtonwood. But we, my pack, we mostly walked.

It was instilled in me from an early age, by my mother, principally, that I had to leave the area to get on. Dad suggested I get a surface job at Parkside, which was not as ludicrous as it sounds, but Mum was having none of it. Flight is what you embraced to find careers and accrue capital, social and monetary. The sensation of life being elsewhere was exacerbated by the absence of a mainline station. You had to change at Wigan or Warrington to get away – this despite the fact the oldest intercity line on the planet runs through the southern outskirts of town.

I will always love St Helens. Many who stayed when I left say it's gone to the dogs. That is their prerogative.

Still, I wonder if St Helens isn't the most declined town in the UK. It's not easy to measure such things, but, by the mid-twentieth century, St Helens had thirty thousand glassworkers and twenty thousand miners, as well as many thousands more in other industries. Today the massive Pilkington Greengate site – which produces float glass, a St Helens invention – employs about 250, the numbers *boosted* in 2024 when another large plant closed for good. There are no working miners. Wholesale and retail are now the main employers; shifting and selling.

St Helens commemorates its colliers at three sites. The Anderton Mining Monument, on a roundabout at the junction of the A58 and the St Helens Linkway, was unveiled in 1994, a year after Parkside closed. It shows the bronze head and shoulders of a miner holding a lump of coal. Supporting the bust is the helical drum of an Anderson Shearer Loader, a cutting machine developed in the 1950s. It was commissioned from the London-based Slovak sculptor Arthur Fleischmann in 1964 for the headquarters of the North-West Division of the National Coal Board in Lowton, and with the demise of the industry was placed at the current site, close to the Ravenhead colliery where Anderton had been general manager. People call the monument 'the miner' or 'th'cutter', though they can't take it in properly while negotiating the traffic.

On another roundabout is *The Landings*, a cast-iron work by Thompson Dagnall, a sculptor originally from Kirkby. Installed in 1995, it shows a muscular collier wielding a pick, a young boy breaking coal and a 'pit brow lass' removing stones from coal at the surface – a family of three, all employed in the coal industry. Dagnall has written, 'The last Lancashire pit closed as I was carving this piece and the last iron foundry, Varleys, shut down just before I had the figures cast.'

The third structure is the best known: *The Dream*, a sixty-six-foot-high elongated young girl's head made from gleaming white dolomite by the Spanish artist Jaume Plensa. Like a solitary moai, the head

                    where tourists seldom tread

stands at the summit of a grassed-over slagheap on the site of the former Sutton Manor colliery, towering over the coastal plain – though not surveying it, as the girl's eyes are closed. Plensa had originally offered a work that looked like a large miner's lamp on a circular plinth, with the title *The Miner's Soul*, but the idea was rejected. The ex-miners preferred a statue that was mythic, allusive, feminine and meditative – a head dreaming instead of a memory of backbreaking work. It reflected, they said, the town's motto: 'Ex Terra Lucem' – 'From the Ground, Light'. The irreverent call it the Knob of the North.

Leavers lament the passing of their towns. But they left them. I'm a tiny contributor to St Helens' emptiness. The town is always on lists of 'left behind' places. I left it behind.

That journey was generic, too. Escaping often is; returning, too. London, Liverpool and Leeds to study, then Buenos Aires to teach, then Patagonia to write. Back to London for another stint, then rural Wales, and pretty Devon. Then Lancashire again.

Once, in Río Turbio, a coal-mining town on the Argentina–Chile border in southern Patagonia, I experienced a powerful nostalgia, laced with déjà vu and edged with something uncanny. The men on the cold morning minibus might have been colliers on a National Coal Board bus to Bold, Sutton Manor or Parkside. But it was the yellowing, scarred hillsides, under the cheerless flag-grey sky, that sent my thoughts homeward. The moment had the time-and-space jolting quality of science fiction; I felt St Helens had been transplanted to the end of the world.

When I visited home from places far- and near-flung, I feasted on nostalgia and on the fickle success of unbelonging. In the middle of the shopping precinct, I'd see my dad from a distance, as a stranger would, long retired now, post-bypass surgery, seated, talking or in silence, with a friend, sometimes a fellow miner.

Industrial towns are chemical reactions, manufactures with built-in obsolescence. Barely controlled energies – and violence – accompany their birth. Their golden ages are very short and their real colours are grey, black and red. Their end is shunned by many, as it is shameful and depressing.

I am sorry the above is fragmentary. I can't quite impose a flow on St Helens. It breaks up as I wander around.

I hadn't planned my walk along the Sankey Canal – the UK's first significant development in infrastructure since the Romans built roads – to coincide with the axing of HS2. But it happened like that.

It was a sunny day. I had been promising myself a hike along the towpath for ages. Between my starting point, at Blackbrook, and Earlestown, only three or so miles, I took a few wrong turns where tangled vegetation blocked the path, and ended up on the road. I don't mind pounding the pavements; a lot of my walking as a teenager was on A-roads.

This first section passed near Burtonwood, where I was born and raised. Vans and lorries thundered by. Memories came fast and intrusively. That field, that light, that horizon; the ineffable markers of place. It was akin to 'beating the bounds', though I felt only a fragile sense of belonging.

Things turned rural and car-free as I approached the Sankey Viaduct, known hereabouts as 'Nine Arches'. Built by George Stephenson in 1830 for his epoch-making Liverpool and Manchester railway, it was, as a red plaque reminded me, the 'earliest major railway viaduct in the world'.

Another red plaque honours the memory of Henry Berry and the canal. They should add a third for the navvies, masons and carpenters who did the hard graft.

Nearby is Earlestown railway station, the oldest in operation, close to the site of the world's first steam railway junction. St Helens is brimful of world's firsts. Passing farmers and miners gaped in awe at the viaduct's soaring arches as it was being erected in the late 1820s. Once opened it became a tourist attraction in its own right.

Beyond the viaduct, the canal was at times quite beautiful, especially when the sun broke through and warmed the green-gold canopy. I passed coarse fishermen, cyclists, dog walkers, four women on horseback. All were friendly, sometimes chatty; the kinds of people I grew up around.

The chaotic, naturally rewilded canal has a lot of birdlife. I saw herons, shags, gulls, coots, hundreds of moorhens, grazing geese, adult swans accompanied by grey moulting cygnets. Dense reed beds provide safety and nesting grounds. The brambles and holly bushes were alive with tits, wrens, robins, blackbirds.

Where the woods retreated, the towpath ran parallel to the west coast mainline – dead quiet due to an ASLEF strike – before guiding me under the M62. I caught a glimpse of Burtonwood's logistics hub and its big blue Ikea – the UK's first, opened in 1987. Close by were the ruins of locks, empty spaces where bascule and swing bridges once stood, and traces of old masonry. I came to a cluster of old buildings, once a bustling maintenance yard, with a pub, limekiln and nearby dry dock. A handsome brick building was dated 1841. On either side were a scrapyard and a car park with a sign advising that dogging is against the law.

As I progressed south the signage was neater, the trail more clearly marked, and littering greatly reduced. I was skirting Warrington, where civic infrastructure is better funded than in St Helens. The park areas around the mainly Jacobean Bewsey Old Hall – which can trace its foundations to just after the Norman conquest – had well-tended lawns and new play areas. I sat down at a picnic bench to eat lunch; I was bombed by conkers falling from horse chestnut trees. I was within wagging distance of my old secondary school, Great Sankey High.

After a cheese barm I set off again. Much of the next section of tow-path was long and linear, but the broad view changed from mellow low-plains bosky to clashing post-industrial. On the far horizon were the cooling towers at decommissioned coal-fired Fiddlers Ferry, one of the great landmarks of the North-West. The towers are scheduled for demolition in 2026. Flat places need drama; the power station will be missed.

I had walked thirteen miles as I passed a tidy marina – dinghies, yachts, skiffs – and was dreaming of the bus stop when, at a break in the woodland on my left, I was gifted a sublime view of the Mersey, glinting at half-tide with waders on the mudbanks and gulls offshore, and the two great bridges beyond: the old 1960s 'Runcorn Bridge' (the Silver Jubilee Bridge), which I crossed en route to childhood holidays in North Wales; and the sweeping span of the Mersey Gateway, which has deservedly scooped engineering awards. The westering sun was gentle and hopeful.

Fifteen miles into the walk, I crossed the canal at Carter House Swing Bridge and entered Widnes by way of an industrial estate. Completists can do a circuit of Spike Island, famous for its chemical plants and a 1990 Stone Roses gig. But I was done. Until June 1951, I would have jumped aboard the *Ditton Dodger* on the St Helens and Runcorn Gap railway, but I had to make do with the number 17 bus, which was a milk-round service; not tedious at all, as I skirted my mum's school, and the homes of my dad and late brother. As I said, beating the bounds – but of memory and life and love.

where tourists seldom tread

Epilogue
Martians and Postcards

Reiterations, connections, echoes, recollections. That's how I have come to know Britain all over again. Before 2021, I was acquainted with a handful of cities, perhaps twenty towns. I knew Buenos Aires better than my native Lancashire. I could find my way around the roads of Patagonia more than I could those of Lincolnshire or Cornwall. I had been to Kamchatka more often than I had been to Thurso, Gateshead or Northern Ireland – that is, I'd been there once. I had an intricate mental map of central London, like other people who have spent significant time there, but its outer rings, spreading and populous, were a blur. Douglas, another UK capital city, was a complete unknown.

The travelling for, and the writing of, *Where Tourists Seldom Tread* (the *Guardian* column and this book) has been enjoyable, edifying, enlightening, the effort almost always rewarded with something of value to my broader education, occasionally a small epiphany.

Some of the towns I visited have overlapping histories. Railways, textiles, soap suds, the sea, New Towns, mining, Roman roads, Civil War battles, radical politics, sports: these are the ties that bind. In the 2020s, they share urgent challenges and vicissitudes: the erosion of footfall, destitution and poverty, homelessness, the disappearance of libraries and department stores. Yearning and missing and remembering are there on every high street. Volunteers protect heritage, educate, open pop-ups and hold communities together.

Towns thrive when there are third places – not home, not work, not nail bars or barber's shops, but places to pass time without spending money. Parks and squares, churchyards and benches, covered places, warm places, they are all vital. Millions are spent trying to regenerate retail. A fraction of that on spaces to relax, read, watch and meet could do so much.

As I decided at the outset, the portraits have been generally positive, trying to see what is to be valued rather than lamented or decried. Nonetheless, a word cloud of my text would find 'sad' and its variants surfacing again and again. This is partly the natural emotion of the traveller. I'm surprised more travelogues aren't full of melancholy. All quests are escapes. Solitariness, rather than sociability, characterises much of my experience of travelling. There's also the reality of British weather, and the cost of things, and the look of poor and loveless people, the rough sleepers, the drug- and drink-dependent in our towns. It rubs off on you.

No regeneration will have any value until the towns and their regions receive the investment they need and deserve. That probably applies to 90 per cent of provincial towns, as well as several cities and many unsung villages. The failure to rebalance the economy and re-distribute wealth underpins every one of my postcards.

My other chief gripe is: demolition – the indiscriminate removal of the cherished. When I had more or less finished the last chapter, I found myself in St Helens again, late in 2025. The wrecking ball had swung like never before and huge swathes of the town had gone. My fantasy – shared in that final postcard – of walking around resurrecting in my mind's eye the shops and streets I grew up on was tested by the gaping holes in the townscape. Apparently, the centre is going to get office space, a '150-bed branded hotel', a market hall (like long-time rival Warrington, like everywhere else), surveilled piazzas, and some retail space to tease back the companies that flitted to out-of-town boxes two decades ago. What, then, will serve as anchors of memory? What will old people recognise in St Helens and what will their grandchildren be able to point to and say: that's where Mam or Grandma danced or worked or shopped? The money for large-scale schemes often comes from London investors. Let's raze Regent Street and Oxford Street – they're pretty tacky these days – and see how that goes down. Renewal is necessary and newbuild vital, but removal of everything that once was is tantamount to an unwonted shredding of the collective life of an entire town, across generations, from ghosts to the unborn.

                    where tourists seldom tread

St Helens is my town. Apologies if I've overlooked similar, or different, crimes in your town.

For all that, I still feel, as a sixty-year-old man, a similar kind of ex-
citement prior to a train trip to Boston or Barrow as I did as a child
before a family outing to Blackpool or Colwyn Bay, or as a teenager
planning to hitchhike with friends to the Lake District. I definitely belong to the travel tribe. I love maps. I read old gazetteers for
pleasure. But there's also an underlying need to see and experience.
It was always there, I think, but in the case of Britain, pushed down
and nudged out by the well-marketed glamour of foreign travel and
our collective national habits.

Travel used to be to undertaken to invade, escape, trade or spy.
Then came Grand Tours: indulgent exploring for elites. Mass tourism
turned it into commercial formulae, chain hotels, well-beaten routes
and prescribed 'highlights'. A five-star package in Brazil is essentially
Blackpool with coconut water and warm seas. So-called independent
travel is five decades old: few places remain that are undescribed,
many are deluged with visitors.

Given all that, surely Britain's bypassed places are due their moment in the sun. Aren't they a ready-made solution to an obvious
problem? I don't understand how anyone can live in a country and
not want to know it. Well, maybe I do. There are no Crap Towns. But
the world is full of Crap Travel, and Crap Travellers.

Martin Parr, who was not one of the latter, and who died while I was
finishing writing this book, said he photographed supermarkets rather
than old churches because the former would disappear while the latter
would be around, largely unchanged, for a long time to come. But he
also followed the crowds. Superstores, every day of the week, throng
like cathedrals once did for a prince's wedding or a bishop's funeral.
Beaches are summertime agoras. Car parks are collective works of art.
Parr saw in the ordinary, banal and 'boring' what everyone else missed.

He was a model artist for anyone who wants to see the familiar with fresh eyes. Now everyone copies him, and that particular Parr-ist filter veers towards cliché. But the trick, I think, is to see the world like Martin Parr without a camera. What if we imagine that everything is interesting? What if we fill the empty places with thoughts and stories? How can we startle a place into life without a ring flash and a fast shutter speed?

One way is to pretend you are a foreign traveller or a Martian, as in the famous Craig Raine poem about the Martian who wrote to tell his friends on the red planet about the wonders of the planet Earth: books are birds, rainfall is TV, time is watches, telephones are haunted, toilets are torture chambers, night-time is dreams and dreams are the best books. Defamiliarisation is not a dodge, a cop-out; it's a means of coming back to what matters.

I was born a mile south of the Liverpool and Manchester railway. When I went fishing with my dad in the Res beside the tracks, I liked to hear the passing trains. I saw the water around my float ripple. No perch were biting. It was the rumble of Deltics and 47s. My first travels were bus trips with him. He thought everywhere was a holiday and, I suppose, if you work underground, as he did, just being under the sun or, at least, the sky, is wondrous. His second wife made him go to Spain, but he really preferred Fleetwood, Rhyl, Bridlington. In the end, we all, searching for enlightenment, go in circles. I've finally realised Dad was right. To come home and, simultaneously, to keep moving is the thing. The only way to know this country and yourself, and take a holiday from time to time that doesn't contribute to the mad, bad circus of climate-breakdown and consumerism, is to look for mystery at every turn, to be a curious stranger in your heartland, and make your own the places where tourists seldom tread.

  where tourists seldom tread

Acknowledgements

I'd like to thank Andy Pietrasik, head of travel at the *Guardian*, for commissioning the series that led to this book.

On the road, the following were generous with their time and thoughts: Suzy Fitzpatrick, formerly of Warrington New Town; Grahame Davies from Wrexham (*New Welsh Review* published an earlier version of that postcard); Ed Isaacs, Kathryn Moore, Andy Howlett and Fiona Cullinan in the Black Country; David Ager at the King Edward Mine Museum near Camborne; Chris de Coulon Berthoud in Gillingham; Charlotte Paxman and Lelia Ferro at Jaywick; Sue Daish in Harwich; Ben Good, Erica Burrows, Ross Keogh and Lisa White in Ipswich; Lorna Reeve in Doncaster; Jane Keightley in Boston; Alex Niven, Paul Stone and Jonpaul Kirvan in Gateshead; Donald Henderson in Wick; Martin Murray, Jay Wilson, Jon Perkins and Kenneth McElroy in Thurso and at John O'Groats; Andrew McKean, Damon Scott, Gavin Divers and the museum team at Paisley; John Irving in Barrow; Donna Fox in Armagh and Frank Roofe and Catherine Scott in Enniskillen; Ruth Keggin Gell in Ramsey; Colin Greenall in St Helens.

I'm grateful to Mid Pennine Arts and the Pendle Radicals for accompanying me in the urban and wild places of Pendle Hill. VisitEngland, VisitScotland and VisitWales assisted with some of the newspaper trips.

Thanks to Mel Bradman, Lizzie Heathcote, Simon Wardell and other sub editors at the *Guardian* for their fact checks, and to Mo Hafeez, Talya Baker, Hamish Ironside and Jo Stimfield at Faber for polishing the final text. All gaps and gaffes are mine.

Permissions

Grateful acknowledgement is made to the publishers for kindly permitting re-use of the following: the epigraph on p. 1 from *The Transparency of Evil: Essays on Extreme Phenomena* by Jean Baudrillard (trans. James Benedict), Verso Books (2009); the lines on p. 18 from *The World Turned Upside Down: Radical Ideas During the English Revolution* by Christopher Hill, Penguin, 1991 © Christopher Hill, 1972, 1975; the line on p. 22 from *Cool Memories II: 1987–1990* by Jean Baudrillard (trans. Chris Turner), Polity (1995); the lyrics on p. 33 from 'Stockport' by Geoff Morrow; the lines on p. 48 from Malcolm Lowry's 'Trinity', from *The Collected Poetry of Malcolm Lowry* by Kathleen Dorothy Scherf, University of British Columbia Press (1988); the verses on p. 77 from 'Black Country', a poem in *Black Country* by Liz Berry, Chatto & Windus, 2014, reprinted by permission of the Random House Group Limited, © Liz Berry, 2014; the quotation from *Londonstani* on pp. 135–6 reprinted by permission of HarperCollins Publishers Ltd © 2007 Gautam Malkani; the Geordie version of 'Caedmon's Hymn' on p. 215 from *Selected Poems* by U. A. Fanthorpe, Enitharmon Press (2013), www.enitharmon.co.uk © The Estate of U. A. Fanthorpe; the epigraph on p. 281 from *Letters from London* by C. L. R. James, Signal Books (2003).

where tourists seldom tread

Further Reading

Warrington

Chapman-Fox, Gordon, 'Warrington-Runcorn New Town Development Plan'
(warringtonruncorn.com/music)

Cooke, Bill, *The Story of Warrington: The Athens of the North* (Matador, 2020)

Fitzpatrick, Suzy, 'Days of the New Town' (daysofthenewtown.wordpress.com)

Moss, Chris, *Lancashire: Exploring the Historic County that Made the Modern World* (Old
Street, 2026)

Tucker, Joe, *The Secret Painter* (Canongate, 2025)

Stockport

Haslam, Dave, *Strawberry and the Big Apple: Grace Jones in Stockport, 1980* (Cōnfingō,
2024)

Birkenhead and New Brighton

Ackerley, Chris and David Large, 'Under the Volcano' (otago.ac.nz/english-linguistics/
english/lowry)

Hawthorne, Nathaniel, *Passages from the English Note-Books* (Strahan & Co., 1870)

'Hear Us' (malcolmlowry.com)

'Ron's Place' (ronsplace.co.uk)

Scherf, Kathleen Dorothy (ed.), *The Collected Poetry of Malcolm Lowry* (University of British
Columbia Press, 1992)

Crewe

Hitchen, Michael, *Crewe in the Days of BR Blue* (Amberley, 2019)

Rear, Bill, *Crewe: Station, Traffic and Footplate Working in the 1950s* (Ian Allan, 1999)

Reed, Brian, *Crewe Locomotive Works and Its Men* (David & Charles, 1985)

Wrexham

Davies, Grahame, *Real Wrexham* (Seren, 2007)

Reid, Teanu and Town, Edward, 'Elihu Yale' (ysrp.yale.edu/elihu-yale)

Wolverhampton, Walsall and Dudley

Berry, Liz, *Black Country* (Chatto & Windus, 2014)

Burn, Gordon, *Best and Edwards* (Faber, 2006)

'Canal and River Trust: West Midlands' (canalrivertrust.org.uk/about-us/where-we-work/west-midlands)

Isaacs, Ed, Instagram profile (instagram.com/edisaacsartist)

Jameson, Fredric, *Marxism and Form* (Princeton University Press, 1971)

Lane, Joel, *The Earth Wire* (Influx Press, 2020)

'The Conservation of Tecton Buildings at Dudley Zoo' (tectons.dudleyzoo.org.uk)

'The New Art Gallery Walsall' (thenewartgallerywalsall.org.uk)

'Walkspace' (walkspace.uk)

Newport

Drysdale, Ann, *Real Newport* (Seren, 2006)

'Newport Rising' (newportrising.co.uk)

Osmond, David, *The Chartist Rambler* (Six Points, 2022)

Redruth and Camborne

'Kresen Kernow' (kresenkernow.org)

'The Capital of Cornish Mining' (cornishmining.org.uk/areas/camborne-redruth-with-portreath)

'The Great Flat Lode' (cornwalltrails.net/main-trails/the-great-flat-lode)

Barnstaple

Barbellion, W. N. P., *The Journal of a Disappointed Man* (Chatto & Windus, 2019)

Hounslow, Croydon, Gillingham, Wokingham, Surbiton, Slough

Atkinson, Rowland, *Alpha City: How London Was Captured by the Super-Rich* (Verso, 2020)

Moss, Chris, *Smoothly from Harrow: A Compendium for the London Commuter* (Blue Guides, 2013)

Noble, Will, *Croydonopolis* (Safe Haven, 2024)

'Oral History Medway' (oralhistorymedway.co.uk)

Jaywick

Darley, Gillian, *Excellent Essex: In Praise of England's Most Misunderstood County* (Old Street, 2019)

Harwich

Falkiner, Suzanne, *Mick: A Life of Randolph Stow* (University of Western Australia Press, 2016)

Ipswich

Howgego, Caleb, 'Ipswich History' (ipswichhistory.com)

'Ipswich Historic Lettering' (ipswich-lettering.co.uk)

'Ipswich Maritime Trust' (ipswichmaritimetrust.org.uk)

Wade, Keith, *Gipeswic: The Anglo-Saxon Town of Ipswich* (Suffolk County Council, 2025)

 where tourists seldom tread

Boston

Turner, Derek, *Edge of England: Landfall in Lincolnshire* (Hurst, 2022)

Verlaine, Paul, *Sagesse* (Librairie Léon Vanier, 1899)

Doncaster

'Doncaster History' (doncasterhistory.wordpress.com)

Tanizaki, Jun'ichirō (trans. Harper, Thomas J. and Seidensticker, Edward G.), *In Praise of Shadows* (Leete's Island Books, 1977)

Waller, Symeon Mark, *The Big Book of Doncaster History* (Doncaster History Publishing, 2012)

Gateshead

Jackson, Dan, *The Northumbrians. North-East England and Its People: A New History* (Hurst, 2019)

Niven, Alex, *The North Will Rise Again: In Search of the Future in Northern Heartlands* (Bloomsbury, 2023)

'Orbis Community' (orbiscommunity.com)

'Vane' (vane.org.uk)

Wick and Thurso

Leith, Ian, *Caithness to Patagonia: Distant Lands and Close Relatives* (Whittles, 2016)

'The Flow Country' (theflowcountry.org.uk)

East Kilbride and Paisley

Byrne, John, *The Slab Boys Trilogy* (Faber, 2003)

Reid, William and Reid, Jim, *Never Understood: The Jesus and Mary Chain* (White Rabbit, 2024)

Williams, Gordon M., *From Scenes Like These* (Secker & Warburg, 1968)

Barrow-in-Furness

Pessoa, F. (author), Cardiello, Antonio and Pizarro, Jerónimo (eds.), The Complete Works of Álvaro de Campos (New Directions, 2023)

Worthen, John, 'Biography of DH Lawrence', Chapter 4 (nottingham.ac.uk/manuscripts andspecialcollections/collectionsindepth/lawrence/extendedbiography/chapter4.aspx)

Zytaruk, George J. and Boulton, James T. (eds.), *The Letters of D. H. Lawrence: Vol. II 1913–16* (Cambridge University Press, 2002)

Armagh and Enniskillen

'Fermanagh Genealogy Centre' (fermanaghgenealogy.org)

Douglas and Ramsey

Carswell, Robert Corteen, *Manannan's Cloak: An Anthology of Manx Literature* (Francis Boutle, 2010)

Nelson and Colne

Hope, Douglas George, *Thomas Arthur Leonard and the Co-operative Holidays Association: Joy in Widest Commonalty Spread* (Cambridge Scholars, 2017)

Liddington, Jill, *The Life and Times of a Respectable Rebel: Selina Cooper, 1864–1946* (Virago, 1984)

Pearson, Harry, *Connie: The Marvellous Life of Learie Constantine* (Abacus, 2018)

'Pendle Press' (pendle-press.co.uk)

'Pendle Radicals' (pendleradicals.org.uk)

Stephenson, Tom (author), Holt, Ann (ed.), *Forbidden Land: Struggle for Access to Mountain and Moorland* (Manchester University Press, 1989)

St Helens

Barker, T. C. and Harris, J. R, *A Merseyside Town in the Industrial Revolution: St Helens 1750–1900* (Frank Cass, 1959)

Forman, Charles, *Industrial Town: Self Portrait of St Helens in the 1920s* (Paladin, 1979)

'Sankey Canal Restoration Society' (scrs.uk)

Stephen Wainwright, 'Sutton Beauty & Heritage' (suttonbeauty.org.uk)

General Books and Websites

'A Vision of Britain Through Time' (visionofbritain.org.uk)

Farley, Paul and Symmons Roberts, Michael, *Edgelands: Journeys into England's True Wilderness* (Jonathan Cape, 2011)

Moss, Chris, 'Where Tourists Seldom Tread', *The Guardian* (theguardian.com/travel/series/where-tourists-seldom-tread)

Nairn, Ian, *Nairn's Towns* (Notting Hill, 2017)

Pragnell, Hubert J., *Industrial Britain: An Architectural History* (Batsford, 2021)

Index

A Certain Ratio, 33
Alderley Edge, 59
Aldershot, 6
Amazon, 15
Armagh, 255–260; apples, 255–6, 259; cathedrals, 257–8; Cú Chulainn, 256–7
Arnold, Matthew, 9
Astley, Rick, 34
Auden, W.H., 81
Avon ladies, 7

Bannau Brycheiniog National Park, 97
Barbellion, W.N.P., 129–30
Barnstaple, 125–130; churches, 127; maritime trade, 126; museum, 128
Barrow-in-Furness, 10, 55, 245–250; armaments factories, 245, 248; Furness Abbey, 249; industry, 246–7
Baudrillard, Jean, 1, 22
Beckett, Samuel, 262
Bede, 211
Bee Gees, 272
Beeching, Dr, 125
Belgravia, 8
Bentham, Jeremy, 18
Berlin, 4
Berry, Liz, 77, 81
Betjeman, John, 146, 148
Birkenhead, 39–49; Cammell Laird, 43; Hamilton Square, 45; Park, 46; Woodside ventilation tower, 44
Black Country, 77; 'Black Country' poem, 77, heavy rock and metal, 84, 86, 92
Blake, Peter, 82
Blossoms (band), 32, 34
Blythe, Ronald, 179
Bolton, 17
Borrow, George, 70
Boston, 189–193; immigration, 190–2; Stump, 189
Boty, Pauline, 82
Bournville model village, 87
Bowie, David, 84, 137, 163, 306
Briggs, Asa, 55, 118

Brighton, 48
Burn, Gordon, 87
Burtonwood, 22; air base 23
Buxton, 31
Byrne, John, 239

Camborne, 6, 113–8; Dulcoath mine, 114–5; Great Flat Lode Trail, 116–118; King Edward Mining Museum, 115–6
Canals, 15, 20, 23, 40, 88–9, 286, 302–3
Canterbury, 6
Carmarthenshire, 3
Catterick, 6
Caulfield, Patrick, 82
Cheshire, 21
Chester, 15, 31
Childish, Billy, 141, 142
Clarion House, 292
Clarke, John Cooper, 59
Clitheroe, 29, 86
Colne, 10, 290, 292, 293–6
Constable, John, 169
Constantine, Learie, 289–90
Cooper, Selina, 291–2
Cornwall: Cornish language, 112; Great Flat Lode, 116–17; overtourism, 118–19; tin mining, 112–16
'Crap Towns', 5
Crewe, 3, 6, 55–61; aviation industry, 59; car manufacturing, 59; Heritage Centre, 58–9; London and North Western Railway, 56–7; see also Webb, Francis
Cromwell, Oliver, 16, 137
Cromwell, Thomas, 176
Croydon, 6, 137–140; airport, 139

Davies, John, 75
Debord, Guy, 44
Debussy, Claude, 193
Demolition, 60, 67, 76, 178, 234, 307, 316
Devon, 3
Dickens, Charles, 140
Dodd, Ken, 271, 278

Doncaster, 3, 6, 199–205; Works, 201–2
Douglas, 271–4; Manx Museum, 273–4, 275–6;
    tourism heyday, 271, 274, 275
Dudley, 87–90; Black Country Living Museum,
    89–90; Castle Hill, 87

East Kilbride, 233–236; Dollan Baths, 234;
    Nae Pasaran, 236; St Bride's church, 234–5
Edinburgh, 6, 45
Edwards, Duncan, 87
English Civil Wars, 16–17, 18
Enniskillen, 260–5

Factory Records, 29
Fanthorpe, U. A., 214–5
Fawcett, Millicent, 56
Felixstowe, 179–80
Fiddlers Ferry, 312
Flâneurs, 4, 135
Florence, 45
Flow Country, 223, 227
Football, 73–4, 82–3, 87, 181–2; 'football
    special' trains, 61
Forster, E. M., 4
Fuller, Thomas, 1

Garden City movement, 40, 233
Gascoigne, Paul, 215
Gateshead, 6, 211–218; Angel of the North, 218;
    Metrocentre, 217; Vane Gallery, 216–7
Gay, John, 127
Gerald of Wales, 68
Get Carter, 215
Gillingham, 141–2
Glasier, Katherine Bruce, 291
Glastonbury, 34
Glyndŵr, Owain, 75
Good Life, The, 146
Graham, James Gillespie, 45
Greater Manchester, 29; *see also* Manchester
György, Dénes, 44

Hamilton, Richard, 82
Happy Mondays, 33
Hartley, J. B., 45
Hartley, Jesse, 45
Harwich, 163–9; Electric Palace Cinema, 163,
    167; Society, 166; Trinity House, 164–5
Haslam, Dave, 33
Havana, 41
Hawthorne, Nathaniel, 41
Herodotus, 1

Hi-de-Hi, 168
Hill, Christopher, 18
Historic England, 9, 191
Home Counties, 144–5
Hounslow, 135–7
Housing estates, 212–3; Plotlands, 156–7,
    Pulteneytown, 225
HS2, 60, 310
Hull, 7

Illustrated London News, 46
Industrial estates, 72, 137, 148–9
Industrial revolution, 5, 84, 90, 91, 111, 118
Ipswich, 5, 175–83; Christchurch Mansion,
    176–8; Maritime Trust, 178–9
Ireland, 47
Irish Republican Army (IRA), 16
Irish Sea, 39
Ironbridge, 16
Isle of Man, 3, 47, 267–79; Maughold, 278–9;
    TT Races, 271, 277

Jackson, Glenda, 43
James, C. L. R., 290
Jaywick, 155–8; Martello towers, 155, 157;
    Plotlands housing, 156–7
Jesus and Mary Chain, 233
Jones, Grace, 33
Joy Division, 33

Karaoke, 34
Keele, 6
Kenya, 3
Knox, Archibald, 275–6

Laird, William, 45
Lampeter, 6
Lancashire, 21, 29, 245, 285
Larkin, Philip, 7
Lawrence, D. H., 245
Lawrence, T. E., 82
Leonard, Thomas Arthur, 294–5
Lever, William Hesketh, 39, 40
Lewis, C. S., 29
Lichtenstein, Roy, 82
Life on Mars (TV series), 31
Liverpool, 38, 41, 44, 45, 47
London, 9; suburbs, 135
Londonstani, 135–6
Look Back in Anger, 101
Lowry, L. S.; 30, 33
Lowry, Malcolm; 47–8

where tourists seldom tread

Machen, Arthur, 104
Malthus, Thomas Robert, 18
Manchester, 9, 29, 33
Manchester Ship Canal, 15, 20, 23, 40
Marat, Jean-Paul, 18
Mayflower, 164
Medway, River, 140
Medway towns, 140–2
Menyhért, Nikolaus, 44
Mersey, River, 15, 31, 44, 46
Middlesbrough, 55
Mitchell and Kenyon, 74
Monty Python, 294
Motorways, 6, 39, 81; M2, 140; M25, 135; M4, 100; M5, 89, 119; M53, 42; M6, 20, 286; M60, 30; M62, 311; M65, 285–6

Nairn, Ian, 4
National Trust, 9
Nelson, 286–92; cotton mills, 287, 288, 295; immigration, 288; socialism, 290–2; Victory V, 287
New Brighton, 47–9, *The Last Resort*, 47
New Towns, 15, 22, 40, 223
Newport, 97–105; Chartists, 97, 102–103; industry, 100; museum and art gallery, 100–1; Pillgwenlly, 99; W. H. Davies, 98–9, 104; Ye Olde Murenger House, 101–2 Newton Abbot, 6
Newton-le-Willows, 15
Nield Chew, Ada, 56

O'Connor, Frank, 260
Offa's Dyke, 71, 76
Office, The, 148
O'Grady, Paul, 43
Orwell, George, 148
Overtourism, 6–7, 118–9, 176

Paisley, 6, 236–240; Ferguslie Park, 239–40; punk music scene, 239; textile industry, 237–8
Paley and Austin (architects), 60
Paris, 4, 33
Parr, Martin, 47, 317–8
Patagonia, 3, 224, 226, 309, 315
Pepys, Samuel, 164–5
Pessoa, Fernando, 249
Pevsner, Nikolaus, 6, 9, 191, 247, 304
Pilgrim's Progress, The, 148
Pontefract, 7
Porridge, 239
Port Sunlight, 39–41

Port Talbot, 6
Preston, 7, 61
Priestley, J. B., 213–4
Priestley, Joseph, 17–8
Pubs, bars and inns, 5, 70, 101, 114, 127, 178, 181–2, 224–5, 246, 264, 278; Greenalls, 303; memory and, 306–7; pub names, 200
Pugin, Edward Welby, 69

Queensway Tunnel, 44

Rafferty, Gerry, 238–9, 240
Railways, 55–61, 163, 201–2, 274–5; Beeching cuts, 125; Liverpool and Manchester Railway, 318
Raine, Craig, 318
Ramsey, 276–8; Grove House, 277
Redruth, 111–3; Kresen Kernow 112
Rimbaud, Arthur, 193
Rowse, Herbert, 44
Royal National Lifeboat Institution, 168, 273

Savage, Lily, 43
Second World War, 5
Shah, Eddy, 16
Shakespeare, Percy, 87
Silverman, Sydney, 292
Slavery, 17, 68, 295
Slough, 148–9
St Helens, 4, 301–12, 316–7; industries, 302–4; mining memorials, 308–9; Parkside Colliery, 30; Pilkingtons, 305–6, 308; Sankey Canal, 303, 309–12; Windleshaw Chantry, 304–5
Stanley family, 16, 273
Stanlow, 39
Starmer, Keir, 248
Stephenson, George, 301, 310
Stephenson, Robert, 217
Stephenson, Tom, 286
Stockport, 6, 29–34; Plaza, 31–2; Pyramid, 29, 34; Strawberry Studios, 33; Underbanks, 32; viaduct, 29, 30
Stow, Randolph, 165
Stratford–upon–Avon, 8
Surbiton, 145–8
Swansea, 7
Szmierek, Anthony, 34

Telford, Thomas, 225
Theroux, Paul, 248
Thomas, Dylan, 7
Thomas the Tank Engine, 273
Thurso, 226–7

Tin mining, 112–13, 114–117
Titanic (ship), 71, 293
Tolstoy, Leo, 16
Totnes, 86
Troubles, the, 255, 260, 264–5
Turner, J. M. W., 86, 165

UNESCO, 7, 4, 223
Usk, River, 97
Ussher, James, 258
Uttoxeter, 6

Vaughan, Frankie, 33
Verlaine, Paul, 192–3

Walsall, 10, 84–87; industry, 85–6; New Art
    Gallery, 86–7
War of the Pacific, 43
Warhol, Andy, 82
Warrington, 15–23, 39, 55, 61, 311; Academy,
    17–18; Bank Quay station, 19, 2, 23;
    Barley Mow pub, 16; Golden Square, 16;
    industry, 18–19, 20–1; New Town, 15, 22;
    road building, 20; Roman Wilderspool, 19;
    Stockton Heath, 22

Webb, Francis, 56, 58
Wells, 6
Wells, H. G., 130
Wesley, John, 258
West Midlands National Park Lab, 91
Wick, 224–6
Widnes, 312
Wigan, 61
Wilkinson, John, 72
Williams, Gordon, 240
Winwick, 15
Wirral, 42, 43, 45, 49
Wokingham, 143–5
Wolf Hall, 176
Wolverhampton, 4, 81–4; Art Gallery, 82; city
    status, 81; industry, 83–4; local artists, 83–4;
    Molineux Stadium, 82
Wood, Victoria, 61
Wordsworth, William, 249, 273
Wrexham, 10, 67–76; brewing, 69–71; city
    status, 67; football, 72–74; HMP Berwyn, 72;
    Marubbi's Temperance Bar, 67; Museum, 74;
    St Giles', 68; Tailor's Quilt, 69, 74

Yale, Elihu, 68

where tourists seldom tread